I0000426

ORGANIZATIONAL SUCCESS AND EFFECTIVE DECISION-MAKING

100 LEADERSHIP MODELS AND STRATEGIES

BY DAN WAITE

GAMIFICATION LEADERSHIP	NONPROFIT LEADERSHIP	IMPROV LEADERSHIP
HACKER LEADERSHIP	SWARM LEADERSHIP	TECH LEADERSHIP
GREAT MAN THEORY	SITUATIONAL LEADERSHIP	AGILE LEADERSHIP
HOLOGRAPHIC LEADERSHIP	TRANSFORMATIONAL LEADERSHIP	PEER LEADERSHIP
LAISSEZ-FAIRE LEADERSHIP	AUTOCRATIC LEADERSHIP	BENEVOLENT DICTATORSHIP
POLITICAL LEADERSHIP	MILITARY LEADERSHIP	LEVEL FIVE LEADERSHIP

100 LEADERSHIP MODELS

RESONANT LEADERSHIP	COACHING LEADERSHIP	EMPATHETIC LEADERSHIP
AI-INTEGRATED LEADERSHIP	MAVERICK LEADERSHIP	IMPROV LEADERSHIP
VISIONARY LEADERSHIP	PACESETTING LEADERSHIP	SUSTAINABLE LEADERSHIP
PARADOXICAL LEADERSHIP	INFLUENCER LEADERSHIP	OPEN-SOURCE LEADERSHIP
STOIC LEADERSHIP	ZEN LEADERSHIP	STARTUP LEADERSHIP
EXISTENTIAL LEADERSHIP	DIALECTICAL LEADERSHIP	SPIRITUAL LEADERSHIP
HUMAN-CANTERED LEADERSHIP	CRISIS LEADERSHIP	HOLACRACY LEADERSHIP
SPORTS LEADERSHIP	DATA-DRIVEN LEADERSHIP	AND MANY, MANY MORE

100 LEADERSHIP MODELS AND STRATEGIES FOR EFFECTIVE DECISION-MAKING FOR ORGANIZATIONAL SUCCESS

BY DAN WAITE

Published by LOCO TEMPUS LIMITED 2025

Cover design by Dan Waite

British Library Cataloguing in Publication Data

A catalogue record for this book is available from the British Library

ISBN: 978-1-917784-00-9

ISBN 978-1-9177840-0-9

9 781917 784009 >

Dan Waite here, CEO of Better Noise Music.

Having worked at Virgin Records, Universal Records, MTV, AEG, BBC, NME and Better Noise Music I have worked for some inspirational leaders.

At Virgin Records the culture and leadership style was built by Sir Richard Branson and was creative and fun, nimble and efficient, at Universal, Sir Lucian Grainge leadership style was different once again and very driven, goal orientated and focusing on the biggest acts on the label. At MTV Bob Bakish had Viacom, CBS & Paramount to juggle, and Bob had a Fortune 500 Leadership quality.

At the BBC Tim Davie's style was suited to managing an enormous company with specific public obligations that a regular company would not need to adhere to with incredible press scrutiny where every move and statement is analysed.

I have to say I've never had a boss like Allen Kovac, an entrepreneur who has only ever worked for himself. He coaches, guides, pushes, give you enough rope, and inspires, and has a similar ethos to Steve Jobs. I have transformed under Allen's leadership.

I hope that during the course of reading this book you will find a leadership style that you can relate to and one that best fits your organization and that other organizational styles may inspire you to adapt and transform though your path to leadership and beyond.

Best of Luck applying these Leadership Models, Dan

This is dedicated to my wife Irena, my family & friends and work colleagues, present and past.

With thanks to Ade Adeluwoye, Nicolas Bate, Sir Richard Branson. Allen Kovac for your trust and guidance as a boss and mentor and Napolean Hill for the advice in spotting opportunity in hard work.

Thank you to inspirational contacts who as a result of their books and classes have me thinking differently, including Rory Sutherland and Will Page.

In memory of my father David Waite.

CHAPTERS

Classic Leadership Theories

1. Great Man Theory
2. Trait Theory
3. Behavioural Theory
4. Contingency Theory
5. Situational Leadership (Hersey-Blanchard)
6. Path-Goal Theory
7. Transactional Leadership
8. Transformational Leadership
9. Laissez-Faire Leadership
10. Autocratic Leadership

Modern Leadership Theories

11. Servant Leadership (Robert Greenleaf)
12. Level 5 Leadership (Jim Collins)
13. Adaptive Leadership (Ronald Heifetz)
14. Authentic Leadership (Bill George)
15. Ethical Leadership
16. Agile Leadership
17. Charismatic Leadership
18. Resonant Leadership
19. Quiet Leadership
20. Empathetic Leadership

Leadership Styles Based on Influence

21. Directive Leadership
22. Participative Leadership
23. Delegative Leadership

24. Democratic Leadership
25. Coaching Leadership
26. Facilitative Leadership
27. Persuasive Leadership
28. Pacesetting Leadership
29. Bureaucratic Leadership
30. Visionary Leadership

Industry-Specific Leadership Models

31. Tech Leadership
32. Military Leadership
33. Healthcare Leadership
34. Educational Leadership
35. Sports Leadership
36. Startup Leadership
37. Political Leadership
38. Corporate Leadership
39. Retail Leadership
40. Nonprofit Leadership

Leadership Models by Psychological Approach

41. Maslow's Hierarchy Leadership
42. McGregor's Theory X and Theory Y
43. Herzberg's Two-Factor Theory
44. Expectancy Theory (Vroom)
45. Self-Determination Theory
46. Emotional Intelligence Leadership (Daniel Goleman)
47. Neuroscience-Based Leadership
48. Behavioural Economics Leadership
49. Social Learning Theory Leadership
50. Cognitive Load Leadership

Leadership in Crisis & Change Management

51. Crisis Leadership
52. Change Management Leadership (Kotter's 8 Steps)
53. VUCA Leadership
54. Antifragile Leadership (Nassim Taleb)
55. Post-Heroic Leadership
56. Distributed Leadership
57. Lean Leadership
58. Fractal Leadership
59. Holacracy Leadership
60. Situational Crisis Communication Theory (SCCT)

Leadership Based on Corporate Culture & Team Dynamics

61. Culture-Driven Leadership
62. Toxic Leadership
63. Shared Leadership
64. Flat Hierarchy Leadership
65. Team-Oriented Leadership
66. Customer-Centric Leadership
67. Purpose-Driven Leadership
68. Adaptive Team Leadership
69. Workplace Diversity Leadership
70. Psychological Safety Leadership

Future & Innovative Leadership Models

71. AI-Integrated Leadership
72. Hybrid Work Leadership
73. Data-Driven Leadership
74. Metaverse Leadership
75. Generational Leadership

76. Sustainable Leadership
77. Human-Cantered Leadership
78. Open-Source Leadership
79. Influencer Leadership
80. Neurodiversity Leadership

Niche & Philosophical Leadership Approaches

81. Stoic Leadership
82. Zen Leadership
83. Existential Leadership
84. Maverick Leadership
85. Paradoxical Leadership
86. Wisdom-Based Leadership
87. Dialectical Leadership
88. Spiritual Leadership
89. Historical Leadership Lessons
90. Transcendent Leadership

Experimental & Unconventional Leadership Models

91. Improv Leadership
92. Gamification Leadership
93. Reverse Leadership
94. Tribal Leadership
95. Hacker Leadership
96. Swarm Leadership
97. Benevolent Dictatorship
98. Open Leadership
99. Peer Leadership
100. Holographic Leadership

Classic Leadership Theories

1. Great Man Theory

Great Man Theory of Leadership: A Breakdown

Theory

The **Great Man Theory** of leadership emerged in the 19th century, proposing that great leaders are born with innate qualities that predestine them for leadership. This theory, championed by historians like Thomas Carlyle, suggests that certain individuals possess extraordinary traits—such as intelligence, charisma, courage, and decisiveness—that set them apart. The idea is that history is shaped by these exceptional individuals, who rise to the occasion during critical moments to lead others toward success.

This perspective assumes that leadership cannot be learned or developed; instead, it is an inherent ability. In its early form, the Great Man Theory primarily focused on political, military, and aristocratic figures, reinforcing the notion that leadership was often hereditary or exclusive to those from privileged backgrounds.

Example

One of the most cited examples of the Great Man Theory in action is **Napoleon Bonaparte**. Rising from relative obscurity, Napoleon displayed remarkable military strategy, vision, and authority, leading France to dominance in

Europe. His natural intelligence, confidence, and decision-making abilities exemplify the idea that certain individuals are simply destined to lead.

Another example is **Winston Churchill**, whose leadership during World War II demonstrated exceptional resilience, charisma, and oratory skill. His ability to inspire and rally the British people in times of crisis aligns with the belief that some leaders possess innate qualities that make them uniquely suited to pivotal historical moments.

Why It Works

The Great Man Theory persists because it aligns with the historical pattern of influential figures shaping the world. It provides a straightforward explanation for leadership by attributing success to innate abilities rather than external factors. Psychological research also suggests that certain personality traits (e.g., extraversion, confidence, decisiveness) correlate strongly with leadership effectiveness, reinforcing the idea that some individuals are naturally predisposed to lead.

Additionally, the theory offers inspiration—many people find the idea of "born leaders" compelling and aspirational, particularly in times of crisis when decisive, heroic figures emerge to guide nations or organizations.

How It Works

The Great Man Theory operates under the assumption that leadership is a product of inherent traits rather than learned behaviour. This suggests that:

- Leaders emerge naturally during crises or critical periods.

- Leadership is exclusive to those possessing specific qualities such as vision, intelligence, and decisiveness.

- Leadership is often linked to historical and political figures who demonstrate extraordinary personal attributes.

Application

Despite its criticisms, elements of the Great Man Theory still influence leadership development today. It is particularly evident in:

- **Political Leadership**: Many political campaigns emphasize a leader's personal qualities rather than policies or experience.

- **Corporate Leadership**: Business icons like Steve Jobs and Elon Musk are often perceived as "visionary leaders" with an almost mythic status.

- **Crisis Leadership**: During emergencies, people often look for strong, confident leaders who exude authority and certainty.

However, modern leadership theories (such as Transformational Leadership or Situational Leadership) emphasize that leadership can also be developed, challenging the exclusivity of the Great Man Theory.

Key Insights

1. **Innate Traits Matter**: While leadership can be developed, certain personality traits and natural abilities provide a strong foundation.

2. **Charisma & Vision Are Powerful**: Exceptional leaders often possess an ability to inspire and influence others naturally.

3. **Situational Context is Important**: While some individuals have leadership potential, the right circumstances are often needed for them to rise to prominence.

4. **Modern Leadership is More Inclusive**: Unlike the traditional Great Man Theory, contemporary leadership models recognize the importance of learning, experience, and collaboration.

While the Great Man Theory has largely been replaced by more nuanced leadership models, its core idea—that some individuals possess extraordinary leadership qualities—remains influential in leadership discourse today.

2. Trait Theory

Trait Theory of Leadership: A Breakdown

Theory

The **Trait Theory of Leadership** suggests that certain individuals possess specific traits that naturally make them effective leaders. Emerging in the early 20th century, this theory builds on the Great Man Theory but offers a more systematic approach by identifying particular characteristics that distinguish leaders from non-leaders.

Researchers like Ralph Stogdill and Gordon Allport explored this theory, concluding that leadership is partly innate but also influenced by situational factors. Unlike the Great Man Theory, which assumes leaders are born, Trait Theory argues that while some traits are inherent, leadership potential can be recognized and developed.

Common traits associated with effective leadership include:

- **Intelligence** (cognitive ability, decision-making skills)
- **Confidence** (self-assurance and decisiveness)
- **Charisma** (ability to inspire and influence others)
- **Integrity** (honesty and ethical behaviour)
- **Emotional Intelligence** (self-awareness, empathy, and interpersonal skills)

- **Resilience** (ability to handle stress and adversity)

The core idea is that individuals with these traits are more likely to emerge as leaders and succeed in leadership roles.

Example

A classic example of Trait Theory in action is **Abraham Lincoln**. His intelligence, integrity, resilience, and ability to communicate effectively made him an exceptional leader during one of the most challenging times in American history—the Civil War.

In the business world, **Elon Musk** exemplifies Trait Theory with his high intelligence, vision, and risk-taking mindset. His confidence, decisiveness, and innovation have positioned him as a dominant leader in industries such as electric vehicles (Tesla) and space exploration (SpaceX).

Why It Works

Trait Theory works because it provides a logical framework for understanding why some individuals naturally rise to leadership positions. Research suggests that people with certain personality traits are more likely to be perceived as leaders and, in turn, more likely to influence and guide others successfully.

Moreover, this theory aligns with psychological assessments that demonstrate links between personality traits and leadership effectiveness. Traits such as extraversion and emotional stability are consistently associated with strong leadership performance.

How It Works

Trait Theory operates under the premise that leadership is largely influenced by personality traits rather than situational or learned behaviour. It suggests:

- Leaders emerge naturally due to their distinct personality traits.

- People with leadership traits are more likely to be placed in leadership roles.

- These traits enable leaders to handle complex situations, inspire teams, and drive success.

- Leadership effectiveness depends on the presence and strength of these key traits.

However, modern interpretations recognize that traits alone do not guarantee leadership success—context, experience, and learned skills also play a role.

Application

Trait Theory is widely used in various leadership development practices:

- **Hiring & Selection**: Organizations use personality assessments (e.g., Big Five Personality Traits, Myers-Briggs Type Indicator) to identify leadership potential.

- **Leadership Training**: Programs focus on enhancing key traits such as confidence, communication, and emotional intelligence.

- **Performance Evaluation**: Leadership effectiveness is often assessed based on traits like decisiveness, integrity, and resilience.

- **Executive Coaching**: High-potential employees receive coaching to strengthen desirable leadership traits.

While Trait Theory is useful in identifying leadership potential, it does not account for the impact of environment, experience, or adaptability—factors that are now emphasized in modern leadership theories.

Key Insights

1. **Certain Traits Are Predictive of Leadership** – Intelligence, confidence, and emotional intelligence are strong indicators of leadership potential.

2. **Traits Alone Do Not Guarantee Success** – Leadership effectiveness depends on experience, adaptability, and external factors.

3. **Trait Development is Possible** – While some traits are innate, others (like communication and resilience) can be developed over time.

4. **Trait Theory Informs Modern Leadership Practices** – Organizations still use personality assessments and leadership development programs based on trait analysis.

While the Trait Theory of Leadership is not the sole explanation for leadership effectiveness, it remains an essential framework for identifying and nurturing future leaders.

3. Behavioural Theory

Behavioural Theory of Leadership: A Breakdown

Theory

The **Behavioural Theory of Leadership** proposes that leadership is not an innate trait but rather a set of learned behaviours that can be developed over time. Unlike earlier theories, such as the Great Man Theory or Trait Theory, which focus on inherent qualities, Behavioural Theory emphasizes **what leaders do** rather than **who they are**.

This theory suggests that effective leadership results from observed and learned behaviours, meaning that anyone can become a leader through training and practice. Psychologists like John B. Watson, B.F. Skinner, and Kurt Lewin played a crucial role in shaping this theory, emphasizing that leadership is shaped by experience, conditioning, and reinforcement.

Two well-known studies that helped define this theory are:

1. **The Ohio State Studies** – Identified two primary leadership behaviours:

    o **Initiating Structure** (task-oriented leadership)

    o **Consideration** (people-oriented leadership)

2. **The University of Michigan Studies** – Differentiated between:

- ○ **Employee-Cantered Leaders** (focused on people and relationships)
- ○ **Production-Cantered Leaders** (focused on tasks and efficiency)

These studies laid the foundation for **leadership styles**, such as democratic, autocratic, and laissez-faire leadership, emphasizing that different behaviours lead to different leadership outcomes.

Example

A strong example of Behavioural Leadership is **Bill Gates**, co-founder of Microsoft. Early in his career, he exhibited a more autocratic and task-focused style, emphasizing efficiency and productivity. However, as he matured as a leader, he adopted more participative behaviours, focusing on collaboration, employee empowerment, and innovation. His leadership transformation supports the idea that leadership behaviours can change and develop over time.

Another example is **Howard Schultz**, former CEO of Starbucks. Schultz practiced a democratic leadership style, actively engaging employees, listening to their feedback, and fostering a people-first culture. His leadership behaviours contributed to Starbucks' success by creating a strong, customer-focused company culture.

Why It Works

Behavioural Theory works because it provides a **flexible and teachable approach** to leadership. Unlike trait-based theories, which assume leadership is innate, this theory suggests that leadership skills can be acquired through observation, practice, and reinforcement.

It also aligns with modern leadership development practices, where individuals can improve their leadership effectiveness by adopting new behaviours. Additionally, this theory helps organizations design leadership training programs that emphasize key behaviours for success.

How It Works

Behavioural Theory operates by categorizing leadership behaviours into different styles and encouraging the adoption of effective behaviours through learning and practice. The key principles include:

- **Observation & Learning** – Leaders can observe successful leadership behaviours and replicate them.

- **Reinforcement & Feedback** – Positive behaviours are reinforced through training, coaching, and experience.

- **Situational Adaptability** – Leaders can adjust their behaviour based on the needs of their team and organization.

- **Focus on Actions Over Traits** – Leadership effectiveness is determined by what leaders do rather than their inherent personality.

Application

Behavioural Theory is widely used in leadership development and organizational management:

- **Leadership Training Programs** – Many companies train leaders to adopt behaviours that drive performance and employee engagement.

- **Performance Management** – Organizations assess leadership effectiveness based on demonstrated behaviours rather than personality traits.

- **Behavioural Assessments** – Tools like the **DISC Personality Assessment** and **Leadership Behaviour Assessment** help leaders understand and improve their behaviours.

- **Coaching & Mentoring** – Leaders refine their behaviours through coaching and continuous feedback.

Key Insights

1. **Leadership is Learned, Not Inherited** – Effective leadership behaviours can be developed through training, practice, and experience.

2. **Actions Define Leadership, Not Personality** – Leadership success is based on behaviour rather than innate traits.

3. **Different Situations Require Different Behaviours** – Leaders must adapt their behaviour based on organizational needs, team dynamics, and external circumstances.

4. **Behaviour Can Be Improved Over Time** – Through observation, reinforcement, and continuous learning, leaders can refine their skills.

Behavioural Theory remains a foundational concept in leadership development, influencing modern approaches such as Transformational and Servant Leadership. Its emphasis on **learning and adaptability** makes it one of the most practical and widely used leadership models today.

4. Contingency Theory

Contingency Theory of Leadership: A Breakdown

Theory

The **Contingency Theory of Leadership** argues that there is no single best way to lead. Instead, effective leadership depends on the situation, the environment, and the relationship between the leader and their team. Unlike Trait Theory (which focuses on inherent qualities) or Behavioural Theory (which emphasizes learned behaviours), Contingency Theory suggests that **the right leadership style depends on specific situational factors**.

Developed by **Fred Fiedler** in the 1960s, this theory introduced the idea that leadership effectiveness is determined by two factors:

1. **Leadership Style** – Leaders are either **task-oriented** (focused on structure, goals, and efficiency) or **relationship-oriented** (focused on people, communication, and team well-being).

2. **Situational Favourableness** – The effectiveness of a leader depends on how favourable the situation is, based on:

   - **Leader-member relations** (trust and respect between the leader and the team)

   - **Task structure** (how clear or ambiguous the task is)

   - **Leader's position power** (the level of authority the leader has)

Fiedler's **Least Preferred Coworker (LPC) Scale** helps determine a leader's natural style. Leaders scoring low on LPC are task-oriented, while those scoring high are relationship-oriented.

Other contingency models, such as **Hersey and Blanchard's Situational Leadership Theory**, expand on this by emphasizing that leaders should adapt their style based on the competence and motivation of their followers.

Example

A historical example of Contingency Theory in action is **Dwight D. Eisenhower** during World War II. As Supreme Commander of the Allied Forces, Eisenhower adapted his leadership style based on the situation. During planning stages, he was **task-oriented**, focusing on strategy and execution. However, when dealing with political allies and maintaining morale, he switched to a **relationship-oriented** approach, fostering collaboration and diplomacy.

In business, **Tim Cook (CEO of Apple)** demonstrates adaptability in leadership. Following Steve Jobs, Cook adjusted his style to focus on teamwork, inclusivity, and operational efficiency rather than Jobs' autocratic and visionary leadership style. His ability to lead based on Apple's evolving needs aligns with Contingency Theory principles.

Why It Works

Contingency Theory works because **it acknowledges that leadership is dynamic**. It rejects the idea of a one-size-fits-all approach and instead emphasizes **flexibility** based on real-world challenges. Leaders who understand the importance of situational adaptation tend to make better decisions and lead more effectively.

Research also supports this model, showing that different environments require different leadership approaches. For example, in times of crisis, **task-oriented leadership** may be most effective, whereas in stable environments, a

relationship-oriented approach fosters long-term engagement.

How It Works

Contingency Theory operates by analysing three main elements:

1. **Identifying Leadership Style** – Leaders assess whether they are task-oriented or relationship-oriented (using tools like the LPC scale).

2. **Assessing Situational Factors** – Leaders evaluate leader-member relations, task structure, and position power to determine situational favourableness.

3. **Matching Leadership Style to the Situation** – If there is a mismatch between a leader's natural style and the situation's demands, adjustments must be made (either by changing leadership style or modifying the situation).

Unlike Behavioural Theory, which assumes leadership behaviours can be universally applied, Contingency Theory insists that leadership success **depends on context**.

Application

Contingency Theory is widely used in:

- **Crisis Management** – Task-oriented leaders thrive in high-pressure environments like emergency response teams or military operations.

- **Corporate Leadership** – CEOs and managers adjust their approach depending on team dynamics and company needs.

- **Project Management** – Leaders determine the best way to manage teams based on project complexity and available resources.

- **Coaching & Mentoring** – Managers use Situational Leadership (a form of Contingency Theory) to tailor their leadership style to employees' skill levels.

Key Insights

1. **No Universal Leadership Style** – Effective leadership is context-dependent; what works in one situation may not work in another.

2. **Situational Awareness is Critical** – Leaders must assess team dynamics, structure, and authority levels before determining their approach.

3. **Leaders Must Adapt or Delegate** – If a leader's natural style does not fit the situation, they must either adjust their behaviour or delegate leadership to someone better suited.

4. **Practical & Flexible Leadership Approach** – This theory provides a real-world perspective, helping leaders make informed decisions based on circumstances rather than rigid leadership principles.

Contingency Theory remains highly relevant today, influencing leadership development programs and organizational decision-making. It reinforces the idea that successful leaders are those who **understand and adapt to their environment.**

5. Situational Leadership (Hersey-Blanchard)

Situational Leadership Theory (Hersey-Blanchard): A Breakdown

Theory

The **Situational Leadership Theory** (SLT), developed by **Paul Hersey and Ken Blanchard**, proposes that effective leadership is not based on a single style but rather on the ability to adapt leadership behaviours to meet the needs of the situation and the people being led. Unlike Trait Theory, which assumes leadership qualities are fixed, or Behavioural Theory, which focuses on consistent leadership actions, Situational Leadership emphasizes **flexibility** in leadership styles based on the readiness (competence and commitment) of followers.

The model outlines four primary leadership styles:

1. **Telling (S1) – High Task, Low Relationship**

    o   The leader provides clear instructions and closely supervises performance.

- Used when followers have low competence and low commitment (new or inexperienced employees).

2. **Selling (S2) – High Task, High Relationship**

   - The leader still directs but also provides encouragement and support.

   - Best for followers with some competence but low confidence or motivation.

3. **Participating (S3) – Low Task, High Relationship**

   - The leader shares decision-making and fosters collaboration.

   - Effective when followers are competent but lack confidence or commitment.

4. **Delegating (S4) – Low Task, Low Relationship**

   - The leader provides minimal supervision and allows employees to take full ownership.

   - Best for followers who are highly competent and highly committed.

The key insight of SLT is that leaders should **diagnose** their team's readiness level and adjust their style accordingly, rather than using a single leadership approach for all situations.

Example

A real-world example of Situational Leadership is **Satya Nadella**, CEO of Microsoft. When he took over leadership, he recognized that Microsoft's employees had high competence but lacked a sense of innovation. Instead of using a directive style, he adopted a **Participating (S3) leadership approach**, focusing on collaboration and empowerment. Over time, as the company regained confidence, he shifted to a **Delegating (S4) style**, allowing senior leaders to drive innovation independently.

Another example is a **football coach** working with a team. A new player with little experience might need a **Telling (S1) approach** with direct instructions. As the player gains confidence, the coach may move to **Selling (S2)** with encouragement, then to **Participating (S3)** by involving the player in decision-making, and finally to **Delegating (S4)** when the player is fully capable of independent performance.

Why It Works

Situational Leadership is effective because it recognizes that leadership is not **one-size-fits-all**. It works because:

- It is **adaptive** to different levels of competence and motivation.

- It helps leaders **develop** their team members by gradually reducing dependency.

- It **improves engagement and motivation** by providing the right level of support.

- It aligns with **real-world leadership challenges**, where different employees require different levels of guidance.

How It Works

The process of applying Situational Leadership involves:

1. **Assessing Readiness** – Determining the competence and commitment level of team members.

2. **Selecting the Appropriate Leadership Style** – Choosing between Telling, Selling, Participating, or Delegating based on the team's needs.

3. **Adapting Over Time** – As employees grow in competence and confidence, leaders shift their style accordingly.

Unlike rigid leadership models, SLT promotes continuous **evaluation and adjustment**, ensuring leaders remain responsive to their team's development.

Application

Situational Leadership is widely used in:

- **Corporate Leadership** – Managers adjust their approach based on employees' skills and confidence levels.

- **Education & Training** – Teachers use different methods to support students at varying levels of understanding.

- **Sports Coaching** – Coaches adapt their guidance based on player experience and motivation.

- **Project Management** – Leaders tailor their supervision depending on project complexity and team capability.

Key Insights

1. **Leadership is Dynamic** – No single leadership style is best; leaders must adapt to the situation.

2. **Readiness Determines Leadership Style** – A team's competence and motivation dictate whether a leader should be directive or supportive.

3. **Situational Leadership Enhances Development** – By shifting styles, leaders help individuals grow into high-performing, independent contributors.

4. **Flexibility is Key to Leadership Success** – The best leaders are those who continuously adjust their approach based on the needs of their people.

Situational Leadership remains one of the most **practical and widely used** leadership models today, helping leaders guide their teams effectively in dynamic and ever-changing environments.

6. Path-Goal Theory

Path-Goal Theory of Leadership: A Breakdown

Theory

The **Path-Goal Theory of Leadership**, developed by **Robert House in 1971**, suggests that a leader's primary role is to **clear the path** for their team to achieve goals by providing direction, support, and motivation. The theory is based on the **Expectancy Theory of Motivation**, which states that individuals are more likely to be motivated when they believe their effort will lead to high performance and desirable rewards.

The **core idea** behind Path-Goal Theory is that leaders should adapt their leadership style based on the needs of their followers and the work environment to enhance productivity and job satisfaction.

The model outlines four **leadership styles**, which leaders use depending on the situation:

1. **Directive Leadership** – Leaders provide clear instructions, expectations, and guidance.

    o Best for unstructured tasks or inexperienced employees who need direction.

2. **Supportive Leadership** – Leaders focus on relationships, well-being, and providing a friendly work environment.

- Effective for stressful or repetitive tasks where morale needs boosting.

3. **Participative Leadership** – Leaders involve employees in decision-making and encourage input.

   - Useful when employees are capable but need motivation and engagement.

4. **Achievement-Oriented Leadership** – Leaders set challenging goals and expect high performance.

   - Ideal for highly competent and motivated employees who thrive under pressure.

The leader's **main role** is to remove obstacles (the "path") that hinder progress and ensure that employees see a clear link between effort and rewards (the "goal").

Example

A strong example of Path-Goal Theory in action is **Elon Musk**, CEO of Tesla and SpaceX. Musk often adopts an **Achievement-Oriented** leadership style, pushing teams to innovate and meet ambitious goals (e.g., launching reusable rockets). However, he also uses **Directive Leadership** in technical areas where precise instructions are required.

Another example is **Mary Barra**, CEO of General Motors. During times of transformation, she has used a **Participative Leadership** approach, engaging employees in decision-making to drive cultural change. Simultaneously, she applies a **Supportive Leadership** style to create an inclusive and motivating work environment.

Why It Works

Path-Goal Theory works because it:

- **Recognizes employee needs** – Different employees require different types of support and motivation.

- **Provides flexibility** – Leaders adjust their approach based on the situation and team dynamics.

- **Increases motivation and performance** – Employees work harder when they see a clear connection between effort and rewards.

- **Reduces workplace obstacles** – Leaders take proactive steps to remove barriers that hinder productivity.

By adapting leadership styles, managers can create the best conditions for success, ensuring their team stays engaged and productive.

How It Works

The Path-Goal Theory follows a **four-step approach**:

1. **Assess the Situation** – Identify employee characteristics (experience, motivation) and task demands (structured vs. unstructured work).

2. **Choose the Right Leadership Style** – Select **Directive, Supportive, Participative, or**

Achievement-Oriented leadership based on what the team needs.

3. **Remove Obstacles** – Identify and eliminate barriers that prevent employees from succeeding (e.g., lack of resources, unclear goals).

4. **Provide Motivation & Rewards** – Ensure employees see that their effort leads to rewards, increasing their commitment and performance.

This **situational approach** ensures that leadership is always relevant and responsive to team dynamics.

Application

Path-Goal Theory is widely used in:

- **Corporate Leadership** – Managers adapt their style to drive employee engagement and productivity.

- **Project Management** – Leaders help teams navigate obstacles and ensure goals are met.

- **Sales & Customer Service** – Sales managers use **Achievement-Oriented Leadership** to motivate high performance.

- **Education & Coaching** – Teachers and coaches use **Supportive Leadership** to boost confidence and learning outcomes.

Key Insights

1. **Leadership is Flexible** – The best leaders adjust their style to match employee needs and workplace conditions.

2. **Removing Barriers is Key** – Leaders should focus on clearing obstacles to help their team succeed.

3. **Motivation Drives Performance** – Employees perform better when they see that effort leads to rewards.

4. **Different Situations Require Different Styles** – A one-size-fits-all approach to leadership does not work; adaptability is essential.

The Path-Goal Theory remains **highly relevant** in today's workplaces, emphasizing that effective leaders **guide, support, and empower** their teams to achieve success.

7. Transactional Leadership

Transactional Leadership: A Breakdown

Theory

Transactional Leadership is a leadership style that focuses on **structure, supervision, and performance**. Rooted in the idea that leadership is based on a system of rewards and punishments, this theory is often associated with **Max Weber** and later expanded by **Bernard Bass** in the 20th century.

Transactional leaders operate within **established systems and processes**, using a clear chain of command and well-defined roles to ensure efficiency. They emphasize **compliance, rules, and task completion**, rewarding employees for meeting expectations and disciplining those who do not.

The core principles of **Transactional Leadership** include:

1. **Clear Expectations** – Leaders define specific goals, processes, and performance standards.

2. **Rewards & Punishments** – Employees are rewarded (e.g., bonuses, recognition) for meeting goals and face consequences (e.g., reprimands, demotions) for underperformance.

3. **Task-Focused Approach** – Leadership is about maintaining order and efficiency rather than fostering creativity or personal development.

4. **Short-Term Goals** – Focus is on achieving immediate objectives rather than long-term vision or innovation.

This model is **hierarchical and directive**, making it highly effective in structured environments that require consistency and control.

Example

A classic example of **Transactional Leadership** is **Jeff Bezos** during Amazon's early years. Bezos implemented a highly structured work environment with strict performance expectations and a strong focus on operational efficiency. Employees were monitored based on key performance indicators (KPIs), and those who met or exceeded targets were rewarded, while underperformance had consequences.

Another example is **military leadership**, where commanders use a clear chain of command and disciplined structure to ensure tasks are completed effectively. Military leaders reward soldiers for following orders and impose penalties for disobedience, aligning perfectly with transactional leadership principles.

Why It Works

Transactional Leadership is effective because it:

- **Creates Stability & Consistency** – By setting clear expectations, employees know what is required of them, reducing ambiguity.

- **Enhances Productivity** – Employees are motivated by tangible rewards, leading to high efficiency.

- **Ensures Compliance & Control** – A structured approach minimizes deviations from procedures, which is crucial in industries like finance, healthcare, and manufacturing.

- **Works Well in Crisis Situations** – In high-pressure environments (e.g., military, emergency services), a directive leadership style ensures rapid decision-making and execution.

How It Works

Transactional Leadership operates through a structured process:

1. **Setting Goals & Expectations** – Leaders define clear performance targets and job responsibilities.

2. **Monitoring Performance** – Employees' work is continuously evaluated based on predefined standards.

3. **Implementing Rewards & Punishments** – Rewards (bonuses, promotions) are given for achieving goals, while failures result in consequences (warnings, demotions).

4. **Maintaining Order & Efficiency** – Leaders ensure that employees follow protocols and complete tasks without deviation.

This model **works best in stable environments** where innovation is less critical than maintaining efficiency and order.

Application

Transactional Leadership is commonly applied in:

- **Corporate Management** – Large organizations use it to maintain efficiency and meet short-term objectives.

- **Military & Law Enforcement** – A command-and-control approach ensures discipline and order.

- **Manufacturing & Production** – Factories rely on strict procedures and performance-based rewards.

- **Customer Service & Sales** – Employees are motivated through commission-based incentives and performance metrics.

Key Insights

1. **Leadership is Based on Structure & Rewards** – Transactional leaders focus on efficiency, clear goals, and performance-based incentives.

2. **Works Best in Stable, Hierarchical Organizations** – This model thrives in environments where tasks are routine and require precision.

3. **Less Focus on Creativity & Innovation** – Unlike Transformational Leadership, which fosters vision

and motivation, Transactional Leadership prioritizes control and short-term results.

4. **Ideal for High-Risk or Performance-Driven Fields** – Industries that require strict compliance (e.g., finance, healthcare, military) benefit the most from this approach.

While **Transactional Leadership is not ideal for innovation-driven industries**, it remains a **highly effective model** for organizations that need **structure, efficiency, and accountability** to drive success.

8. Transformational Leadership

Transformational Leadership: A Breakdown

Theory

Transformational Leadership is a leadership model that emphasizes **inspiring, motivating, and empowering** followers to exceed expectations and achieve long-term success. Introduced by **James MacGregor Burns** in 1978 and later expanded by **Bernard Bass**, this theory contrasts with **Transactional Leadership**, which focuses on maintaining structure and order through rewards and punishments.

Transformational leaders go beyond managing day-to-day tasks; they create a **vision**, instil **purpose**, and encourage innovation and personal growth. They build strong emotional connections with their teams, fostering trust and motivation.

The four key components of **Transformational Leadership** are:

1. **Idealized Influence (Role Model)** – Leaders act with integrity, setting an example that inspires respect and trust.

2. **Inspirational Motivation (Vision & Purpose)** – Leaders articulate a compelling vision that excites and motivates their team.

3. **Intellectual Stimulation (Encouraging Innovation)** – Leaders challenge assumptions, encourage problem-solving, and promote creative thinking.

4. **Individualized Consideration (Personal Development)** – Leaders mentor and support employees, helping them reach their full potential.

This leadership style **creates engaged, self-motivated teams** that strive for excellence and continuous improvement.

Example

One of the best examples of **Transformational Leadership** is **Steve Jobs**, co-founder of Apple. Jobs had a powerful vision for innovation and excellence, inspiring employees to push creative boundaries. He challenged conventional thinking, encouraged intellectual stimulation, and fostered a company culture driven by passion and innovation.

Another example is **Oprah Winfrey**, who has inspired millions through her leadership in media and philanthropy. Her ability to connect with people, share a compelling vision, and empower others has made her a global transformational leader.

Why It Works

Transformational Leadership works because it:

- **Increases Employee Engagement** – People feel inspired and motivated when they believe in a larger purpose.

- **Encourages Innovation** – By fostering intellectual stimulation, employees feel empowered to think outside the box.

- **Builds Strong Relationships** – Individualized support strengthens trust and loyalty.

- **Drives Long-Term Success** – Organizations that adopt transformational leadership often achieve sustained growth and adaptability.

Studies show that transformational leaders enhance **job satisfaction, team performance, and organizational commitment**, making it one of the most effective leadership styles.

How It Works

Transformational Leadership follows these steps:

1. **Define a Vision** – Leaders establish a compelling and meaningful purpose.

2. **Inspire & Communicate** – Leaders use storytelling and communication to share their vision.

3. **Encourage Innovation** – Employees are given the freedom and support to develop creative solutions.

4. **Mentor & Develop People** – Leaders provide coaching, feedback, and opportunities for professional growth.

This model is **adaptive and people-cantered**, making it highly effective in dynamic industries.

Application

Transformational Leadership is widely applied in:

- **Business & Entrepreneurship** – CEOs drive innovation and inspire teams to disrupt industries.

- **Education & Academia** – Teachers and professors encourage critical thinking and personal growth.

- **Politics & Social Movements** – Leaders like Martin Luther King Jr. have used this model to inspire change.

- **Technology & Startups** – Leaders foster innovation in fast-changing industries.

Key Insights

1. **Leaders Inspire, Not Just Manage** – The focus is on vision, passion, and motivation rather than control.

2. **Encourages Long-Term Growth** – Transformational leadership builds innovative and adaptable organizations.

3. **Empowers Individuals** – By recognizing employees' potential, leaders create high-performing teams.

4. **Requires Emotional Intelligence** – Leaders must be self-aware, empathetic, and excellent communicators.

Transformational Leadership is one of the **most effective leadership styles**, creating highly engaged, forward-thinking teams that drive innovation and long-term success.

9. Laissez-Faire Leadership

Laissez-Faire Leadership: A Breakdown

Theory

Laissez-Faire Leadership is a **hands-off leadership style** where leaders provide minimal direction and allow employees to make decisions independently. The term **"laissez-faire"** is French for **"let it be"**, emphasizing autonomy and self-regulation.

This leadership model is characterized by:

- **Minimal supervision** – Leaders provide resources but do not closely monitor progress.

- **High autonomy** – Employees have the freedom to set their own goals and strategies.

- **Limited intervention** – Leaders step in only when necessary or requested.

Laissez-Faire Leadership is most effective in environments where employees are **highly skilled, self-motivated, and experienced**, allowing them to work independently without constant guidance.

The concept was first identified by **Kurt Lewin** in his 1939 study on leadership styles. He found that Laissez-Faire leaders had the least involvement in decision-making, which could lead to either **high productivity (if employees were competent)** or **chaos (if they lacked direction).**

Example

A notable example of **Laissez-Faire Leadership** is **Warren Buffett**, CEO of Berkshire Hathaway. Buffett trusts his managers to run their businesses independently, stepping in only when critical decisions are needed. This approach allows highly capable executives to operate without micromanagement, fostering innovation and accountability.

Another example is **Google's early work culture**, where employees were given **"20% time"** to pursue passion projects without direct oversight. This approach led to innovations like Gmail and Google Maps, demonstrating the power of autonomy in creative environments.

Why It Works

Laissez-Faire Leadership works because it:

- **Encourages innovation** – Employees have the freedom to experiment and develop creative solutions.

- **Increases job satisfaction** – Autonomy leads to higher engagement and motivation among skilled workers.

- **Fosters accountability** – Employees take ownership of their work and decisions.

- **Reduces bureaucracy** – Fewer layers of management speed up decision-making.

Studies show that this leadership style **enhances productivity in knowledge-based industries** where employees are experts in their field. However, it can fail in environments where employees lack experience or need clear direction.

How It Works

Laissez-Faire Leadership operates through:

1. **Delegation** – Leaders assign tasks but provide minimal guidance.

2. **Trust & Empowerment** – Employees are given full authority over their work.

3. **Resource Provision** – Leaders ensure teams have the tools they need but do not interfere.

4. **Periodic Check-ins** – Instead of daily oversight, leaders step in only when necessary.

This leadership model is **most effective in high-performing teams** but can lead to disorganization if used in the wrong setting.

Application

Laissez-Faire Leadership is widely used in:

- **Technology & Innovation** – Companies like Google and Tesla encourage independent thinking.

- **Research & Development** – Scientists and engineers thrive with minimal restrictions.

- **Creative Industries** – Artists, designers, and writers work best with full autonomy.

- **Startups & Entrepreneurship** – Founders often allow teams to take ownership of projects.

Key Insights

1. **Best for Skilled & Self-Motivated Teams** – Works well when employees have expertise and require little supervision.

2. **Encourages Innovation & Creativity** – Autonomy leads to groundbreaking ideas and problem-solving.

3. **Not Suitable for Every Workplace** – Inexperienced or unmotivated teams may struggle without clear direction.

4. **Leaders Must Still Provide Support** – While hands-off, leaders must ensure resources and occasional guidance are available.

Laissez-Faire Leadership is **powerful in the right context** but requires **self-disciplined, capable teams** to be truly effective.

10. Autocratic Leadership

Autocratic Leadership: A Breakdown

Theory

Autocratic Leadership is a leadership style where a single leader holds absolute control over decision-making, with little to no input from team members. Also known as **authoritarian leadership**, this model is characterized by **centralized power, strict rules, and direct supervision**.

Autocratic leaders:

- Make **unilateral decisions** without consulting their team.

- Expect **strict compliance** with rules and procedures.

- Maintain **clear hierarchical authority**, leaving little room for employee autonomy.

- Provide **structured guidance** and close supervision.

This leadership approach has been widely studied since **Kurt Lewin's** 1939 research on leadership styles. He found that autocratic leadership fosters **high efficiency** in situations requiring control but can lead to **low employee morale** in less structured environments.

Autocratic leadership is best suited for situations where:

- **Quick decision-making is crucial.**

- **Strict compliance with policies is required.**

- **The leader possesses superior knowledge or expertise.**

While often criticized for being rigid, autocratic leadership can be effective when applied in the right context.

Example

A classic example of **Autocratic Leadership** is **Steve Jobs**, the co-founder of Apple. Known for his perfectionism and demanding leadership style, Jobs made key product decisions himself, set strict performance standards, and expected his team to follow his vision without debate. His authoritarian approach led to breakthrough innovations like the iPhone and MacBook, showcasing how this leadership style can drive success when paired with expertise and vision.

Another example is **military leadership**, where commanding officers must make fast, high-stakes decisions without consulting subordinates. In these environments, quick, decisive leadership is critical for maintaining order and achieving mission success.

Why It Works

Autocratic Leadership is effective because it:

- **Enables Quick Decision-Making** – With a single decision-maker, responses to crises or urgent situations are immediate.

- **Creates Clear Direction & Structure** – Employees know exactly what is expected of them.

- **Ensures Consistency & Compliance** – In regulated industries (e.g., healthcare, military, finance), strict adherence to rules is necessary.

- **Works Well with Inexperienced Teams** – Employees who lack knowledge or confidence benefit from strong guidance.

However, this leadership style can be demotivating in creative or highly skilled workplaces, where employees value autonomy and innovation.

How It Works

Autocratic Leadership operates through:

1. **Strict Hierarchical Structure** – The leader holds top-down control, with little delegation.

2. **Decision-Making Without Consultation** – The leader relies on their own expertise to make quick, firm decisions.

3. **Close Supervision & Monitoring** – Employees follow detailed instructions with limited independence.

4. **Clear Rules & Expectations** – Tasks and goals are predefined, minimizing ambiguity.

This model **thrives in high-pressure environments** but requires balance to avoid excessive control and resistance from employees.

Application

Autocratic Leadership is commonly applied in:

- **Military & Law Enforcement** – Fast, authoritative decisions are necessary for success.

- **Manufacturing & Construction** – Strict processes ensure safety and efficiency.

- **Crisis Management** – Leaders must take immediate control to navigate emergencies.

- **Large Corporations with Bureaucratic Structures** – Ensures compliance with strict regulations.

Key Insights

1. **Best for High-Stakes or High-Control Environments** – This leadership style excels in situations requiring **precision, order, and discipline**.

2. **Can Increase Efficiency but Reduce Morale** – While autocratic leadership ensures consistency, **it can stifle creativity and motivation**.

3. **Requires a Skilled Leader** – If the leader lacks expertise or vision, **their decisions can be detrimental** to the organization.

4. **Needs Balance to Avoid Resistance** – Effective autocratic leaders must **know when to involve employees** in decision-making to maintain engagement.

While **Autocratic Leadership is not ideal for every situation**, it remains an **essential leadership model** in structured, high-stakes, or compliance-driven industries where strong control is necessary.

Modern Leadership Theories

11. Servant Leadership (Robert Greenleaf)

Servant Leadership: A Breakdown

Theory

Servant Leadership is a leadership model that prioritizes **serving others first**, rather than exercising power or authority. Developed by **Robert Greenleaf** in 1970, this theory suggests that **the best leaders are servants first**, meaning they focus on the **growth, well-being, and success of their team** before their own ambitions.

Unlike traditional leadership models that emphasize hierarchy and control, **Servant Leadership** is based on:

- **Empathy and active listening** – Leaders understand the needs of their team members.

- **Empowerment and development** – They help employees reach their full potential.

- **Community building** – The focus is on collaboration rather than individual power.

- **Ethical leadership** – Decision-making is guided by integrity, fairness, and trust.

Servant leaders **inspire loyalty, trust, and commitment** by ensuring their team members feel valued and supported. This leadership model is **highly people-cantered**, making it effective in environments where collaboration, innovation, and employee engagement are crucial.

Example

One of the best examples of **Servant Leadership** is **Herb Kelleher**, co-founder and former CEO of Southwest Airlines. Kelleher believed that **employees come first**, arguing that if workers are treated well, they will provide excellent customer service, ultimately benefiting the company. His leadership style led to a highly engaged workforce, a strong company culture, and long-term success.

Another example is **Mahatma Gandhi**, who led India's independence movement through **selfless service, non-violence, and moral leadership**. He put the needs of his people first, showing how Servant Leadership extends beyond business into social and political change.

Why It Works

Servant Leadership works because it:

- **Increases employee engagement** – People feel valued and are more motivated.

- **Builds trust and loyalty** – Employees and followers feel genuinely supported.

- **Encourages long-term success** – A focus on people creates sustainable growth.

- **Fosters a positive work culture** – Ethical leadership leads to high morale and collaboration.

Research shows that Servant Leadership leads to **higher employee satisfaction, lower turnover, and improved organizational performance** because employees feel respected and empowered.

How It Works

Servant Leadership follows a **people-first approach**:

1. **Listening & Empathy** – Leaders actively listen to team members' concerns.

2. **Developing Others** – They mentor and coach employees to help them grow.

3. **Sharing Power** – Decision-making is inclusive, allowing employees to contribute.

4. **Leading by Example** – Leaders demonstrate ethical behaviour and humility.

5. **Creating a Vision** – The leader focuses on the greater good rather than personal gain.

By **serving others first**, leaders **inspire teams to be highly engaged, productive, and innovative**.

Application

Servant Leadership is widely used in:

- **Corporate Leadership** – Companies like Starbucks and Southwest Airlines adopt this model to create strong work cultures.

- **Education & Nonprofits** – Schools and NGOs focus on empowering individuals and communities.

- **Healthcare & Public Services** – Patient-focused leadership improves care and efficiency.

- **Social Movements & Religious Organizations** – Ethical and people-driven leadership is crucial in these areas.

Key Insights

1. **Great Leaders Serve First** – The best leaders prioritize their people, not their own status.

2. **Employee Growth = Organizational Growth** – When employees are supported, the organization thrives.

3. **Trust & Ethics Matter** – Servant Leaders inspire long-term commitment and integrity.

4. **Works Best in Collaborative Cultures** – This model thrives where teamwork, respect, and shared vision are valued.

Servant Leadership remains one of the **most impactful leadership styles**, focusing on **empowering, inspiring, and developing others** for long-term success.

12. Level 5 Leadership (Jim Collins)

Level 5 Leadership: A Breakdown

Theory

Level 5 Leadership, introduced by **Jim Collins** in his book *Good to Great (2001)*, describes the **highest level of leadership capability**. Collins' research found that companies that made the leap from being "good" to "great" were led by **Level 5 Leaders**—executives who combined **personal humility with professional will**.

Unlike traditional leadership models that emphasize charisma, dominance, or control, Level 5 Leadership is based on **selflessness, resilience, and a deep commitment to long-term success**.

Collins identified five levels of leadership, with **Level 5 being the pinnacle**:

1. **Highly Capable Individual** – Possesses skills and knowledge to contribute effectively.

2. **Contributing Team Member** – Works well in a team setting to achieve goals.

3. **Competent Manager** – Organizes people and resources efficiently.

4. **Effective Leader** – Builds commitment to a vision and motivates teams to achieve high performance.

5. **Level 5 Executive** – Combines humility and fierce determination to drive long-term success.

A **Level 5 Leader** is not focused on personal recognition but instead works **selflessly** to ensure the organization's success **beyond their tenure**. They set up **strong successors**, creating sustainable greatness rather than relying on their own presence.

Example

A prime example of **Level 5 Leadership** is **Tim Cook**, CEO of Apple. After taking over from Steve Jobs, Cook did not try to replicate Jobs' high-profile, visionary leadership style. Instead, he **led with humility, focused on operational excellence**, and strengthened Apple's long-term growth strategy. His quiet but determined leadership helped Apple continue its dominance while maintaining ethical and sustainable business practices.

Another example is **Darwin E. Smith**, former CEO of Kimberly-Clark, whom Collins highlights in *Good to Great*. Smith, despite being an unassuming leader, transformed the company into an industry powerhouse by making tough decisions, such as selling paper mills to focus on consumer products like Kleenex and Huggies. His **humble but relentless** approach exemplifies Level 5 Leadership.

Why It Works

Level 5 Leadership works because it:

- **Eliminates Ego-Driven Leadership** – Leaders prioritize the company's success over personal recognition.

- **Ensures Long-Term Growth** – These leaders focus on sustainable, strategic decisions.

- **Builds Strong Teams** – Instead of demanding loyalty, they **develop future leaders**.

- **Creates Resilient Organizations** – Companies thrive even after the leader steps down.

Research shows that Level 5 Leadership **significantly improves organizational performance** by fostering **commitment, accountability, and a culture of excellence**.

How It Works

Level 5 Leadership follows a **dual approach**:

1. **Personal Humility** – Level 5 Leaders:

    o Avoid the spotlight and credit others for success.

    o Accept responsibility for failures and challenges.

    o Focus on **organizational impact** rather than personal gain.

2. **Unwavering Determination** – They:

    o Make bold, strategic decisions for long-term success.

- o Maintain a **relentless commitment** to improvement.

- o Work hard behind the scenes, ensuring lasting impact.

This leadership style fosters **strong, independent organizations** that thrive well beyond a leader's tenure.

Application

Level 5 Leadership is widely applied in:

- **Corporate Leadership** – CEOs focused on **sustainable success** rather than personal fame.

- **Nonprofits & Social Enterprises** – Leaders who prioritize impact over personal status.

- **Government & Public Policy** – Ethical leaders driving long-term change.

- **Startups & Entrepreneurship** – Founders who build **lasting companies**, not just short-term hype.

Key Insights

1. **Great Leaders Are Humble Yet Relentless** – They put the organization first but **drive success with quiet determination**.

2. **Sustainable Growth Requires Selflessness** – Level 5 Leaders build strong foundations **beyond their tenure**.

3. **Success Comes from the Right Mindset** – It's not about power, but about **impact, resilience, and legacy**.

4. **Long-Term Vision Over Short-Term Wins** – Level 5 Leaders **prioritize enduring greatness over quick success**.

Level 5 Leadership remains **one of the most effective leadership models**, proving that **humility and determination** are more powerful than charisma alone.

13. Adaptive Leadership (Ronald Heifetz)

Adaptive Leadership: A Breakdown

Theory

Adaptive Leadership, developed by **Ronald Heifetz** and colleagues at Harvard University, is a leadership model that focuses on navigating complex, changing environments. Unlike traditional leadership models that emphasize authority and stability, **Adaptive Leadership** helps organizations and individuals **adjust to new challenges, uncertainty, and disruptions**.

This model differentiates between:

- **Technical Challenges** – Problems with known solutions that can be solved with existing knowledge and authority.

- **Adaptive Challenges** – Problems that require new learning, experimentation, and shifts in values or behaviours.

Adaptive leaders **do not simply dictate solutions**; they **mobilize people to confront difficult realities**, encouraging innovation, collaboration, and shared responsibility.

The core principles of **Adaptive Leadership** include:

1. **Diagnosing the System** – Identifying adaptive vs. technical challenges.

2. **Regulating Distress** – Managing discomfort while pushing for necessary change.

3. **Giving the Work Back to the People** – Encouraging team ownership over solutions.

4. **Protecting Leadership Voices from Below** – Encouraging diverse perspectives and ideas.

Adaptive Leadership is crucial in industries or situations where **rapid change, disruption, and uncertainty** require leaders to guide transformation rather than enforce rigid solutions.

Example

A strong example of **Adaptive Leadership** is **Satya Nadella**, CEO of Microsoft. When he took over, Microsoft was struggling with innovation and workplace culture. Rather than imposing top-down directives, he encouraged **cultural transformation**, promoted a growth mindset, and shifted Microsoft towards cloud computing. His approach allowed Microsoft to **adapt to market changes and regain industry leadership**.

Another example is **Dr. Anthony Fauci**, who used Adaptive Leadership principles during public health crises, including the COVID-19 pandemic. Given the **uncertain and evolving nature** of the crisis, he **adjusted strategies based on new data**, communicated transparently, and navigated resistance while guiding public health policies.

Why It Works

Adaptive Leadership is effective because it:

- **Encourages Learning & Innovation** – Leaders embrace change and seek new solutions.

- **Builds Resilience** – Organizations and individuals become better at handling uncertainty.

- **Engages Teams in Problem-Solving** – Employees take responsibility, fostering commitment.

- **Creates Lasting Change** – Rather than offering quick fixes, leaders guide **deep transformation**.

This model **thrives in complex, uncertain environments** where traditional leadership approaches fail to address evolving challenges.

How It Works

Adaptive Leadership operates through a structured yet flexible process:

1. **Identify Adaptive Challenges** – Distinguish between technical and adaptive problems.

2. **Create a Safe but Challenging Environment** – Allow teams to feel **safe enough to experiment** but challenged enough to grow.

3. **Empower People to Find Solutions** – Shift responsibility from the leader to the team.

4. **Experiment & Adapt** – Leaders encourage continuous **testing, feedback, and course correction**.

5. **Maintain a Long-Term Perspective** – Focus on sustainable change rather than short-term gains.

Unlike **autocratic or transactional leadership models**, Adaptive Leadership **relies on collaboration, learning, and shared accountability**.

Application

Adaptive Leadership is widely used in:

- **Technology & Business Innovation** – Tech firms like Microsoft and Google thrive by constantly adapting to market changes.

- **Public Policy & Healthcare** – Leaders in government and medicine must navigate shifting regulations and new challenges.

- **Crisis Management** – Organizations facing **disruptive change** need leaders who embrace complexity.

- **Education & Nonprofits** – Schools and social organizations must continuously evolve to meet changing needs.

Key Insights

1. **Leadership is About Adapting, Not Controlling** – The best leaders **navigate uncertainty rather than impose rigid solutions**.

2. **Change Requires Discomfort** – Effective transformation involves **pushing people out of their comfort zones while supporting them**.

3. **Leaders Must Encourage Experimentation** – Instead of providing answers, leaders must **help teams discover solutions**.

4. **Adaptive Leadership is a Continuous Process** – It's not a one-time fix but an **ongoing effort to evolve and improve**.

Adaptive Leadership is one of the **most relevant leadership models** in today's fast-changing world, enabling leaders to **guide organizations through disruption, complexity, and transformation.**

14. Authentic Leadership (Bill George)

Authentic Leadership: A Breakdown

Theory

Authentic Leadership, developed by **Bill George** in his book *Authentic Leadership: Rediscovering the Secrets to Creating Lasting Value (2003)*, is a leadership model that emphasizes **genuine, ethical, and self-aware leadership**. Unlike traditional leadership styles that focus on authority or influence, **Authentic Leadership is built on trust, transparency, and personal integrity**.

Bill George identified five key dimensions of **Authentic Leadership**:

1. **Self-Awareness** – Leaders understand their values, emotions, and motivations.

2. **Relational Transparency** – They openly share thoughts and feelings, fostering trust.

3. **Balanced Processing** – They consider different perspectives before making decisions.

4. **Internalized Moral Perspective** – They act according to strong ethical values rather than external pressures.

5. **Mission-Driven** – They focus on long-term impact rather than short-term gains.

Authentic leaders are **self-reflective, empathetic, and purpose-driven**, ensuring that their leadership **aligns with their values** while inspiring and developing others.

Example

A strong example of **Authentic Leadership** is **Howard Schultz**, the former CEO of Starbucks. Schultz built Starbucks not just as a business but as a company rooted in ethical leadership, employee well-being, and customer experience. He openly shared his personal journey and values, ensuring Starbucks remained **mission-driven, socially responsible, and people-focused**.

Another example is **Oprah Winfrey**, whose leadership in media and philanthropy is guided by authenticity, transparency, and a deep sense of purpose. By being open about her struggles, values, and beliefs, Oprah has built trust and loyalty among her audience and business partners.

Why It Works

Authentic Leadership is effective because it:

- **Builds trust and credibility** – People follow leaders they believe in.

- **Inspires commitment and engagement** – Employees are more motivated when working for a leader who genuinely cares.

- **Fosters ethical decision-making** – Leaders act based on integrity rather than external pressure.

- **Encourages long-term growth** – Sustainable success is prioritized over short-term wins.

Research suggests that **Authentic Leadership improves employee satisfaction, engagement, and loyalty**, making it a powerful leadership approach in **modern, purpose-driven organizations**.

How It Works

Authentic Leadership operates through a structured yet **genuine** approach:

1. **Develop Self-Awareness** – Leaders continuously reflect on their strengths, weaknesses, and motivations.

2. **Live by Core Values** – Decision-making is guided by integrity and ethics.

3. **Be Transparent and Open** – Leaders share their stories, experiences, and challenges to build trust.

4. **Listen and Consider Multiple Perspectives** – They encourage open dialogue and feedback.

5. **Lead with Purpose** – Their leadership is driven by **a clear mission** rather than personal ambition.

This model **creates emotionally intelligent leaders** who **connect deeply with their teams,** fostering loyalty and a strong organizational culture.

Application

Authentic Leadership is widely applied in:

- **Corporate Leadership** – Ethical CEOs who prioritize employee well-being and mission-driven goals.

- **Nonprofits & Social Enterprises** – Leaders who focus on long-term impact and social responsibility.

- **Media & Public Influence** – Figures like Oprah Winfrey who build trust through transparency.

- **Healthcare & Education** – Sectors where leadership must be **trustworthy, mission-driven, and compassionate**.

Key Insights

1. **Authenticity Builds Influence** – True leadership comes from **genuine self-awareness and ethical action**.

2. **Trust is the Foundation of Leadership** – Transparency and honesty foster loyalty.

3. **Values Drive Decision-Making** – Authentic leaders stay true to **internal principles, not external pressures**.

4. **Sustainable Success Requires Purpose** – Companies and teams thrive when leadership is **mission-driven** rather than profit-driven.

Authentic Leadership is **one of the most impactful leadership models**, proving that **integrity, transparency, and self-awareness are key to lasting influence and success.**

15. Ethical Leadership

Ethical Leadership: A Breakdown

Theory

Ethical Leadership is a leadership approach cantered on **morality, integrity, fairness, and social responsibility**. Ethical leaders prioritize doing what is right over personal gain, fostering an environment of **trust, accountability, and transparency** within their organizations.

Ethical Leadership is guided by the belief that leaders should:

1. **Lead by Example** – Demonstrate ethical behaviour in all decisions and actions.

2. **Promote Fairness & Justice** – Treat all employees and stakeholders with honesty and respect.

3. **Encourage Ethical Decision-Making** – Create a culture where integrity is valued.

4. **Hold Themselves & Others Accountable** – Take responsibility for both successes and failures.

5. **Prioritize the Greater Good** – Focus on **long-term impact** rather than short-term profits.

This model is rooted in **virtue ethics, deontology, and consequentialism**, emphasizing **moral responsibility and the social impact** of leadership decisions. Ethical

Leadership is essential in environments where trust, reputation, and values play a crucial role in success.

Example

A powerful example of **Ethical Leadership** is **Paul Polman**, the former CEO of Unilever. Polman transformed Unilever's business strategy by focusing on **sustainability, corporate social responsibility, and ethical business practices**. Instead of prioritizing short-term shareholder profits, he focused on **long-term environmental and social impact**, setting new industry standards for ethical leadership.

Another example is **Nelson Mandela**, who led South Africa through its transition from apartheid with **forgiveness, integrity, and moral conviction**. Rather than seeking personal revenge, Mandela prioritized reconciliation and ethical governance, demonstrating the power of ethical leadership in political transformation.

Why It Works

Ethical Leadership is effective because it:

- **Builds Trust & Credibility** – Employees and stakeholders respect leaders who act with integrity.

- **Enhances Employee Engagement** – People feel motivated and loyal when they work for a leader who upholds ethical values.

- **Reduces Corruption & Misconduct** – A culture of accountability discourages unethical behaviour.

- **Fosters Long-Term Success** – Companies with strong ethical leadership often have **higher sustainability and brand loyalty**.

Studies show that organizations with ethical leadership experience **higher employee satisfaction, lower turnover, and better stakeholder relationships**.

How It Works

Ethical Leadership is practiced through:

1. **Defining Core Values** – Establishing a clear moral code for decision-making.

2. **Demonstrating Integrity** – Leading by example and maintaining transparency.

3. **Encouraging Ethical Behaviour** – Rewarding integrity and addressing unethical conduct.

4. **Making Fair & Just Decisions** – Ensuring all stakeholders are treated with fairness.

5. **Balancing Profit with Responsibility** – Prioritizing social impact alongside financial success.

This approach fosters a **values-driven culture**, ensuring that ethical considerations remain at the heart of business and leadership decisions.

Application

Ethical Leadership is widely applied in:

- **Corporate Governance** – CEOs and executives fostering transparency and accountability.

- **Public Service & Government** – Leaders making decisions that serve society ethically.

- **Nonprofits & Social Enterprises** – Organizations prioritizing ethical missions over profits.

- **Healthcare & Education** – Sectors where ethical responsibility is critical.

Key Insights

1. **Integrity & Trust Define Ethical Leaders** – Leadership is about doing what's right, not just what's profitable.

2. **Ethical Leaders Inspire Loyalty & Commitment** – Employees and stakeholders respect leaders who prioritize fairness.

3. **Accountability is Crucial** – Ethical leaders **take responsibility** for both successes and failures.

4. **Ethical Leadership Drives Long-Term Success** – Companies and organizations that embrace ethical leadership are more sustainable and respected.

Ethical Leadership remains **one of the most impactful leadership models**, proving that **leading with integrity fosters trust, success, and long-term value.**

16. Agile Leadership

Agile Leadership: A Breakdown

Theory

Agile Leadership is a modern leadership model that emphasizes **flexibility, collaboration, adaptability, and continuous learning**. Rooted in **Agile methodologies**, which originated in software development, Agile Leadership has expanded into a broader framework applicable across industries.

The core idea of Agile Leadership is that traditional, hierarchical leadership approaches **fail in fast-changing environments**. Instead, Agile Leaders:

1. **Embrace Change** – They see uncertainty as an opportunity rather than a threat.

2. **Empower Teams** – They encourage autonomy and decentralize decision-making.

3. **Encourage Experimentation** – They promote iterative improvements and innovation.

4. **Focus on Customer Value** – Decisions are made based on delivering maximum value.

5. **Lead with Transparency & Collaboration** – Open communication fosters trust and agility.

Agile Leadership is particularly **valuable in volatile, uncertain, complex, and ambiguous (VUCA) environments**, where rapid adaptation is critical.

Example

A strong example of **Agile Leadership** is **Elon Musk**, CEO of Tesla and SpaceX. Musk embraces **rapid innovation cycles, decentralizes decision-making, and iterates continuously**, allowing his companies to outpace traditional competitors. For example, SpaceX's reusable rocket technology was achieved through **continuous testing, learning, and iteration**, aligning with Agile principles.

Another example is **Satya Nadella**, CEO of Microsoft. Under his leadership, Microsoft shifted from a rigid, siloed organization to a more **collaborative, innovative, and adaptable company**, embracing Agile methodologies in product development and company culture.

Why It Works

Agile Leadership is effective because it:

- **Enhances Adaptability** – Organizations can respond quickly to market changes.

- **Empowers Employees** – Team members take ownership, increasing engagement.

- **Promotes Innovation** – Iterative processes encourage constant improvement.

- **Improves Decision-Making** – Decentralized decision-making speeds up responses.

- **Creates Resilient Organizations** – Businesses become more sustainable in dynamic markets.

Studies show that companies practicing Agile Leadership outperform competitors in **growth, innovation, and employee engagement**, making it a powerful leadership model in today's fast-paced world.

How It Works

Agile Leadership operates through several key principles:

1. **Adopting a Growth Mindset** – Leaders encourage learning and adaptation.

2. **Empowering Self-Organizing Teams** – Employees have the freedom to make decisions.

3. **Iterative Decision-Making** – Leaders focus on quick, incremental improvements.

4. **Prioritizing Customer & Employee Feedback** – Continuous feedback loops improve outcomes.

5. **Encouraging Open Communication** – Transparency fosters collaboration and trust.

Unlike traditional top-down leadership, Agile Leaders **distribute authority, encourage innovation, and embrace continuous change**.

Application

Agile Leadership is widely applied in:

- **Technology & Startups** – Fast-paced environments require adaptability.

- **Corporate Transformation** – Large organizations adopt Agile to stay competitive.

- **Product Development** – Agile methodologies drive faster, customer-focused innovation.

- **Healthcare & Crisis Management** – Rapid adaptation is crucial in high-stakes fields.

Key Insights

1. **Agility is a Mindset, Not Just a Process** – True Agile Leaders **embrace change and uncertainty**.

2. **Empowerment Drives Innovation** – Decentralized leadership leads to **faster decision-making and better solutions**.

3. **Continuous Learning is Essential** – Agile Leaders **prioritize feedback, iteration, and adaptability**.

4. **Agile Leadership Fosters Long-Term Success** – Organizations that **embrace agility remain resilient and competitive** in dynamic markets.

Agile Leadership is **one of the most relevant leadership models today**, enabling leaders and organizations to **thrive in unpredictable, fast-changing environments**.

17. Charismatic Leadership

Charismatic Leadership: A Breakdown

Theory

Charismatic Leadership is a leadership style where leaders inspire and influence followers through their **personal charm, vision, and strong communication skills**. Unlike traditional leadership models that focus on structure or processes, **Charismatic Leadership relies on a leader's personality, confidence, and ability to emotionally connect with their team**.

Charismatic leaders often possess:

1. **A Compelling Vision** – They articulate a bold, inspiring future.

2. **Strong Communication Skills** – They captivate audiences and inspire action.

3. **Confidence & Presence** – Their energy and passion command attention.

4. **Emotional Connection** – They forge deep relationships with followers.

5. **Risk-Taking & Innovation** – They challenge the status quo and push boundaries.

Sociologist **Max Weber** first introduced **Charismatic Authority**, distinguishing it from **traditional and bureaucratic leadership**. Modern scholars like **Robert**

House expanded the concept, emphasizing that **charisma alone is not enough**—it must be paired with ethical leadership and sound decision-making.

Example

A well-known example of **Charismatic Leadership** is **Dr. Martin Luther King Jr.** His ability to **deliver powerful speeches, connect emotionally with people, and inspire social change** made him one of history's most influential leaders. His famous *"I Have a Dream"* speech united millions around the civil rights movement, demonstrating the power of **charisma in leadership**.

Another example is **Elon Musk**, who has built a global following through his **bold vision for the future, innovative mindset, and engaging presence**. Musk's charisma helps attract top talent, secure investor confidence, and drive revolutionary projects in space exploration (SpaceX) and electric vehicles (Tesla).

Why It Works

Charismatic Leadership is effective because it:

- **Inspires & Motivates Teams** – Employees and followers feel emotionally connected to the leader's vision.

- **Builds Strong Loyalty & Commitment** – People believe in the leader and their cause, driving dedication.

- **Encourages Innovation & Risk-Taking** – Charismatic leaders push boundaries and inspire bold action.

- **Creates a Unifying Vision** – Helps teams or organizations rally around a common goal.

Research shows that charismatic leaders **increase team morale, engagement, and performance**, making this leadership style particularly effective in **challenging or transformational environments**.

How It Works

Charismatic Leadership follows several key principles:

1. **Developing a Powerful Vision** – The leader clearly communicates a **bold, inspiring future**.

2. **Building Emotional Connections** – They engage with people on a personal, emotional level.

3. **Leading with Passion & Confidence** – Their enthusiasm inspires action and commitment.

4. **Challenging the Status Quo** – They encourage risk-taking and new ideas.

5. **Leveraging Storytelling & Communication** – They use compelling narratives to **rally support** and influence followers.

Unlike **transactional leaders**, who focus on systems and rewards, charismatic leaders **inspire action through influence and vision**.

Application

Charismatic Leadership is widely applied in:

- **Politics & Social Movements** – Leaders like **Barack Obama and Nelson Mandela** inspired change through vision and charisma.

- **Entrepreneurship & Business** – Visionary leaders like **Steve Jobs and Richard Branson** used charisma to build strong brands.

- **Motivational Speaking & Public Influence** – Figures like **Tony Robbins** leverage charisma to inspire millions.

- **Crisis & Change Management** – Charismatic leaders can **unify and mobilize teams** in times of uncertainty.

Key Insights

1. **Charisma Alone is Not Enough** – It must be backed by **ethical decision-making and real results**.

2. **Emotional Connection Drives Influence** – People follow leaders they **connect with personally**.

3. **A Clear Vision is Essential** – Charismatic leaders must define and **consistently communicate their mission**.

4. **Charismatic Leadership is Powerful, But Risky** – If misused, it can lead to **over-dependence on the leader or unethical behaviour** (e.g., dictatorships).

Charismatic Leadership is **one of the most influential leadership styles**, capable of **driving movements, businesses, and innovations**, but it requires **responsibility, authenticity, and ethical leadership** to create lasting success.

18. Resonant Leadership

Resonant Leadership: A Breakdown

Theory

Resonant Leadership, introduced by **Richard Boyatzis and Annie McKee** in their book *Resonant Leadership (2005)*, is a leadership model that focuses on **emotional intelligence, mindfulness, and positive relationships** to create lasting impact. This leadership style is based on the idea that **leaders who connect deeply with their teams create an environment of trust, engagement, and high performance**.

Unlike traditional leadership styles that focus purely on decision-making or authority, **Resonant Leadership prioritizes emotional connection and well-being**. It revolves around the concept of **resonance**, meaning leaders **vibrate emotionally** with their teams, fostering positivity and commitment.

The key components of **Resonant Leadership** include:

1. **Emotional Intelligence (EI)** – Leaders understand and manage their emotions while empathizing with others.

2. **Mindfulness** – They are self-aware and present, making thoughtful decisions.

3. **Hope & Optimism** – They inspire others by focusing on possibilities and growth.

4. **Compassion** – They genuinely care about the well-being of their teams.

Resonant leaders **create positive workplace cultures, motivate employees, and drive sustainable success by maintaining strong emotional connections with their people.**

Example

A well-known example of **Resonant Leadership** is **Jacinda Ardern**, former Prime Minister of New Zealand. Her **empathetic and emotionally intelligent leadership** was evident during the Christchurch mosque attacks and the COVID-19 pandemic. She communicated with **authenticity, compassion, and resilience**, building trust and unity among citizens.

Another example is **Satya Nadella**, CEO of Microsoft. Since taking over leadership, Nadella has fostered **a culture of collaboration, emotional intelligence, and innovation**, shifting Microsoft's workplace culture from rigid and competitive to **empathetic and inclusive**. His leadership has **boosted employee morale and corporate performance**.

Why It Works

Resonant Leadership is effective because it:

- **Enhances Employee Engagement** – Employees feel valued, leading to higher productivity.

- **Builds Trust & Loyalty** – Teams connect with leaders who show genuine care.

- **Reduces Burnout & Stress** – Mindfulness and emotional intelligence create a healthier work environment.

- **Encourages Creativity & Collaboration** – Positive emotional environments drive innovation.

Studies show that emotionally intelligent leaders create **more motivated, productive, and resilient organizations**, making Resonant Leadership highly effective in modern workplaces.

How It Works

Resonant Leadership follows a structured yet **emotionally-driven approach**:

1. **Cultivating Emotional Intelligence** – Leaders develop self-awareness and empathy.

2. **Practicing Mindfulness** – They remain fully present and thoughtful in interactions.

3. **Inspiring Hope & Optimism** – They create a vision that motivates and uplifts.

4. **Leading with Compassion** – They build relationships based on trust and care.

5. **Sustaining Positive Energy** – Leaders manage their emotions to **avoid burnout and maintain resonance with their teams.**

Unlike **authoritarian or transactional leaders, resonant leaders prioritize human connection, well-being, and emotional alignment.**

Application

Resonant Leadership is widely applied in:

- **Corporate Leadership** – CEOs fostering positive workplace cultures.

- **Healthcare & Education** – Sectors where emotional intelligence is crucial for leadership.

- **Crisis & Change Management** – Leaders maintaining emotional stability during uncertainty.

- **Team Development & Coaching** – Building high-trust, engaged teams.

Key Insights

1. **Emotional Intelligence is a Leadership Superpower** – Leaders who understand emotions **build stronger, more engaged teams.**

2. **Mindfulness Prevents Burnout** – Leaders who are **self-aware and present** create healthier work environments.

3. **Resonance Drives Motivation & Success** – Employees perform better when they feel connected to their leaders.

4. **Sustainable Leadership Requires Emotional Alignment** – Leaders must **balance their own energy and well-being** to lead effectively.

Resonant Leadership is one of the **most impactful leadership models**, proving that **empathy, emotional intelligence, and connection are essential for building engaged, high-performing organizations**.

19. Quiet Leadership

Quiet Leadership: A Breakdown

Theory

Quiet Leadership is a leadership model that challenges the traditional notion that leaders must be loud, dominant, or highly charismatic to be effective. Instead, **Quiet Leaders lead through thoughtful actions, deep listening, and strategic influence rather than commanding authority**.

This concept has been explored in **David Rock's book *Quiet Leadership* (2006)** and overlaps with the ideas presented in **Susan Cain's *Quiet: The Power of Introverts in a World That Can't Stop Talking* (2012)**. The core belief of **Quiet Leadership** is that great leaders can be **reserved, reflective, and supportive** while still driving **meaningful change and inspiring others**.

Key characteristics of **Quiet Leadership** include:

1. **Deep Listening & Observational Skills** – Rather than speaking often, Quiet Leaders carefully observe and listen before acting.

2. **Empowering Others** – They support and develop their teams by guiding them toward their own insights and solutions.

3. **Leading by Example** – Instead of making bold declarations, they model **integrity, patience, and resilience**.

4. **Strategic Thinking** – They take a thoughtful, **long-term approach** to problem-solving and decision-making.

5. **Emotional Intelligence & Humility** – They lead with self-awareness, compassion, and modesty.

Quiet Leadership is **not about avoiding leadership responsibilities**; rather, it focuses on **influencing others through thoughtful action and empowerment instead of dominance and command**.

Example

A great example of **Quiet Leadership** is **Tim Cook, CEO of Apple**. Unlike his predecessor, the highly charismatic Steve Jobs, Cook is a **reserved, thoughtful leader** who prefers to make decisions carefully and empower his team rather than command the spotlight. His leadership style has helped Apple **continue its success while fostering a culture of collaboration and sustainability**.

Another example is **Mahatma Gandhi**, whose leadership was based on **peaceful resistance, deep listening, and leading by example** rather than force or aggression. His **quiet yet powerful influence** helped lead India to independence and continues to inspire leaders worldwide.

Why It Works

Quiet Leadership is effective because it:

- **Encourages Deep Thinking & Innovation** – Leaders who listen and reflect create space for **better ideas and thoughtful decision-making**.

- **Empowers Employees** – Rather than micromanaging, Quiet Leaders allow their teams to grow and **develop their own leadership abilities**.

- **Builds Trust & Loyalty** – Employees respect leaders who lead with **integrity, humility, and quiet confidence**.

- **Reduces Conflict & Improves Communication** – A calm, composed leadership approach **creates a collaborative and respectful work environment**.

Research suggests that introverted and quiet leaders often excel in **highly creative, knowledge-based, and emotionally complex workplaces**, where deep thinking and collaboration matter more than dominance.

How It Works

Quiet Leadership follows a **subtle yet effective process**:

1. **Listening First, Speaking Last** – Leaders gather insights before making decisions.

2. **Asking the Right Questions** – Instead of giving direct orders, they help others **find their own solutions**.

3. **Leading Through Actions, Not Words** – Their leadership is demonstrated through **consistency, patience, and thoughtful decision-making**.

4. **Encouraging Team Autonomy** – They empower employees by **trusting them to take ownership** of their work.

5. **Creating a Safe, Low-Ego Culture** – Their humility and emotional intelligence **foster collaboration and innovation**.

Unlike **Charismatic or Autocratic Leadership**, Quiet Leaders **don't seek attention or impose authority**— instead, they create **lasting impact through subtle, consistent, and meaningful actions**.

Application

Quiet Leadership is widely applied in:

- **Corporate Leadership** – Leaders like **Tim Cook** foster collaborative and sustainable cultures.

- **Education & Coaching** – Teachers and mentors who guide through thoughtful reflection.

- **Nonprofits & Social Movements** – Leaders like **Gandhi** inspire change without force.

- **Technology & Innovation** – Many introverted leaders in **Silicon Valley** use Quiet Leadership to drive progress.

Key Insights

1. **Leadership is Not About Volume, But Impact –** **Quiet Leaders inspire through thoughtful action, not loud words.**

2. **Listening is a Powerful Leadership Tool** – Deep listening **builds trust, engagement, and innovation.**

3. **Empowerment Creates Stronger Teams** – By **guiding rather than commanding**, Quiet Leaders develop future leaders.

4. **Quiet Leadership is Ideal for Complex, Knowledge-Based Work** – It thrives in **creative, strategic, and emotionally intelligent environments.**

Quiet Leadership proves that **leadership doesn't require being the loudest voice in the room**—sometimes, the most powerful leaders **lead with silence, wisdom, and steady influence.**

20. Empathetic Leadership

Empathetic Leadership: A Breakdown

Theory

Empathetic Leadership is a leadership style that prioritizes **understanding, compassion, and emotional intelligence** to build strong, engaged teams. Unlike traditional leadership models that focus on authority or efficiency, **Empathetic Leadership is cantered on human connection, active listening, and recognizing the emotions of others**.

At its core, **Empathetic Leadership** involves:

1. **Active Listening** – Leaders genuinely listen to employees' concerns and perspectives.

2. **Emotional Awareness** – They recognize and validate the emotions of their team members.

3. **Compassionate Decision-Making** – They make choices that consider the well-being of their employees.

4. **Building Trust & Psychological Safety** – They create an environment where employees feel safe to express themselves.

5. **Balancing Empathy with Accountability** – While supportive, they still maintain high standards and expectations.

This leadership model is rooted in **Daniel Goleman's Emotional Intelligence framework**, which identifies **empathy as a key leadership trait** that enhances collaboration, morale, and productivity.

Example

A strong example of **Empathetic Leadership** is **Satya Nadella, CEO of Microsoft**. When he took over in 2014, he shifted Microsoft's culture from rigid and competitive to **empathetic, inclusive, and growth-oriented**. He introduced policies that emphasized **employee well-being, learning, and collaboration**, leading to increased innovation and profitability.

Another example is **Jacinda Ardern**, former Prime Minister of New Zealand. Her leadership during crises, such as the Christchurch mosque attacks and the COVID-19 pandemic, demonstrated **genuine empathy, emotional intelligence, and strong communication**, fostering national unity and trust.

Why It Works

Empathetic Leadership is effective because it:

- **Enhances Employee Engagement** – Employees feel **valued and heard**, leading to higher motivation.

- **Builds Trust & Loyalty** – Workers are more likely to stay with leaders who care about their well-being.

- **Improves Team Collaboration** – Open communication fosters teamwork and problem-solving.

- **Reduces Burnout & Stress** – Supportive work environments lead to better mental health.

- **Boosts Productivity & Innovation** – Employees feel safe to share new ideas and take creative risks.

Studies show that **leaders with high empathy create workplaces with lower turnover rates, better performance, and higher employee satisfaction**.

How It Works

Empathetic Leadership follows a **people-first approach**:

1. **Develop Emotional Intelligence** – Leaders practice **self-awareness, empathy, and active listening**.

2. **Prioritize Open Communication** – They encourage honest conversations and feedback.

3. **Support Employee Well-Being** – They recognize challenges and offer flexibility when needed.

4. **Lead with Compassion & Fairness** – They make decisions that balance business goals with employee needs.

5. **Encourage a Culture of Empathy** – They model and promote empathy at all levels of the organization.

Unlike **transactional leadership**, which focuses on rewards and punishments, **Empathetic Leadership fosters intrinsic motivation and emotional commitment**.

Application

Empathetic Leadership is widely applied in:

- **Corporate Leadership** – CEOs like **Satya Nadella** prioritize culture and employee well-being.

- **Healthcare & Education** – Leaders in these fields must balance emotional care with performance.

- **Nonprofits & Social Enterprises** – Empathy-driven organizations focus on **people-first missions**.

- **Diversity & Inclusion Initiatives** – Leaders create equitable workplaces by **understanding diverse experiences**.

Key Insights

1. **Empathy is a Leadership Strength, Not a Weakness** – It builds **trust, engagement, and performance**.

2. **Listening is as Important as Leading** – Leaders must **understand before making decisions**.

3. **Empathy Drives Long-Term Success** – Companies with empathetic leaders have **stronger cultures and lower turnover**.

4. **Empathy Must Be Balanced with Accountability** – Leaders must **be supportive while maintaining high standards**.

Empathetic Leadership proves that **leading with heart creates stronger, more resilient, and more successful organizations**.

Leadership Styles Based on Influence

21. Directive Leadership

Directive Leadership: A Breakdown

Theory

Directive Leadership is a leadership style where the leader provides **clear instructions, closely supervises tasks, and expects compliance** from their team. It is a highly **structured and authoritative** approach that focuses on efficiency, precision, and maintaining order.

This model is rooted in **task-oriented leadership theories**, including **Path-Goal Theory (Robert House)**, which suggests that directive leaders provide **specific guidance and set clear expectations** to help their team achieve goals. Unlike participative leadership, where employees have input, directive leadership **centralizes decision-**

making and ensures that employees follow defined procedures.

Key characteristics of **Directive Leadership** include:

1. **Clear Instructions & Expectations** – Leaders define roles, responsibilities, and goals.

2. **Close Supervision & Control** – Employees' performance is monitored to ensure alignment.

3. **Strict Rule Enforcement** – Compliance with policies and procedures is emphasized.

4. **Fast Decision-Making** – The leader makes quick, decisive choices without broad consultation.

5. **Minimal Employee Autonomy** – Decisions and processes are dictated by the leader.

Directive Leadership is most effective in **high-risk, high-precision, or emergency-driven environments**, where structure and discipline are essential.

Example

A classic example of **Directive Leadership** is **military leadership**. In combat or crisis situations, soldiers rely on **clear, direct orders from commanding officers,** as hesitation or misinterpretation could lead to failure or loss of life.

Another example is **Jeff Bezos in Amazon's early years.** Bezos enforced **rigorous performance expectations and clear operational processes**, ensuring that Amazon's rapid scaling was controlled, efficient, and highly disciplined. His direct leadership style helped Amazon **establish dominance in e-commerce through structure and operational excellence**.

Why It Works

Directive Leadership is effective because it:

- **Creates Clarity & Structure** – Employees know exactly what is expected of them.

- **Enhances Efficiency & Productivity** – Eliminates ambiguity, leading to faster execution.

- **Works Well in Crisis or High-Stakes Situations** – Quick, decisive action is critical in emergency services, military, and fast-paced industries.

- **Reduces Errors & Inconsistencies** – Ensures strict adherence to policies and standards.

Studies show that **directive leadership is highly effective in structured environments** where consistency, compliance, and precision are crucial.

How It Works

Directive Leadership operates through **strict oversight and clear guidance**:

1. **Establish Clear Objectives** – The leader defines goals and performance expectations.

2. **Communicate Instructions Precisely** – Clear, direct communication minimizes confusion.

3. **Monitor & Enforce Compliance** – Employees are closely supervised to ensure adherence.

4. **Make Quick, Decisive Calls** – The leader makes all major decisions without delegation.

5. **Maintain Order & Discipline** – Rules are strictly followed to ensure operational success.

Unlike **participative leadership**, directive leadership **prioritizes control over collaboration**, making it ideal for hierarchical organizations.

Application

Directive Leadership is widely used in:

- **Military & Emergency Services** – Leaders must make **immediate, high-stakes decisions**.

- **Manufacturing & Industrial Work** – Consistency and adherence to protocols are essential.

- **Healthcare & Surgical Teams** – Precision and compliance reduce risks in medical procedures.

- **Fast-Growth Startups & Logistics** – Leaders set clear processes to ensure **scalability and efficiency**.

Key Insights

1. **Best for High-Structure Environments** – Works well in industries where **rules, efficiency, and compliance are priorities**.

2. **Effective in Crisis Management** – When quick decisions are needed, **directive leadership provides clarity and control**.

3. **Can Limit Employee Engagement** – Overuse of directive leadership may **reduce creativity and motivation** in dynamic workplaces.

4. **Requires Strong Leadership Skills** – Leaders must **balance authority with fairness** to maintain morale.

While **Directive Leadership is not ideal for innovation-driven industries**, it remains one of the **most effective leadership styles for maintaining order, precision, and control in structured environments**.

22. Participative Leadership

Participative Leadership: A Breakdown

Theory

Participative Leadership, also known as **Democratic Leadership**, is a leadership model where leaders actively involve their team members in **decision-making, problem-solving, and goal-setting**. This approach values **collaboration, transparency, and employee input**, creating a sense of ownership and engagement within the team.

Unlike **Directive Leadership**, which centralizes decision-making, **Participative Leadership distributes authority**, allowing employees to contribute ideas and take part in shaping organizational strategies. This model is rooted in **Lewin's Leadership Styles (1939)** and further expanded by **Likert's System 4 Leadership Model**, which emphasizes **group participation as a key driver of success**.

Key principles of **Participative Leadership** include:

1. **Encouraging Team Input** – Leaders seek and value contributions from employees.

2. **Shared Decision-Making** – Employees have a say in strategies, policies, and problem-solving.

3. **Open Communication** – Transparent discussions create trust and alignment.

4. **Empowerment & Accountability** – Employees feel responsible for outcomes.

5. **Collaboration Over Hierarchy** – Authority is distributed rather than centralized.

This leadership style **fosters creativity, motivation, and long-term organizational success**, making it highly effective in environments that require innovation and employee engagement.

Example

A strong example of **Participative Leadership** is **Google's workplace culture**. Google encourages employees to **share ideas, participate in decision-making, and collaborate on innovative projects**. Their open culture has led to **breakthrough innovations like Gmail, Google Maps, and AI-driven technology**, demonstrating how participative leadership drives creativity.

Another example is **Howard Schultz, former CEO of Starbucks**. Schultz involved employees in shaping Starbucks' corporate vision, policies, and benefits programs, ensuring that all stakeholders had a voice. His participative approach **enhanced employee satisfaction, brand loyalty, and customer experience**.

Why It Works

Participative Leadership is effective because it:

- **Increases Employee Engagement** – Employees feel valued and motivated.

- **Encourages Innovation & Creativity** – Open discussions lead to **better ideas and problem-solving**.

- **Builds Trust & Loyalty** – Transparency and shared decision-making **increase team commitment**.

- **Improves Job Satisfaction** – Employees have greater control over their work.

- **Leads to Better Decisions** – Diverse perspectives help leaders make **informed, well-rounded choices**.

Studies show that companies with participative leadership **have higher retention rates, stronger team performance, and more resilient workplace cultures**.

How It Works

Participative Leadership follows a **collaborative decision-making process**:

1. **Encouraging Open Dialogue** – Leaders actively seek input from employees.

2. **Facilitating Group Discussions** – Ideas are explored collectively before decisions are made.

3. **Empowering Teams** – Employees take ownership of projects and outcomes.

4. **Providing Guidance, Not Control** – Leaders offer support rather than micromanagement.

5. **Recognizing & Rewarding Contributions** – Acknowledging employee input **reinforces engagement and trust**.

Unlike **Autocratic Leadership**, which enforces top-down control, Participative Leadership **thrives in dynamic, knowledge-driven industries where teamwork and collaboration drive success**.

Application

Participative Leadership is widely applied in:

- **Technology & Innovation** – Companies like **Google, Apple, and Microsoft** foster participative work cultures.

- **Education & Academia** – Universities and schools encourage **collaborative decision-making** among educators.

- **Healthcare & Public Policy** – Medical and government leaders involve teams in shaping policies and procedures.

- **Nonprofits & Social Enterprises** – Organizations use participative leadership to ensure community-driven impact.

Key Insights

1. **Empowering Employees Leads to Higher Performance** – Teams work harder when they **feel heard and valued**.

2. **Collaboration Creates Better Solutions** – A diversity of ideas leads to **smarter, more innovative decisions**.

3. **Trust is Essential for Participative Leadership** – Leaders must **balance authority with openness**.

4. **Not Always Ideal for Crisis Situations** – Participative leadership is effective **in stable environments**, but in emergencies, **quick decision-making may be required**.

Participative Leadership is **one of the most effective leadership models for fostering engagement, innovation, and long-term organizational success**, proving that **leaders who listen create stronger, more resilient teams**.

23. Delegative Leadership

Delegative Leadership: A Breakdown

Theory

Delegative Leadership, also known as **Laissez-Faire Leadership**, is a leadership model where leaders **entrust decision-making, task execution, and problem-solving to their team members** with minimal direct supervision. Unlike directive leadership, which emphasizes control and structure, **delegative leaders provide autonomy, trusting employees to manage their responsibilities independently**.

This leadership style is based on the idea that **competent, self-motivated employees thrive when given freedom**. It is rooted in **Kurt Lewin's 1939 leadership study**, where **laissez-faire leadership** was identified as a model that fosters creativity and independence when used with skilled teams.

Key characteristics of **Delegative Leadership** include:

1. **High Trust & Autonomy** – Employees are given authority over their work.

2. **Minimal Direct Supervision** – Leaders step in only when needed.

3. **Encouragement of Innovation** – Teams are free to explore creative solutions.

4. **Decentralized Decision-Making** – Employees have control over their processes.

5. **Leader as a Guide, Not a Micromanager** – Support is available but not enforced.

While **Delegative Leadership works well with highly skilled teams**, it can **fail in unstructured environments where employees lack experience or motivation**.

Example

A great example of **Delegative Leadership** is **Warren Buffett, CEO of Berkshire Hathaway**. Buffett **delegates decision-making to his managers**, trusting them to run subsidiaries independently. His hands-off approach allows **skilled leaders to drive business success without micromanagement**.

Another example is **Google's early innovation strategy**. Google allowed employees **"20% time"** to work on personal projects, leading to the creation of **Gmail, Google Maps, and AdSense**. By trusting employees to manage their own work, Google fostered a culture of **self-driven creativity and breakthrough innovation**.

Why It Works

Delegative Leadership is effective because it:

- **Empowers Employees** – Workers feel valued and motivated when trusted with autonomy.

- **Encourages Innovation & Creativity** – Freedom leads to **new ideas and problem-solving**.

- **Reduces Managerial Bottlenecks** – Leaders can focus on strategic goals instead of micromanaging.

- **Boosts Employee Growth & Accountability** – Employees develop **independence and leadership skills**.

Studies show that **delegative leadership is highly effective in R&D, tech, and creative industries**, where autonomy **fuels innovation and efficiency**.

How It Works

Delegative Leadership follows a **structured but flexible approach**:

1. **Selecting the Right People** – Leaders ensure **employees are skilled, self-motivated, and responsible**.

2. **Defining Clear Goals & Expectations** – While hands-off, leaders set **clear objectives**.

3. **Providing Resources & Support** – Teams have the tools they need but **make their own decisions**.

4. **Stepping In Only When Needed** – Leaders intervene **if guidance or crisis management is required**.

5. **Evaluating Performance** – Outcomes are assessed to ensure autonomy is productive.

Unlike **Autocratic Leadership**, which demands strict control, **Delegative Leadership trusts employees to own their work**, making it ideal for fast-moving industries.

Application

Delegative Leadership is widely applied in:

- **Technology & Startups** – Companies like **Google, Tesla, and Apple** foster innovation through autonomy.

- **Creative Industries** – Designers, writers, and filmmakers work best with **independent creative freedom**.

- **Academia & Research** – Scientists and researchers operate **with minimal supervision** to explore discoveries.

- **Corporate Management** – Executives like **Warren Buffett** empower managers to run divisions independently.

Key Insights

1. **Delegation Requires Trust & Competence** – This model **only works with self-motivated, skilled employees**.

2. **Innovation Flourishes with Autonomy** – Freedom allows **creative problem-solving and breakthrough ideas**.

3. **Not Ideal for Unstructured Environments** – If teams **lack experience or accountability**, productivity can decline.

4. **Leaders Must Still Set Clear Expectations** – Delegation doesn't mean **abandoning leadership; it means guiding without micromanaging**.

Delegative Leadership proves that autonomy, trust, and responsibility drive performance—but only when leaders **delegate effectively** to capable, motivated teams.

24. Democratic Leadership

Democratic Leadership: A Breakdown

Theory

Democratic Leadership, also known as **Participative Leadership**, is a leadership model where **leaders encourage team input, shared decision-making, and open communication**. Unlike autocratic leadership, which centralizes authority, democratic leadership values **collaboration, inclusivity, and collective problem-solving**.

This leadership model is rooted in **Kurt Lewin's 1939 leadership studies**, which identified democratic leadership as one of the most effective leadership styles for **fostering innovation, engagement, and productivity**. It is based on the principle that **employees perform better when they feel valued, heard, and involved in decision-making**.

Key characteristics of **Democratic Leadership** include:

1. **Encouraging Team Input** – Leaders actively seek opinions before making decisions.

2. **Shared Decision-Making** – Authority is distributed rather than centralized.

3. **Transparent Communication** – Open discussions ensure clarity and trust.

4. **Employee Empowerment** – Employees have autonomy and ownership over their work.

5. **Collaboration & Inclusivity** – The team works together towards a shared vision.

While **Democratic Leadership fosters innovation and morale**, it requires **strong facilitation skills and well-structured discussions** to prevent delays in decision-making.

Example

A well-known example of **Democratic Leadership** is **Google's leadership approach**. Google's work culture encourages employees to contribute ideas and participate in decision-making. Employees have **opportunities to present ideas, engage in brainstorming sessions, and influence company policies**. This approach has led to innovations like **Google Search improvements, AI advancements, and employee-driven projects like Gmail and Google Maps**.

Another example is **President John F. Kennedy**, who utilized **Democratic Leadership during the Cuban Missile Crisis**. He encouraged discussion among advisors, military officials, and experts before making strategic decisions, ultimately leading to a diplomatic resolution instead of war.

Why It Works

Democratic Leadership is effective because it:

- **Boosts Employee Engagement** – Employees feel valued, increasing motivation.

- **Encourages Innovation & Creativity** – Open discussions lead to better ideas.

- **Strengthens Team Collaboration** – Transparency and trust build strong relationships.

- **Improves Decision-Making** – Diverse perspectives lead to well-rounded solutions.

- **Builds a Positive Work Culture** – Employees feel ownership over their contributions.

Research shows that **Democratic Leadership leads to higher productivity, job satisfaction, and team cohesion**, making it ideal for dynamic and creative environments.

How It Works

Democratic Leadership operates through **structured collaboration and inclusivity**:

1. **Encouraging Open Dialogue** – Leaders actively listen and seek team input.

2. **Facilitating Group Decision-Making** – Decisions are made through discussion and consensus.

3. **Empowering Employees** – Team members have autonomy to take initiative.

4. **Providing Guidance, Not Control** – Leaders support rather than dictate.

5. **Recognizing & Rewarding Contributions** – Acknowledging team efforts fosters motivation.

Unlike **Autocratic Leadership**, where leaders dictate decisions, Democratic Leadership thrives on **group participation and shared responsibility**.

Application

Democratic Leadership is widely applied in:

- **Technology & Innovation** – Companies like **Google and Apple** use participative decision-making.

- **Education & Research** – Universities and schools encourage **collaborative problem-solving**.

- **Public Policy & Government** – Leaders like **John F. Kennedy and Barack Obama** emphasized inclusivity.

- **Corporate Teams & Startups** – Businesses leverage team input to drive innovation.

Key Insights

1. **Involvement Leads to Higher Performance** – Employees are more productive when they **feel heard and valued**.

2. **Collaboration Improves Decision-Making** – Multiple perspectives **enhance innovation and reduce blind spots**.

3. **Trust & Transparency are Essential** – Successful democratic leaders **foster open communication**.

4. **Not Ideal for Crisis Situations** – In emergencies, quick decisions may be needed instead of long discussions.

Democratic Leadership is **one of the most effective leadership styles,** fostering **collaboration, engagement, and innovation,** making it ideal for **modern workplaces that value inclusivity and teamwork.**

25. Coaching Leadership

Coaching Leadership: A Breakdown

Theory

Coaching Leadership is a leadership style that focuses on **developing individuals, enhancing skills, and fostering long-term professional growth**. Unlike autocratic or transactional leadership, which prioritizes performance metrics, Coaching Leadership emphasizes **mentorship, guidance, and personalized support** to help employees reach their full potential.

This model is rooted in **Daniel Goleman's Emotional Intelligence framework**, which highlights coaching as one of the six key leadership styles. Coaching Leaders act as **mentors rather than authority figures**, guiding employees through **self-discovery, goal-setting, and continuous learning**.

Key characteristics of **Coaching Leadership** include:

1. **Personalized Development** – Leaders help employees identify strengths, weaknesses, and career aspirations.

2. **Ongoing Feedback & Encouragement** – Constructive feedback is given in a supportive, growth-oriented manner.

3. **Emphasis on Learning & Growth** – Employees are encouraged to develop new skills and take on challenges.

4. **Building a Trust-Based Relationship** – Leaders foster strong bonds through **empathy, transparency, and support**.

5. **Long-Term Vision Over Short-Term Results** – Coaching focuses on **sustained success rather than immediate performance**.

Coaching Leadership is **highly effective in organizations that value talent development, innovation, and continuous learning.**

Example

A strong example of **Coaching Leadership** is **Satya Nadella, CEO of Microsoft**. When he took over, Microsoft's rigid, competitive culture was hindering growth. Nadella **shifted the company's focus to a learning-oriented, growth mindset**, encouraging employees to embrace challenges and innovation. His leadership transformed Microsoft into a **more agile, inclusive, and forward-thinking organization**.

Another example is **Phil Jackson**, the legendary basketball coach of the Chicago Bulls and LA Lakers. Instead of simply instructing his players, he **focused on developing their mental resilience, teamwork, and leadership abilities**, helping players like Michael Jordan and Kobe Bryant maximize their potential.

Why It Works

Coaching Leadership is effective because it:

- **Boosts Employee Engagement & Motivation** – Employees feel **valued and empowered**.

- **Enhances Skill Development** – Continuous learning creates **high-performing, adaptable teams**.

- **Increases Retention & Loyalty** – Employees stay longer in organizations that **invest in their growth**.

- **Fosters Innovation & Problem-Solving** – Encourages **creative thinking and independent decision-making**.

- **Creates Stronger Team Relationships** – Trust and mentorship improve **team cohesion and morale**.

Studies show that companies with **coaching-focused leadership cultures** have **higher employee satisfaction, better retention, and greater long-term success**.

How It Works

Coaching Leadership follows a **mentorship-based approach**:

1. **Identifying Strengths & Areas for Growth** – Leaders **assess employee potential** and set personalized goals.

2. **Providing Regular Feedback & Support** – Employees receive **constructive feedback** and encouragement.

3. **Encouraging Self-Reflection & Growth** – Employees are guided to **find their own solutions.**

4. **Empowering Employees to Take Initiative** – They gain **confidence and independence** in decision-making.

5. **Celebrating Progress & Milestones** – Recognizing achievements reinforces **motivation and commitment.**

Unlike **directive leadership**, which dictates actions, Coaching Leadership **guides employees to discover their own path to success.**

Application

Coaching Leadership is widely applied in:

- **Corporate Leadership & HR Development** – Companies invest in **leadership training and mentorship programs.**

- **Education & Academia** – Teachers and professors guide **students through personalized learning experiences.**

- **Sports & Team Management** – Coaches focus on **skill development and mental strength.**

- **Entrepreneurship & Startups** – Founders mentor employees to **foster innovation and leadership skills**.

Key Insights

1. **Coaching Leadership Focuses on Growth, Not Control** – Leaders **mentor rather than dictate**.

2. **Feedback & Encouragement Drive Performance** – Employees **thrive in supportive, trust-based environments**.

3. **Long-Term Development Creates Stronger Teams** – Investing in **people leads to sustained success**.

4. **Not Ideal for High-Stakes, Fast-Paced Environments** – Coaching works best when **learning and growth are prioritized over immediate results**.

Coaching Leadership is **one of the most effective models for developing talent, fostering engagement, and creating resilient organizations**, proving that **investing in people leads to long-term success**.

26. Facilitative Leadership

Facilitative Leadership: A Breakdown

Theory

Facilitative Leadership is a leadership style that focuses on **empowering teams, fostering collaboration, and guiding decision-making through shared responsibility**. Instead of commanding authority or making unilateral decisions, **Facilitative Leaders act as catalysts**, creating an environment where individuals work together to achieve common goals.

This leadership model is rooted in **systems thinking, participative leadership, and emotional intelligence**, emphasizing that leaders should **remove barriers, provide resources, and guide discussions rather than dictate outcomes. Facilitative Leadership thrives in dynamic, team-based environments where problem-solving, innovation, and adaptability are essential.**

Key characteristics of **Facilitative Leadership** include:

1. **Encouraging Participation** – Leaders ensure all voices are heard in decision-making.

2. **Building Consensus** – They help teams reach **mutual agreements** while balancing different perspectives.

3. **Empowering Others** – Employees take **ownership of their roles and contributions**.

4. **Removing Obstacles** – Leaders identify and eliminate **barriers that hinder collaboration and progress**.

5. **Active Listening & Emotional Intelligence** – They ensure discussions remain productive and inclusive.

Unlike **directive leadership, which enforces control, Facilitative Leadership relies on trust, dialogue, and engagement to drive success.**

Example

A strong example of **Facilitative Leadership** is **Satya Nadella, CEO of Microsoft**. When he took over in 2014, he shifted Microsoft's leadership culture from **rigid and competitive to collaborative and inclusive**. Nadella encouraged **teamwork, open communication, and employee empowerment**, leading to Microsoft's resurgence in cloud computing and AI-driven innovation.

Another example is **Mary Barra, CEO of General Motors**, who transformed GM's leadership style by **fostering open dialogue, cross-functional collaboration, and employee-driven innovation**. Her facilitative approach helped GM **embrace electric vehicle technology and industry transformation.**

Why It Works

Facilitative Leadership is effective because it:

- **Encourages Team Engagement & Ownership** – Employees feel **more motivated and invested** in outcomes.

- **Enhances Problem-Solving & Innovation** – **Diverse perspectives** lead to better decision-making.

- **Builds Trust & Stronger Relationships** – Open dialogue fosters **loyalty and collaboration**.

- **Improves Adaptability in Complex Environments** – Teams can **quickly adjust to new challenges**.

- **Reduces Conflict & Strengthens Consensus** – **Balanced discussions prevent resistance and disengagement**.

Studies show that **Facilitative Leadership improves workplace collaboration, innovation, and employee satisfaction**, particularly in **knowledge-driven and team-based industries**.

How It Works

Facilitative Leadership follows a **structured but inclusive approach**:

1. **Creating an Open & Inclusive Environment** – Leaders ensure all team members feel **safe to contribute**.

2. **Encouraging Discussion & Input** – Ideas are explored collaboratively before decisions are made.

3. **Guiding (Not Controlling) Conversations** – Leaders help teams **navigate discussions and resolve conflicts**.

4. **Providing Tools & Resources** – Employees receive **support, training, and autonomy** to execute tasks.

5. **Ensuring Accountability & Follow-Through** – Teams commit to **decisions and take ownership of results**.

Unlike **autocratic leadership**, which demands obedience, **Facilitative Leadership allows teams to drive decision-making while the leader ensures structure and progress**.

Application

Facilitative Leadership is widely applied in:

- **Technology & Innovation Teams** – Encouraging cross-functional collaboration in companies like **Microsoft and Google**.

- **Education & Training** – Teachers and coaches guide students toward self-directed learning.

- **Healthcare & Public Policy** – Collaborative decision-making ensures **patient-cantered care and policy development**.

- **Corporate Strategy & Change Management** – Leaders guide organizations through **transformation while involving employees in the process**.

Key Insights

1. **Leaders Act as Guides, Not Controllers** – The focus is on **facilitating teamwork and problem-solving, not enforcing rules**.

2. **Collaboration Strengthens Decision-Making** – The best solutions come from **diverse input and group consensus**.

3. **Empowering Employees Drives Performance** – People perform better when **they feel valued and included**.

4. **Works Best in Flexible, Knowledge-Based Industries** – Ideal for **dynamic environments where adaptability and innovation are crucial**.

Facilitative Leadership is one of the **most effective models for fostering teamwork, innovation, and long-term organizational success**, proving that **leaders who facilitate, rather than dictate, create more engaged and high-performing teams**.

27. Persuasive Leadership

Persuasive Leadership: A Breakdown

Theory

Persuasive Leadership is a leadership style that relies on **influence, communication, and logical reasoning** to guide and motivate others. Unlike **autocratic leadership**, which commands obedience, **Persuasive Leadership** focuses on **convincing, inspiring, and guiding teams through well-articulated arguments and emotional appeal**.

This leadership model is rooted in **Aristotle's principles of persuasion—ethos (credibility), pathos (emotional connection), and logos (logical reasoning)**—which help leaders gain trust, inspire action, and drive decision-making. Persuasive leaders do not **force compliance**; instead, they **use influence, credibility, and emotional intelligence** to align teams with their vision.

Key characteristics of **Persuasive Leadership** include:

1. **Strong Communication Skills** – Leaders articulate ideas clearly and persuasively.

2. **Emotional Intelligence & Empathy** – They **connect with people on an emotional level**.

3. **Logical & Rational Approach** – Decisions are backed by facts, reasoning, and data.

4. **Influence Over Authority** – They **motivate rather than dictate**.

5. **Adaptability & Open-Mindedness** – They consider different viewpoints to **refine their arguments and strategies**.

Persuasive Leadership is highly effective in environments that require **buy-in from stakeholders, negotiation, and influence-based decision-making**.

Example

A great example of **Persuasive Leadership** is **Steve Jobs**, co-founder of Apple. Jobs was not just a visionary; he was a master persuader. His **compelling storytelling, passion, and ability to frame ideas in an inspiring way** convinced employees, investors, and customers to believe in Apple's vision. His **legendary product launches, marketing campaigns, and leadership strategies** were all rooted in persuasive influence.

Another example is **Barack Obama**, whose leadership style was built on **powerful oratory, emotional intelligence, and logical persuasion**. His ability to connect with audiences, build trust, and **convince people through well-crafted arguments** made him an effective leader.

Why It Works

Persuasive Leadership is effective because it:

- **Builds Trust & Credibility** – People follow leaders they **respect and believe in**.

- **Motivates & Engages Employees** – Emotional connection fosters **loyalty and commitment**.

- **Encourages Open Dialogue** – Teams feel heard and **more willing to accept new ideas**.

- **Drives Change & Innovation** – Persuasive leaders help teams **overcome resistance to change**.

- **Works in Complex Decision-Making** – Logic, reasoning, and storytelling **make decision-making smoother and more impactful**.

Studies show that leaders who use **persuasion instead of authority** create **more motivated, engaged, and high-performing teams**.

How It Works

Persuasive Leadership follows a **structured yet flexible approach**:

1. **Establish Credibility (Ethos)** – Leaders demonstrate expertise, trustworthiness, and confidence.

2. **Connect Emotionally (Pathos)** – They **use storytelling and empathy to make ideas relatable**.

3. **Use Logical Reasoning (Logos)** – Decisions are backed by **facts, research, and rational arguments**.

4. **Listen & Adapt** – Persuasive leaders engage in dialogue, **adjusting their message to gain support**.

5. **Reinforce & Inspire Action** – They **communicate consistently, motivating teams to take action**.

Unlike **directive leadership**, which enforces authority, **Persuasive Leadership encourages voluntary commitment through influence and trust**.

Application

Persuasive Leadership is widely applied in:

- **Business & Marketing** – Leaders like **Steve Jobs and Elon Musk** use persuasion to sell ideas.

- **Politics & Public Speaking** – Figures like **Barack Obama and Martin Luther King Jr.** inspire movements through persuasion.

- **Corporate & Executive Leadership** – Persuasive CEOs convince **stakeholders, investors, and teams** to align with company goals.

- **Change Management & Innovation** – Leaders **persuade teams to adopt new strategies and innovations**.

Key Insights

1. **Persuasion is More Powerful Than Authority** – Influence **creates deeper commitment than force**.

2. **Emotional Connection Strengthens Leadership** – **People follow leaders they relate to and trust**.

3. **Logic & Credibility Build Confidence** – Facts, reasoning, and expertise **make persuasion more effective**.

4. **Great Leaders Are Great Communicators** –
    Mastering persuasion helps leaders inspire action
    and drive change.

Persuasive Leadership is one of the **most effective**
leadership styles in today's world, proving that **leaders**
who communicate with passion, reason, and trust can
move people, shape ideas, and drive success.

28. Pacesetting Leadership

Pacesetting Leadership: A Breakdown

Theory

Pacesetting Leadership is a high-performance leadership
style where the leader sets ambitious goals and expects
employees to **match their speed, efficiency, and**
excellence. These leaders lead by example, demonstrating
a strong work ethic, **high standards, and a relentless drive**
for results.

This model is rooted in **Daniel Goleman's Emotional**
Intelligence framework, where Pacesetting Leadership is
identified as one of the six key leadership styles. **While**
effective in high-performing teams, this style can also
create stress if expectations are too demanding.

Key characteristics of **Pacesetting Leadership** include:

1. **High Performance Expectations** – Leaders demand excellence from themselves and their teams.

2. **Leading by Example** – They work hard and expect employees to follow their lead.

3. **Fast-Paced Execution** – The focus is on **speed, efficiency, and continuous improvement**.

4. **Minimal Supervision** – Leaders trust employees to be self-motivated and **keep up with their pace**.

5. **Immediate Performance Corrections** – If someone falls behind, leaders intervene quickly.

While Pacesetting Leadership works **well in goal-oriented, fast-moving industries**, it can lead to **burnout and decreased morale if overused**.

Example

A strong example of **Pacesetting Leadership** is **Elon Musk, CEO of Tesla and SpaceX**. Musk is known for his **high expectations, fast-paced decision-making, and relentless pursuit of innovation**. He expects employees to work long hours, solve complex problems quickly, and **deliver breakthrough innovations under intense deadlines**.

Another example is **Jeff Bezos during Amazon's early years**, where he set aggressive growth targets, pushed employees to deliver results, and personally maintained a high work ethic, demanding **customer obsession and operational excellence**.

Why It Works

Pacesetting Leadership is effective because it:

- **Drives Rapid Results** – Teams move faster and achieve **ambitious goals**.

- **Encourages Excellence & Precision** – Employees strive to **meet high standards**.

- **Works Well with Highly Skilled Teams** – Competent, self-motivated employees **thrive in fast-paced environments**.

- **Leverages the Leader's Expertise** – Employees follow a **highly capable and driven leader**.

Studies show that **this leadership style works best in high-performance, results-driven industries**, but **can demotivate employees if expectations become unrealistic**.

How It Works

Pacesetting Leadership follows an **intense, performance-focused approach**:

1. **Setting High Standards & Expectations** – Leaders establish **challenging performance goals**.

2. **Leading by Example** – They demonstrate the **work ethic and speed they expect from others**.

3. **Providing Minimal Supervision** – Employees are trusted to **self-manage and deliver results**.

4. **Quickly Addressing Underperformance** – Leaders intervene immediately when **performance slips**.

5. **Focusing on Speed & Efficiency** – The emphasis is on **delivering fast, high-quality results**.

Unlike **coaching leadership**, which prioritizes employee growth, **Pacesetting Leadership prioritizes speed, execution, and immediate impact**.

Application

Pacesetting Leadership is widely applied in:

- **Technology & Startups** – Leaders like **Elon Musk and Jeff Bezos** push for rapid innovation.

- **Finance & Consulting** – High-performance environments require **precision and speed**.

- **Product Development & Engineering** – Teams are expected to **deliver cutting-edge solutions under pressure**.

- **Sales & Performance-Based Industries** – Employees thrive in **fast-paced, goal-driven cultures**.

Key Insights

1. **High Standards Drive Excellence** – When used correctly, **this style pushes teams to achieve breakthrough results**.

2. **Best for Skilled, Self-Motivated Employees** – Works in industries where **employees thrive under pressure**.

3. **Can Lead to Burnout** – If overused, **this leadership style can create stress and lower morale**.

4. **Balance is Key** – Combining Pacesetting Leadership with **coaching or democratic leadership** can enhance sustainability.

Pacesetting Leadership is **one of the most effective styles in high-performance environments**, proving that **leaders who set the pace can inspire success—but only if they manage expectations wisely**.

29. Bureaucratic Leadership

Bureaucratic Leadership: A Breakdown

Theory

Bureaucratic Leadership is a structured and rule-based leadership model where leaders focus on **establishing policies, enforcing procedures, and maintaining hierarchy** to ensure organizational stability and efficiency. This leadership style is ideal for environments that require **strict compliance, risk management, and consistency in operations**.

This model is heavily influenced by **Max Weber's Bureaucratic Theory of Management**, which emphasizes that **clear structures, defined roles, and hierarchical control create efficiency and order**. Bureaucratic Leadership prioritizes **discipline, standardization, and accountability** to maintain smooth operations.

Key characteristics of **Bureaucratic Leadership** include:

1. **Strict Adherence to Rules & Policies** – Leaders enforce guidelines and protocols.

2. **Clear Chain of Command** – Authority and responsibilities are well-defined.

3. **Standardized Processes** – Workflows are structured to ensure efficiency and compliance.

4. **Impersonal Decision-Making** – Decisions are based on **policies rather than personal judgment.**

5. **Low Flexibility & High Control** – Leaders **minimize deviations from procedures** to ensure consistency.

While **Bureaucratic Leadership is not innovation-driven**, it is **highly effective in organizations where security, compliance, and operational control are paramount.**

Example

A strong example of **Bureaucratic Leadership** is **government institutions**. In public administration, bureaucratic systems ensure that **laws, regulations, and**

procedures are followed uniformly, reducing the risk of corruption or favouritism.

Another example is **NASA**, where bureaucratic leadership ensures **strict adherence to safety regulations, operational procedures, and mission protocols**. Given the high risks involved in space exploration, NASA's bureaucratic structure is **necessary for precision, consistency, and risk mitigation**.

Why It Works

Bureaucratic Leadership is effective because it:

- **Creates Organizational Stability** – Well-defined structures reduce confusion and inefficiencies.

- **Ensures Compliance & Risk Management** – Strict adherence to rules minimizes legal and operational risks.

- **Maintains Consistency & Reliability** – Standardized processes ensure **uniformity in execution**.

- **Works Well in Large, Complex Organizations** – Bureaucratic structures help manage **large-scale operations efficiently**.

Studies show that **bureaucratic leadership is ideal for industries where safety, regulatory compliance, and operational precision are critical**.

How It Works

Bureaucratic Leadership follows a **rigid, control-oriented approach**:

1. **Establishing Clear Policies & Procedures** – Leaders create strict operational guidelines.

2. **Enforcing Hierarchical Structure** – Employees follow a **clear chain of command**.

3. **Prioritizing Standardization** – Workflows remain **consistent and repeatable**.

4. **Making Decisions Based on Rules** – Leaders follow **protocols rather than personal judgment**.

5. **Minimizing Flexibility** – Leaders avoid **unnecessary changes to maintain control**.

Unlike **transformational leadership**, which fosters innovation, **bureaucratic leadership prioritizes stability, order, and rule enforcement**.

Application

Bureaucratic Leadership is widely applied in:

- **Government & Public Administration** – Ensuring **legal and regulatory compliance**.

- **Healthcare & Pharmaceuticals** – Standardizing **medical procedures, patient safety, and drug regulations**.

- **Manufacturing & Engineering** – Following **strict quality control and safety standards**.

- **Finance & Banking** – Enforcing **security, compliance, and risk management policies**.

Key Insights

1. **Best for High-Control Environments** – This style **ensures consistency and minimizes risk** in regulated industries.

2. **Standardization Reduces Errors** – Strict rules **create efficiency and reliability**.

3. **Can Limit Creativity & Flexibility** – Bureaucratic systems **may stifle innovation** in dynamic industries.

4. **Works Best in Large Organizations** – It is **effective for large, complex entities** that require structured governance.

Bureaucratic Leadership is **one of the most effective models for structured, high-compliance industries**, proving that **strong processes, clear hierarchy, and strict rule enforcement lead to efficiency and risk management**.

30. Visionary Leadership

Visionary Leadership: A Breakdown

Theory

Visionary Leadership is a leadership model where leaders inspire and guide their teams by articulating a **clear, compelling vision of the future**. These leaders are **forward-thinking, innovative, and transformational**, focusing on long-term goals rather than short-term objectives. Visionary leaders **energize and align** their teams by communicating a strong sense of purpose and direction.

This model is rooted in **Transformational Leadership Theory (James MacGregor Burns & Bernard Bass)** and draws from **Daniel Goleman's Emotional Intelligence framework**, where visionary leadership is identified as one of the six key leadership styles.

Key characteristics of **Visionary Leadership** include:

1. **A Compelling Future Vision** – Leaders articulate **a bold and inspiring goal** for the organization.

2. **Emotional Intelligence & Influence** – They connect **deeply with people's values and aspirations**.

3. **Encouraging Innovation & Risk-Taking** – Visionary leaders **embrace change and challenge the status quo**.

4. **Building Strong Team Alignment** – They ensure everyone **understands and commits to the vision**.

5. **Long-Term, Purpose-Driven Focus** – Their leadership **extends beyond immediate results** to **lasting impact**.

Unlike **Transactional Leadership**, which focuses on maintaining processes, **Visionary Leadership thrives on transformation, inspiration, and innovation**.

Example

A great example of **Visionary Leadership** is **Elon Musk, CEO of Tesla & SpaceX**. Musk's vision for **a sustainable future with electric vehicles and interplanetary colonization** has driven Tesla's dominance in the EV market and SpaceX's advancements in space exploration. His **ability to communicate a futuristic vision, inspire his teams, and push technological boundaries** exemplifies visionary leadership.

Another example is **Steve Jobs, co-founder of Apple**. Jobs envisioned **a world where technology is intuitive, beautifully designed, and accessible**. His visionary approach led to the development of **the iPhone, iPad, and Mac**, revolutionizing the tech industry.

Why It Works

Visionary Leadership is effective because it:

- **Inspires Motivation & Commitment** – Employees feel **connected to a greater purpose**.

- **Encourages Innovation & Creativity** – Teams **think beyond conventional solutions**.

- **Provides Clear Direction in Uncertain Times** – A strong vision **keeps organizations focused** amid change.

- **Attracts & Retains Top Talent** – People want to **work for inspiring leaders** with bold ambitions.

Studies show that **organizations with visionary leaders outperform competitors by fostering innovation, employee engagement, and long-term growth**.

How It Works

Visionary Leadership follows a **future-oriented, inspiration-driven approach**:

1. **Defining a Clear Vision** – Leaders **articulate an exciting and ambitious future goal**.

2. **Communicating with Passion & Clarity** – They use **storytelling and emotional appeal** to inspire belief.

3. **Empowering Teams to Innovate** – Employees are encouraged **to take risks and challenge norms**.

4. **Aligning Strategy with the Vision** – Organizational decisions are **guided by the larger mission**.

5. **Sustaining Momentum & Adaptability** – Leaders ensure that **the vision evolves with industry changes**.

Unlike **Directive Leadership**, which focuses on control, **Visionary Leadership thrives on inspiration, trust, and long-term thinking.**

Application

Visionary Leadership is widely applied in:

- **Technology & Innovation** – Companies like **Tesla, Apple, and Google** rely on bold leadership.

- **Entrepreneurship & Startups** – Founders **set ambitious goals** to disrupt industries.

- **Social & Political Movements** – Leaders like **Martin Luther King Jr.** inspired transformational change.

- **Corporate Strategy & Transformation** – CEOs lead **companies through industry shifts and digital revolutions.**

Key Insights

1. **A Strong Vision Creates Loyalty & Passion** – People commit to **leaders who inspire them.**

2. **Innovation & Bold Thinking Drive Change** – Visionary leaders **challenge conventional limits.**

3. **Communication & Emotional Intelligence Are Key** – A vision must **resonate deeply with teams.**

4. **Vision Without Execution is Useless** – Visionary leaders **must balance inspiration with action.**

Visionary Leadership is **one of the most powerful leadership models**, proving that **leaders who inspire, innovate, and think long-term create lasting impact and transformation**.

Industry-Specific Leadership Models

31. Tech Leadership

Tech Leadership: A Breakdown

Theory

Tech Leadership is a leadership model that focuses on **guiding technology-driven teams, fostering innovation, and driving digital transformation**. Unlike traditional leadership models, Tech Leadership **blends technical expertise, strategic vision, and people management** to navigate the rapidly evolving technological landscape.

This leadership model is rooted in principles of **Transformational Leadership, Agile Leadership, and Servant Leadership**, ensuring that teams are both **technically capable and strategically aligned**. A **Tech Leader is not just a manager but a visionary who bridges the gap between technology and business goals.**

Key characteristics of **Tech Leadership** include:

1. **Technical Proficiency & Innovation Mindset** – Leaders must understand **emerging technologies** and anticipate industry trends.

2. **Agile & Adaptive Thinking** – They **embrace change, pivot quickly, and support iterative development.**

3. **Empowering Cross-Functional Teams** – Effective tech leaders **bridge the gap between engineers, product managers, designers, and business teams.**

4. **Customer-Centric & Scalable Thinking** – Ensuring that **technological solutions align with market needs and future scalability.**

5. **Security, Ethics, & Compliance Awareness** – Leaders **balance rapid innovation with cybersecurity, privacy, and regulatory compliance.**

Tech Leadership is **essential in industries where digital transformation, automation, and AI are reshaping how businesses operate.**

Example

A strong example of **Tech Leadership** is **Sundar Pichai, CEO of Google & Alphabet.** Under his leadership, Google has made massive strides in **AI, cloud computing, and digital services.** Pichai fosters an **innovation-driven culture** while ensuring that technology aligns with user needs and business strategy.

Another example is **Elon Musk**, who has used **Tech Leadership principles** to drive disruptive innovation at **Tesla, SpaceX, and Neuralink.** Musk combines **deep technical knowledge with a bold vision**, pushing teams to **develop groundbreaking technologies in electric vehicles, space travel, and AI.**

Why It Works

Tech Leadership is effective because it:

- **Encourages Innovation & Scalability** – Leaders drive teams to **explore cutting-edge solutions** and **future-proof technology**.

- **Bridges the Gap Between Technology & Business** – Aligns **technical advancements with market demands**.

- **Drives Agile Decision-Making** – Leaders **adapt quickly to industry shifts and disruptions**.

- **Fosters High-Performing Teams** – Employees thrive in an **environment of experimentation, autonomy, and learning**.

- **Enhances Problem-Solving** – Leaders **promote a fail-fast, learn-fast mindset** that accelerates growth.

Studies show that **companies with strong tech leadership outperform competitors by driving digital transformation, talent retention, and long-term innovation**.

How It Works

Tech Leadership follows a **dynamic and iterative approach**:

1. **Developing a Vision for Technology** – Leaders **identify future trends and align them with business strategy**.

2. **Building & Empowering Skilled Teams** – Hiring, mentoring, and supporting **highly technical professionals.**

3. **Driving Agile & Lean Methodologies** – Focusing on **fast iterations, minimal viable products (MVPs), and continuous improvement.**

4. **Creating an Open & Learning Culture** – Encouraging **knowledge sharing, upskilling, and collaboration.**

5. **Managing Risks & Ethical Considerations** – Balancing **rapid innovation with security, compliance, and responsible AI.**

Unlike **directive leadership, which focuses on control, Tech Leadership thrives on empowerment, trust, and adaptability.**

Application

Tech Leadership is widely applied in:

- **Software Development & AI** – Leading teams in **machine learning, cybersecurity, and enterprise software.**

- **Startups & Digital Transformation** – Driving **disruptive innovation in fintech, edtech, and healthtech.**

- **Product Development & UX Design** – Ensuring seamless integration between technology and user experience.

- **IT & Cloud Computing** – Managing **scalable, secure infrastructure and cloud-based solutions.**

Key Insights

1. **Technology Alone is Not Enough** – Tech leaders **must combine technical expertise with strategic thinking.**

2. **Agility is Critical in Tech Leadership** – The **fast-changing nature of tech requires constant adaptation.**

3. **Empowering Teams Drives Innovation** – Leaders **foster collaboration, autonomy, and skill development.**

4. **Scalability & Ethical Leadership Matter** – **Long-term success depends on sustainable, responsible innovation.**

Tech Leadership is **one of the most impactful leadership models**, proving that **vision, adaptability, and technical expertise are key to shaping the future of technology and business.**

32. Military Leadership

Military Leadership: A Breakdown

Theory

Military Leadership is a structured, disciplined leadership model that emphasizes **hierarchical command, strategic decision-making, teamwork, and adaptability in high-pressure environments**. It is built on principles such as **authority, duty, discipline, resilience, and accountability**, ensuring that teams operate with precision and efficiency.

Military Leadership is guided by several core principles:

1. **Mission-First Mentality** – The mission or objective takes precedence over individual interests.

2. **Chain of Command & Authority** – A strict hierarchy ensures clear lines of communication and responsibility.

3. **Discipline & Accountability** – Leaders and subordinates are held to high ethical and performance standards.

4. **Adaptability & Decision-Making Under Pressure** – Leaders must make quick, effective decisions in uncertain situations.

5. **Servant Leadership & Team Loyalty** – Effective military leaders support and protect their teams while expecting commitment in return.

This leadership style **balances directive, transformational, and servant leadership**, allowing leaders to **command with authority while inspiring loyalty and fostering teamwork**.

Example

A powerful example of **Military Leadership** is **General Dwight D. Eisenhower**, Supreme Allied Commander during World War II. Eisenhower effectively managed large, multinational forces, balancing **strategy, coordination, and leadership under immense pressure**. His ability to **make decisive choices, motivate troops, and adapt to rapidly changing conditions** exemplifies strong military leadership.

Another example is **Admiral William H. McRaven**, a U.S. Navy SEAL officer who led special operations forces. His leadership philosophy, outlined in his famous "Make Your Bed" speech, emphasizes **discipline, resilience, and leading by example**—core elements of military leadership.

Why It Works

Military Leadership is effective because it:

- **Provides Clear Structure & Direction** – A well-defined chain of command eliminates confusion.

- **Fosters Discipline & Resilience** – High expectations create **mentally and physically strong teams**.

- **Enhances Decision-Making Under Pressure** – Leaders are trained to **act quickly and effectively in crises**.

- **Builds Trust & Team Cohesion** – Soldiers and personnel develop **strong loyalty and accountability**.

- **Encourages Strategic Thinking & Adaptability** – Military leaders assess **risks, threats, and evolving challenges** efficiently.

Research shows that **military leadership principles are highly transferable to business, crisis management, and public administration**, as they create **disciplined, adaptable, and results-driven teams**.

How It Works

Military Leadership follows a **structured yet flexible approach**:

1. **Establishing a Clear Mission** – Leaders define the mission, objectives, and operational strategy.

2. **Training & Readiness** – Continuous training ensures **teams are prepared for any scenario**.

3. **Executing with Precision & Control** – Orders are given and executed with discipline.

4. **Adaptation & Quick Decision-Making** – Leaders pivot strategies based on evolving conditions.

5. **Accountability & Leadership by Example** – Leaders **set the standard for integrity and performance**.

Unlike **participative leadership, which encourages broad input**, Military Leadership **thrives on decisive action and hierarchical efficiency.**

Application

Military Leadership is widely applied in:

- **Defence & Law Enforcement** – Used in **military, police, and emergency response teams.**

- **Corporate Leadership & Crisis Management** – CEOs and executives apply **military principles in high-stakes decision-making.**

- **Government & Public Service** – Leaders use military leadership tactics in **policy-making, logistics, and national security.**

- **Sports & Team Management** – Coaches implement **military-style discipline and strategy to build high-performing teams.**

Key Insights

1. **Discipline & Structure Drive Success** – Military leaders **enforce discipline to create reliable, efficient teams.**

2. **Leadership is About Service & Accountability** – The best leaders **support their teams while maintaining high standards.**

3. **Quick, Decisive Action is Critical** – Military leaders **must think and act fast in high-risk situations.**

4. **Training & Preparedness Define Great Leadership**
   – Leaders who **prioritize readiness and adaptability excel in any environment**.

Military Leadership is **one of the most effective leadership models**, proving that **strategy, discipline, and adaptability create strong, resilient teams capable of achieving critical objectives under any circumstances**.

33. Healthcare Leadership

Healthcare Leadership: A Breakdown

Theory

Healthcare Leadership is a specialized leadership model focused on **guiding healthcare organizations, professionals, and systems to provide high-quality patient care, improve efficiency, and adapt to rapidly changing medical advancements**. Unlike traditional leadership styles, Healthcare Leadership requires a **balance between clinical expertise, strategic management, and ethical decision-making**.

This model integrates elements of **Transformational Leadership, Servant Leadership, and Adaptive Leadership** to navigate complex healthcare environments. Healthcare leaders must ensure **patient-cantered care, regulatory compliance, operational efficiency, and staff well-being** while managing challenges like **technological advancements, public health crises, and policy changes**.

Key characteristics of **Healthcare Leadership** include:

1. **Patient-Cantered Approach** – Ensuring **quality, safety, and accessibility of care.**

2. **Evidence-Based Decision-Making** – Using **medical research and data** to inform policies.

3. **Interdisciplinary Collaboration** – Bridging **doctors, nurses, administrators, and policymakers.**

4. **Ethical & Compassionate Leadership** – Maintaining **integrity, transparency, and empathy** in decision-making.

5. **Resilience & Crisis Management** – Leading through **health crises, pandemics, and emergency situations.**

Unlike **corporate leadership, which focuses solely on profitability**, Healthcare Leadership **balances financial sustainability with ethical healthcare delivery.**

Example

A powerful example of **Healthcare Leadership** is **Dr. Anthony Fauci**, former director of the National Institute of Allergy and Infectious Diseases (NIAID).** His leadership during the COVID-19 pandemic emphasized **evidence-based guidance, crisis management, and transparent**

communication, ensuring public trust and global collaboration in fighting the pandemic.

Another example is **Dr. Atul Gawande**, a surgeon and public health leader who advocates for **systematic improvements in patient safety, medical protocols, and ethical healthcare reform**. His leadership has **transformed surgical practices and policy implementation worldwide**.

Why It Works

Healthcare Leadership is effective because it:

- **Ensures High-Quality Patient Care** – Leaders prioritize **safety, efficiency, and ethical treatment**.

- **Improves Team Collaboration & Morale** – Effective leadership fosters **communication and trust among healthcare professionals**.

- **Enhances Crisis Preparedness** – Leaders **respond swiftly to medical emergencies and public health threats**.

- **Encourages Innovation & Medical Advancements** – **Research-driven leadership improves healthcare systems**.

- **Navigates Regulatory & Policy Challenges** – Leaders **balance clinical excellence with compliance and financial constraints**.

Studies show that **strong healthcare leadership improves patient outcomes, reduces medical errors, and increases healthcare provider satisfaction.**

How It Works

Healthcare Leadership follows a **structured yet adaptable approach**:

1. **Defining Clear Health Objectives** – Leaders establish **patient care goals and hospital policies.**

2. **Enhancing Communication & Teamwork** – Promoting **collaboration among medical staff, administrators, and policymakers.**

3. **Data-Driven Decision-Making** – Implementing **evidence-based strategies to improve healthcare delivery.**

4. **Managing Resources Efficiently** – Optimizing **hospital operations, budgets, and medical technology.**

5. **Fostering Continuous Learning & Innovation** – Encouraging **medical education, research, and process improvements.**

Unlike **directive leadership, which enforces top-down decisions, Healthcare Leadership thrives on adaptability, ethical considerations, and multidisciplinary teamwork.**

Application

Healthcare Leadership is widely applied in:

- **Hospitals & Healthcare Systems** – Managing **medical staff, patient care, and operational efficiency**.

- **Public Health & Policy-Making** – Leading initiatives in **disease prevention, vaccination programs, and healthcare access**.

- **Medical Research & Innovation** – Advancing **new treatments, medical technology, and patient care models**.

- **Crisis & Disaster Management** – Coordinating responses to **pandemics, natural disasters, and emergency situations**.

Key Insights

1. **Leadership in Healthcare Requires Ethical Responsibility** – Patient well-being must always be the **top priority**.

2. **Collaboration Strengthens Healthcare Systems – Doctors, nurses, and administrators must work together for efficiency**.

3. **Adaptability is Essential in Healthcare Leadership** – Leaders **must respond to medical and technological advancements**.

4. **Crisis Management & Resilience Define Strong Leaders** – Healthcare leaders **must remain composed and strategic during health emergencies**.

Healthcare Leadership is **one of the most impactful leadership models**, proving that **a combination of medical expertise, ethical responsibility, and strategic thinking leads to better patient care and stronger healthcare systems**.

34. Educational Leadership

Educational Leadership: A Breakdown

Theory

Educational Leadership is a leadership model that focuses on **guiding, managing, and transforming educational institutions to enhance student learning, teacher effectiveness, and overall school performance**. Unlike corporate leadership, which emphasizes profit, **Educational Leadership prioritizes academic excellence, student development, and institutional improvement**.

This model integrates elements of **Transformational Leadership, Servant Leadership, and Instructional Leadership**, ensuring that school leaders **create a vision, foster collaboration, and implement policies that improve education systems. Effective educational leaders inspire teachers, engage students, and establish a culture of continuous learning.**

Key characteristics of **Educational Leadership** include:

1. **Student-Cantered Approach** – Ensuring that **all decisions focus on student growth and success**.

2. **Teacher Support & Professional Development** – Providing **mentorship, training, and resources for educators**.

3. **Strategic Policy Implementation** – Managing **curriculum, assessment methods, and institutional regulations**.

4. **Building Community & Stakeholder Engagement** – Involving **teachers, parents, and local organizations** in school improvement.

5. **Data-Driven Decision-Making** – Using **academic performance metrics and research to inform strategies**.

Unlike **bureaucratic leadership, which enforces rigid policies, Educational Leadership thrives on innovation, collaboration, and evidence-based decision-making**.

Example

A strong example of **Educational Leadership** is **Michelle Rhee**, former Chancellor of Washington, D.C. Public Schools. Rhee **implemented major reforms to improve teacher quality, standardized testing, and student performance**, focusing on **accountability, data-driven decision-making, and professional development for educators**.

Another example is **Sir Ken Robinson**, a thought leader in education who advocated for **creativity, personalized learning, and modernizing traditional education systems.** His leadership approach emphasized **rethinking education to prepare students for the future rather than following outdated models.**

Why It Works

Educational Leadership is effective because it:

- **Improves Student Learning Outcomes** – Schools with strong leadership **see higher graduation rates and better academic performance.**

- **Enhances Teacher Satisfaction & Performance** – When teachers **receive guidance, training, and support**, they teach more effectively.

- **Encourages Innovation in Teaching** – Leaders promote **new teaching strategies, technology integration, and modern learning approaches.**

- **Strengthens School-Community Relationships** – Engaged stakeholders **contribute to better educational environments.**

- **Adapts to Changing Educational Needs** – Leaders **respond to curriculum changes, policy reforms, and technological advancements.**

Studies show that **schools with effective leadership consistently outperform those with weak leadership, proving its direct impact on student achievement.**

How It Works

Educational Leadership follows a **structured yet adaptable approach**:

1. **Establishing a Clear Vision** – Leaders define a **mission for student success and institutional growth**.

2. **Empowering Teachers & Staff** – Providing **resources, mentorship, and professional development opportunities**.

3. **Implementing Research-Based Strategies** – Using **data and best practices to improve instruction and management**.

4. **Building a Positive School Culture** – Encouraging **collaboration, inclusivity, and student engagement**.

5. **Ensuring Accountability & Continuous Improvement** – Leaders **evaluate student outcomes, teacher performance, and institutional effectiveness regularly**.

Unlike **directive leadership, which focuses on control, Educational Leadership thrives on empowerment, adaptability, and vision-driven strategies**.

Application

Educational Leadership is widely applied in:

- **K-12 School Administration** – Principals and school leaders manage **curriculum, staff, and student welfare**.

- **Higher Education Management** – University leaders oversee **academic programs, faculty development, and institutional policies**.

- **Education Policy & Reform** – Policymakers shape **national and regional education standards**.

- **Teacher Training & Professional Development** – Educational leaders **mentor and guide future educators**.

Key Insights

1. **Leadership Directly Impacts Student Success** – **Strong educational leadership transforms schools and universities**.

2. **Empowering Teachers Leads to Better Learning Environments** – When **teachers receive guidance and resources, student outcomes improve**.

3. **Data & Research Are Essential for Decision-Making** – Leaders **use academic performance metrics to guide policies**.

4. **Education Must Continuously Evolve** – Leaders must **embrace change, technology, and new teaching methods**.

Educational Leadership is **one of the most impactful leadership models**, proving that **strong vision, strategic decision-making, and collaboration can create world-class education systems that empower both students and teachers.**

35. Sports Leadership

Sports Leadership: A Breakdown

Theory

Sports Leadership is a leadership model that focuses on **motivating, guiding, and developing teams or individual athletes to achieve peak performance.** It combines **strategic decision-making, psychological motivation, and team management** to foster success in highly competitive environments. Unlike corporate leadership, which prioritizes business growth, **Sports Leadership emphasizes discipline, resilience, teamwork, and mental strength.**

This leadership style integrates elements of **Transformational Leadership, Servant Leadership, and Situational Leadership**, depending on the needs of the athletes and the team. A great sports leader is not only focused on winning but also on **developing character, teamwork, and long-term success.**

Key characteristics of **Sports Leadership** include:

1. **Vision & Goal Setting** – Establishing **clear performance objectives for the team or athlete.**

2. **Discipline & Accountability** – Enforcing **training schedules, ethics, and high-performance standards.**

3. **Motivation & Inspiration** – Keeping athletes **mentally strong and committed to success.**

4. **Adaptability & Game Strategy** – Adjusting **tactics based on competition, injuries, and team dynamics.**

5. **Emotional Intelligence & Communication** – Understanding **athletes' mindsets and building strong team relationships.**

Unlike **authoritative leadership, which relies on strict control, Sports Leadership balances discipline with empowerment to help athletes reach their full potential.**

Example

A strong example of **Sports Leadership** is **Phil Jackson, former NBA coach of the Chicago Bulls and LA Lakers.** Known for his **Zen leadership approach, psychological motivation, and ability to build trust,** Jackson led Michael Jordan and Kobe Bryant to multiple championships by **fostering team cohesion and mental discipline.**

Another example is **Sir Alex Ferguson, legendary manager of Manchester United.** His leadership focused on **strategic thinking, player development, and adaptability,** creating a winning culture that led to **13 Premier League titles and two Champions League trophies.**

Why It Works

Sports Leadership is effective because it:

- **Builds Team Cohesion & Trust** – Players perform better when they **trust their coach and teammates.**

- **Enhances Mental Resilience** – Leaders help athletes **overcome failure, pressure, and adversity.**

- **Optimizes Performance** – Strategic leadership **ensures peak physical and tactical execution.**

- **Encourages Personal & Professional Growth** – Athletes develop **both on and off the field.**

- **Creates a Winning Culture** – A strong leader **fosters a mindset of excellence and commitment.**

Studies show that **teams with strong leadership consistently outperform rivals due to better motivation, discipline, and teamwork.**

How It Works

Sports Leadership follows a **structured yet adaptable approach**:

1. **Setting Clear Goals & Expectations** – Defining **winning strategies and performance metrics.**

2. **Building Trust & Communication** – Ensuring **strong relationships between coaches and athletes.**

3. **Motivating & Mentoring Players** – Using **psychological coaching and motivation techniques**.

4. **Tactical & Strategic Planning** – Analysing **competition and adjusting game plans**.

5. **Instilling Discipline & Work Ethic** – Ensuring **consistent training, preparation, and mindset development**.

Unlike **transactional leadership, which focuses on rewards**, **Sports Leadership relies on intrinsic motivation and team spirit**.

Application

Sports Leadership is widely applied in:

- **Professional & Amateur Sports Teams** – Managing **athletes, team dynamics, and strategies**.

- **Youth & Development Coaching** – Fostering **future sports talent with mentorship and discipline**.

- **Olympic & Elite Athlete Training** – Developing **mental and physical excellence for high-performance sports**.

- **Corporate Team-Building & Leadership Training** – Using **sports principles to improve business teamwork**.

Key Insights

1. **Leadership Determines Team Success** – The **right coach can turn underperformers into champions.**

2. **Motivation & Psychology Are Just as Important as Skill** – **Winning is a mindset as much as a skillset.**

3. **Adaptability & Strategy Win Games** – Great leaders **adjust tactics based on competition and challenges.**

4. **Discipline & Resilience Are Core Pillars** – Success comes from **hard work, preparation, and mental toughness.**

Sports Leadership is **one of the most dynamic leadership models**, proving that **strong vision, motivation, and strategy create champions on and off the field.**

36. Startup Leadership

Startup Leadership: A Breakdown

Theory

Startup Leadership is a leadership model designed for **entrepreneurs and business founders** navigating the fast-paced, high-risk environment of startups. Unlike traditional corporate leadership, which emphasizes stability and structure, **Startup Leadership focuses on agility, innovation, risk-taking, and rapid decision-making**.

Startup Leadership integrates elements of **Transformational Leadership, Agile Leadership, and Servant Leadership**, ensuring that leaders can **inspire teams, adapt to market changes, and build scalable business models**. A startup leader must be a **visionary, strategist, and motivator**, capable of making quick decisions while fostering a culture of resilience and innovation.

Key characteristics of **Startup Leadership** include:

1. **Vision & Purpose-Driven Leadership** – Founders articulate **a bold mission to inspire teams and investors**.

2. **Risk-Taking & Adaptability** – Leaders must **navigate uncertainty and pivot when necessary**.

3. **Lean & Agile Decision-Making** – Prioritizing **speed, experimentation, and rapid iterations**.

4. **Team Empowerment & Culture Building** – Creating a collaborative, high-energy startup environment.

5. **Customer-Centric & Scalable Thinking** – Focusing on **market fit, user feedback, and growth potential**.

Unlike **bureaucratic leadership, which emphasizes structure, Startup Leadership thrives on flexibility, creativity, and fast execution**.

Example

A great example of **Startup Leadership** is **Elon Musk, CEO of Tesla & SpaceX**. Musk has **pioneered disruptive industries by taking bold risks, maintaining a futuristic vision, and pushing his teams to innovate rapidly**. His leadership has enabled Tesla to dominate the electric vehicle market and SpaceX to revolutionize space travel.

Another example is **Brian Chesky, co-founder of Airbnb**. Despite scepticism, Chesky led Airbnb through **regulatory challenges, global expansion, and the COVID-19 crisis**, demonstrating **resilience, adaptability, and customer-focused leadership**.

Why It Works

Startup Leadership is effective because it:

- **Drives Rapid Innovation** – Encourages experimentation, iteration, and creative problem-solving.

- **Builds Strong, Motivated Teams** – Startups require passionate, mission-driven employees.

- **Encourages Market Disruption** – Leaders challenge traditional industries with bold ideas.

- **Adapts Quickly to Challenges** – Leaders **embrace failure as part of growth and pivot strategies fast**.

- **Attracts Investors & Customers** – A strong, visionary leader **builds trust and credibility in the market**.

Studies show that **successful startups often have founders with strong leadership capabilities, resilience, and customer-driven innovation**.

How It Works

Startup Leadership follows a **fast-moving, execution-driven approach**:

1. **Defining a Clear Vision & Mission** – Leaders **align the team around a compelling purpose**.

2. **Building a Lean, Agile Team** – Hiring **multi-skilled, adaptable individuals** who thrive in uncertainty.

3. **Executing Fast & Learning from Failures** – Launching **minimum viable products (MVPs) and iterating based on feedback**.

4. **Securing Funding & Managing Resources** – Balancing **growth with financial sustainability**.

5. **Scaling & Sustaining Culture** – As startups grow, leaders must **retain core values and team cohesion**.

Unlike **corporate leadership, which focuses on structured growth, Startup Leadership requires speed, bold decision-making, and resilience in the face of uncertainty**.

Application

Startup Leadership is widely applied in:

- **Tech Startups & Innovation Hubs** – Founders lead breakthroughs in **AI, fintech, biotech, and SaaS**.

- **E-Commerce & Digital Platforms** – Startups like **Airbnb, Uber, and Shopify** scale through agile leadership.

- **Social Enterprises & Impact Startups** – Leaders drive **mission-based, sustainable businesses**.

- **High-Growth Ventures & VC-Backed Companies** – Startup leaders **manage fast expansion and investor expectations**.

Key Insights

1. **Speed & Execution Define Success** – Startups must **move fast, test ideas, and iterate continuously**.

2. **Adaptability is a Core Strength** – The ability to **pivot and embrace failure separates successful leaders from the rest**.

3. **Culture & Vision Matter** – A strong startup leader **creates an inspiring, mission-driven environment**.

4. **Customer & Market Fit Are Essential** – The best leaders **focus on delivering real value, not just raising funds**.

Startup Leadership is **one of the most demanding leadership models**, proving that **vision, adaptability, and bold execution are key to building groundbreaking businesses**.

37. Political Leadership

Political Leadership: A Breakdown

Theory

Political Leadership is a leadership model focused on **governing, influencing public opinion, and making policy decisions to guide societies, organizations, or nations**. Unlike corporate leadership, which emphasizes profitability and operational efficiency, **Political Leadership prioritizes public service, diplomacy, negotiation, and decision-making for the greater good**.

Political Leadership incorporates elements of **Transformational Leadership, Charismatic Leadership, and Servant Leadership**, depending on the leader's governing style. It requires **vision, strategic communication, crisis** management, and the ability to unite diverse groups under a common goal.

Key characteristics of **Political Leadership** include:

1. **Vision & Policy-Driven Governance** – Leaders articulate **long-term strategies for social and economic development.**

2. **Public Communication & Influence** – Leaders **shape public opinion through rhetoric, media, and political discourse.**

3. **Negotiation & Diplomacy** – Effective political leaders **build alliances, resolve conflicts, and balance stakeholder interests.**

4. **Crisis Management & Decision-Making** – Handling **national emergencies, economic challenges, and global issues.**

5. **Ethical Responsibility & Accountability** – Balancing **power with public trust and transparency.**

Unlike **autocratic leadership, which enforces control through authority**, Political Leadership thrives on **influence, persuasion, and coalition-building.**

Example

A strong example of **Political Leadership** is **Nelson Mandela, former President of South Africa.** Mandela led **post-apartheid reconciliation efforts through vision, diplomacy, and a commitment to justice.** His leadership emphasized **unity, peace, and democratic values**, making him an internationally respected political leader.

Another example is **Franklin D. Roosevelt (FDR), the 32nd U.S. President**. Facing the **Great Depression and World War II**, FDR demonstrated **strategic crisis management, policy innovation (New Deal), and inspirational communication (Fireside Chats)** to restore economic stability and public confidence.

Why It Works

Political Leadership is effective because it:

- **Mobilizes Large Populations** – Leaders inspire and **unite people toward common goals.**

- **Balances Power & Governance** – Ensures **stability through laws, policies, and public institutions.**

- **Manages Crises & Uncertainty** – Leaders make **decisive, impactful choices during emergencies.**

- **Encourages Diplomacy & Global Relations** – Successful leaders **navigate international politics and economic agreements.**

- **Influences Long-Term Social & Economic Growth** – Policies **shape infrastructure, education, and global development.**

Research shows that **effective political leadership leads to social progress, economic growth, and national stability, while weak leadership results in unrest and dysfunction**.

How It Works

Political Leadership follows a **strategic and people-centric approach**:

1. **Setting a National or Organizational Vision** – Leaders **define long-term goals and policy priorities.**

2. **Building Coalitions & Negotiating Policy** – Engaging **political parties, institutions, and the public.**

3. **Communicating Effectively with Citizens** – Using **speeches, debates, and media to inform and persuade.**

4. **Making Tough Decisions Under Pressure** – **Handling conflicts, crises, and policy trade-offs with resilience.**

5. **Ensuring Transparency & Public Trust** – Leaders maintain **ethical standards and democratic accountability.**

Unlike **corporate leadership, which focuses on profit-driven strategy, Political Leadership must consider public welfare, ethics, and governance complexities.**

Application

Political Leadership is widely applied in:

- **Government & Public Policy** – Leaders **govern nations, states, and local communities.**

- **International Diplomacy** – Politicians negotiate **treaties, trade agreements, and global peace efforts**.

- **Social Movements & Activism** – Figures like **Martin Luther King Jr.** and **Malala Yousafzai** lead **political change**.

- **Nonprofits & Global Organizations** – Leaders in **NGOs and the UN drive policy for social impact**.

Key Insights

1. **Political Leadership Shapes History** – Great leaders **influence laws, culture, and economic structures for generations**.

2. **Public Trust is Essential – Without transparency and ethical leadership, instability and corruption arise**.

3. **Crisis Management Defines Strong Leaders** – Political leaders **must act decisively during wars, pandemics, and economic downturns**.

4. **Diplomacy & Negotiation Are Key Skills** – Leaders **must balance different viewpoints to achieve stability and progress**.

Political Leadership is **one of the most complex yet impactful leadership models**, proving that **influence, strategic governance, and ethical responsibility define national and global success**.

38. Corporate Leadership

Corporate Leadership: A Breakdown

Theory

Corporate Leadership is a leadership model that focuses on **guiding businesses, managing stakeholders, and driving organizational success through strategic decision-making, innovation, and strong company culture**. Unlike leadership in non-business sectors, **Corporate Leadership balances profitability, operational efficiency, employee engagement, and long-term sustainability**.

Corporate Leadership integrates elements of **Transformational Leadership, Servant Leadership, and Strategic Leadership**, ensuring that leaders can **motivate teams, make data-driven decisions, and navigate economic complexities**. Effective corporate leaders shape **company vision, culture, and financial health**, ensuring businesses remain competitive.

Key characteristics of **Corporate Leadership** include:

1. **Vision & Strategy** – Leaders **define business goals, market positioning, and long-term growth plans**.

2. **Financial & Operational Acumen** – Strong understanding of **profitability, cost management, and efficiency**.

3. **Talent Development & Team Building** – Ensuring employees are engaged, trained, and aligned with corporate values.

4. **Ethical Decision-Making & Corporate Responsibility** – Balancing profit motives with social and environmental considerations.

5. **Adaptability & Crisis Management** – Leaders must pivot strategies during economic shifts, market disruptions, or crises.

Unlike **bureaucratic leadership, which focuses on rigid structures, Corporate Leadership thrives on innovation, people management, and continuous improvement.**

Example

A great example of **Corporate Leadership** is **Satya Nadella, CEO of Microsoft**. When he took over in 2014, he transformed Microsoft's culture from **rigid and competitive to collaborative and growth-focused**. His leadership prioritized **cloud computing, AI, and open-source partnerships**, making Microsoft one of the most valuable companies globally.

Another example is **Indra Nooyi, former CEO of PepsiCo**. Nooyi led **corporate transformation by focusing on sustainability, healthier products, and global expansion**, demonstrating that corporate leaders must balance **business growth with corporate responsibility**.

Why It Works

Corporate Leadership is effective because it:

- **Drives Organizational Growth & Profitability** – Leaders set strategies that **increase revenue and market share.**

- **Builds Strong Company Culture** – Employee engagement and motivation **improve retention and performance.**

- **Encourages Innovation & Agility** – Companies **adapt to new markets, trends, and technologies.**

- **Strengthens Stakeholder Trust** – Ethical and transparent leadership **builds investor, employee, and customer confidence.**

- **Ensures Long-Term Sustainability** – Leaders **balance financial success with social and environmental impact.**

Research shows that **companies with strong leadership outperform competitors, innovate faster, and retain top talent more effectively.**

How It Works

Corporate Leadership follows a **strategic, people-centric approach:**

1. **Setting a Clear Business Vision** – Leaders align **teams with corporate goals and market trends.**

2. **Leading Through Data & Innovation** – Using analytics, AI, and market research to inform decisions.

3. **Developing & Empowering Employees** – Fostering leadership pipelines, training, and professional growth.

4. **Managing Risk & Economic Uncertainty** – Navigating **financial crises, regulatory changes, and global competition**.

5. **Ensuring Corporate Responsibility & Ethics** – Implementing **ESG (Environmental, Social, Governance) strategies**.

Unlike **directive leadership, which enforces strict rules**, **Corporate Leadership empowers employees and fosters a vision-driven culture**.

Application

Corporate Leadership is widely applied in:

- **Multinational Corporations** – Leaders guide **global expansion, innovation, and financial management**.

- **Startups & Scaling Companies** – Founders transition from **entrepreneurs to strategic business leaders**.

- **Tech & Innovation Industries** – Companies like **Apple, Amazon, and Tesla thrive on visionary corporate leadership**.

- **Finance & Banking Sectors** – Leaders focus on **risk management, investment strategies, and economic forecasting**.

Key Insights

1. **Corporate Leadership Shapes Global Markets** – **Strong leaders define industry trends and economic growth**.

2. **People-First Leadership Drives Success** – Engaged employees **fuel innovation and productivity**.

3. **Ethics & Transparency Build Corporate Trust** – Reputation is critical for **long-term sustainability**.

4. **Agility & Innovation Are Non-Negotiable** – Leaders must **constantly adapt to new technologies and market shifts**.

Corporate Leadership is **one of the most influential leadership models**, proving that **vision, strategy, and people management are key to building resilient, future-ready businesses**.

39. Retail Leadership

Retail Leadership: A Breakdown

Theory

Retail Leadership is a leadership model focused on **managing retail operations, enhancing customer experience, driving sales, and leading frontline teams effectively**. Unlike corporate leadership, which emphasizes strategic planning and long-term growth, **Retail Leadership requires a combination of operational efficiency, employee engagement, and adaptability in a fast-paced environment**.

This model incorporates elements of **Transactional Leadership, Servant Leadership, and Transformational Leadership**, ensuring that leaders can **motivate employees, optimize retail performance, and respond to changing consumer behaviours**. Successful retail leaders focus on **customer satisfaction, staff development, and financial performance** while adapting to **technological advancements and market trends**.

Key characteristics of **Retail Leadership** include:

1. **Customer-Centric Focus** – Ensuring that **customer experience and satisfaction drive all decisions**.

2. **Sales & Performance Management** – Setting and monitoring **sales targets, promotions, and key performance indicators (KPIs).**

3. **Team Development & Employee Engagement** – Training, **motivating, and retaining frontline retail employees.**

4. **Operational Efficiency & Inventory Control** – Managing **stock levels, supply chains, and store organization.**

5. **Adaptability & Innovation** – Adjusting to **seasonal trends, digital transformation, and competitive pressures.**

Unlike **bureaucratic leadership, which relies on rigid structures**, **Retail Leadership thrives on agility, customer focus, and dynamic team management.**

Example

A great example of **Retail Leadership** is **Howard Schultz, former CEO of Starbucks.** Schultz transformed Starbucks into a **global brand by focusing on customer experience, employee satisfaction, and consistent store quality.** His leadership **reinvented the coffeehouse culture, emphasizing premium service, employee benefits, and store atmosphere.**

Another example is **Doug McMillon, CEO of Walmart**, who led **Walmart's digital transformation, improving e-commerce operations while maintaining in-store**

efficiency. His leadership has helped **Walmart stay competitive against Amazon in the retail industry**.

Why It Works

Retail Leadership is effective because it:

- **Enhances Customer Loyalty & Experience** – Happy customers **return, increasing long-term sales and brand reputation**.

- **Drives Employee Engagement & Retention** – Motivated employees **provide better service and improve store efficiency**.

- **Improves Sales & Profitability** – Data-driven leadership **optimizes sales strategies and operational costs**.

- **Encourages Innovation & Adaptability** – Retail leaders must **respond to shifting consumer preferences and technology**.

- **Strengthens Brand Identity & Culture** – A strong **brand image and leadership culture attract both employees and customers**.

Studies show that **retail companies with strong leadership have higher employee retention, better customer satisfaction, and improved financial performance**.

How It Works

Retail Leadership follows a **customer and team-driven approach**:

1. **Creating a Strong Customer Experience** – Leaders ensure that **store layout, product availability, and service meet customer expectations.**

2. **Training & Empowering Employees** – Developing **sales associates, store managers, and team leaders to enhance productivity.**

3. **Monitoring Sales Performance & KPIs** – Using **data analytics to track trends, inventory, and revenue growth.**

4. **Implementing Digital & Omnichannel Strategies** – Integrating **e-commerce, mobile shopping, and in-store experiences.**

5. **Ensuring Operational Excellence** – Managing **supply chains, staffing, and cost-efficiency in retail stores.**

Unlike **directive leadership, which prioritizes top-down control, Retail Leadership empowers frontline employees to deliver outstanding customer service.**

Application

Retail Leadership is widely applied in:

- **Brick-and-Mortar Retail Stores** – Leading teams in **fashion, grocery, department stores, and specialty retailers.**

- **E-Commerce & Digital Retail** – Managing **online shopping platforms, supply chains, and customer service**.

- **Franchise & Multi-Store Operations** – Overseeing **multiple locations while ensuring brand consistency**.

- **Luxury & High-End Retail** – Providing **personalized shopping experiences and premium service**.

Key Insights

1. **Retail Leadership is Customer-Driven – Leaders must focus on delivering a seamless shopping experience**.

2. **Employee Motivation Translates to Business Success** – Happy, well-trained employees **enhance customer interactions**.

3. **Adaptability is Essential in Retail** – Market trends, **technology, and consumer behaviour constantly evolve**.

4. **Retail Leadership Must Balance Operations & Innovation** – Efficiency and creativity are both key **to long-term retail success**.

Retail Leadership is **one of the most dynamic leadership models**, proving that **strong vision, customer focus, and team empowerment drive retail success in an ever-changing industry**.

40. Nonprofit Leadership

Nonprofit Leadership: A Breakdown

Theory

Nonprofit Leadership is a leadership model focused on **mission-driven impact, stakeholder engagement, and resource management to serve communities and drive social change.** Unlike corporate leadership, which prioritizes profitability, **Nonprofit Leadership emphasizes purpose, sustainability, and community impact over financial gain.**

This model integrates elements of **Servant Leadership, Transformational Leadership, and Adaptive Leadership,** ensuring that nonprofit leaders can **inspire teams, mobilize resources, and navigate challenges such as funding constraints and policy changes.** Effective nonprofit leaders **balance strategic vision, ethical leadership, and grassroots engagement** to fulfil their organization's mission.

Key characteristics of **Nonprofit Leadership** include:

1. **Mission-Driven Decision-Making** – Leaders focus on **advancing social causes rather than maximizing revenue.**

2. **Stakeholder & Community Engagement** – Collaborating with **donors, volunteers, policymakers, and beneficiaries.**

3. **Financial Sustainability & Fundraising** – Securing **grants, donations, and partnerships to maintain operations.**

4. **Ethical & Transparent Governance** – Ensuring **accountability, compliance, and responsible stewardship of resources.**

5. **Advocacy & Public Influence** – Raising awareness and **shaping policies to create systemic change.**

Unlike **transactional leadership, which is goal and profit-driven, Nonprofit Leadership thrives on inspiration, collaboration, and long-term impact.**

Example

A great example of **Nonprofit Leadership** is **Malala Yousafzai, co-founder of the Malala Fund.** She has led efforts to **advocate for girls' education worldwide, mobilizing resources, influencing policymakers, and inspiring millions to support the cause.** Her leadership showcases **resilience, storytelling, and strategic advocacy** to drive nonprofit success.

Another example is **Bill Drayton, founder of Ashoka**, a nonprofit that supports **social entrepreneurs worldwide.** His leadership has **empowered thousands of changemakers to implement innovative solutions for**

social issues, proving that nonprofit leadership can have a global impact.

Why It Works

Nonprofit Leadership is effective because it:

- **Inspires Purpose & Commitment** – Employees and volunteers **stay engaged due to the meaningful mission.**

- **Builds Strong Community & Donor Relationships** – Nonprofits **rely on trust, transparency, and collaboration.**

- **Drives Sustainable Social Change** – Leaders create **long-term impact through policy advocacy and community programs.**

- **Maximizes Limited Resources** – Effective leaders **leverage partnerships, volunteers, and grants efficiently.**

- **Adapts to Social & Economic Challenges** – Nonprofits must **navigate funding shifts, policy changes, and crises.**

Studies show that **strong nonprofit leadership results in higher donor retention, volunteer engagement, and long-term organizational sustainability.**

How It Works

Nonprofit Leadership follows a **mission-focused, people-cantered approach:**

1. **Defining a Clear Vision & Mission** – Leaders ensure that **every decision aligns with the organization's purpose**.

2. **Engaging & Empowering Teams** – Encouraging **volunteer participation, staff development, and leadership growth**.

3. **Building Strategic Partnerships** – Collaborating with **governments, corporations, and other nonprofits**.

4. **Fundraising & Financial Management** – Securing **grants, donors, and sponsorships to sustain operations**.

5. **Advocating for Social & Policy Change** – Using **research, media, and campaigns to raise awareness and influence legislation**.

Unlike **corporate leadership, which focuses on competitive advantage**, **Nonprofit Leadership fosters cooperation, advocacy, and collective impact**.

Application

Nonprofit Leadership is widely applied in:

-   **Human Rights & Advocacy Organizations** – Groups like **Amnesty International and the Malala Fund**.

-   **Community & Social Services** – Nonprofits providing **education, healthcare, and disaster relief**.

- **Environmental & Sustainability Initiatives** – Organizations focused on **climate change, conservation, and clean energy**.

- **Philanthropy & Charitable Foundations** – Managing **grants, funding programs, and social investments**.

Key Insights

1. **Mission is the Core of Leadership** – Every decision must align with **the nonprofit's purpose and social impact goals**.

2. **People & Partnerships Drive Success** – Collaboration with **volunteers, donors, and communities is essential**.

3. **Sustainability Requires Strategic Fundraising** – Leaders must **balance financial responsibility with mission-driven goals**.

4. **Nonprofit Leaders Must Be Resilient & Adaptive** – Changing policies, funding shifts, and global crises require **flexibility and long-term vision**.

Nonprofit Leadership is **one of the most purpose-driven leadership models**, proving that **vision, collaboration, and ethical leadership can create meaningful, lasting social impact**.

Leadership Models by Psychological Approach

41. Maslow's Hierarchy Leadership

Maslow's Hierarchy Leadership: A Breakdown

Theory

Maslow's Hierarchy Leadership is a leadership model based on **Abraham Maslow's Hierarchy of Needs theory**, which suggests that individuals are motivated by five levels of needs: **physiological, safety, love/belonging, esteem, and self-actualization**. This leadership model applies Maslow's psychological framework to **employee motivation, engagement, and development** within an organization.

The core idea is that **leaders must understand and fulfil these needs to create a productive, motivated workforce**. Unlike traditional leadership styles that focus only on performance, **Maslow's Hierarchy Leadership prioritizes well-being, personal growth, and fulfilment as drivers of success**.

Key characteristics of **Maslow's Hierarchy Leadership** include:

1. **Addressing Basic Needs First** – Ensuring employees have **fair wages, job security, and a safe work environment**.

2. **Fostering a Sense of Belonging** – Encouraging **teamwork, collaboration, and strong workplace culture.**

3. **Building Employee Confidence** – Recognizing achievements and **providing opportunities for skill development.**

4. **Encouraging Growth & Self-Actualization** – Helping employees **reach their highest potential through leadership opportunities and innovation.**

5. **Creating a People-Cantered Organization** – Ensuring leadership **focuses on individual well-being and long-term development.**

Unlike **transactional leadership, which focuses on rewards and penalties, Maslow's Hierarchy Leadership emphasizes intrinsic motivation and human-cantered management.**

Example

A great example of **Maslow's Hierarchy Leadership** is **Richard Branson, founder of Virgin Group.** He believes in **prioritizing employee well-being, fostering a sense of belonging, and encouraging creativity and self-expression.** His leadership philosophy aligns with Maslow's model, ensuring employees **feel valued and empowered.**

Another example is **Patagonia's leadership approach,** where the company **focuses on employee work-life balance, environmental responsibility, and a strong community-driven culture.** By meeting employees' higher-level needs, Patagonia has built a **loyal, purpose-driven workforce**.

Why It Works

Maslow's Hierarchy Leadership is effective because it:

- **Creates Highly Engaged Employees** – People are **more motivated when their needs are met**.

- **Fosters a Positive Work Culture** – Employees feel **valued, secure, and part of a community**.

- **Encourages Innovation & Growth** – Self-actualized employees **drive creativity and problem-solving**.

- **Increases Retention & Loyalty** – Companies that **prioritize employee well-being** experience lower turnover.

- **Leads to Sustainable Success** – Organizations **thrive long-term by investing in their people**.

Studies show that **organizations applying Maslow's principles have higher job satisfaction, productivity, and employee retention**.

How It Works

Maslow's Hierarchy Leadership follows a **progressive, people-first approach**:

1. **Meeting Basic Needs (Physiological & Safety)** – Providing **fair salaries, job security, and a healthy work environment**.

2. **Building Social Connections (Belongingness)** – Encouraging **team collaboration, inclusivity, and company culture**.

3. **Boosting Confidence & Recognition (Esteem Needs)** – Offering **positive feedback, promotions, and leadership opportunities**.

4. **Empowering Employees to Achieve Their Potential (Self-Actualization)** – Encouraging **creativity, autonomy, and career growth**.

Unlike **authoritative leadership, which focuses on strict control**, Maslow's Hierarchy Leadership supports individual development and emotional well-being.

Application

Maslow's Hierarchy Leadership is widely applied in:

- **Corporate & People-Centric Companies** – Organizations that prioritize **employee engagement and workplace culture**.

- **Startups & Innovation-Driven Teams** – Encouraging **creativity, autonomy, and leadership development**.

- **Education & Nonprofit Organizations** – Fostering **personal growth and a strong sense of purpose**.

- **Healthcare & Service Industries** – Ensuring **emotional and professional support for employees**.

Key Insights

1. **Employees Perform Best When Their Needs Are Met** – Addressing **physiological, emotional, and professional needs leads to better engagement**.

2. **Belonging & Recognition Improve Retention** – A strong workplace culture **reduces turnover and increases loyalty**.

3. **Self-Actualization Drives Innovation** – Employees **who feel fulfilled contribute to creative solutions and long-term success**.

4. **Leadership Should Be People-Centric** – Organizations thrive when **leaders focus on employee well-being and holistic development**.

Maslow's Hierarchy Leadership proves that **investing in people leads to higher performance, stronger loyalty, and long-term organizational success.**

42. McGregor's Theory X and Theory Y

McGregor's Theory X and Theory Y Leadership: A Breakdown

Theory

McGregor's Theory X and Theory Y is a leadership model developed by **Douglas McGregor in 1960** that categorizes two distinct ways leaders perceive and manage employees. It is based on the idea that a leader's assumptions about human nature shape their leadership style and management approach.

- **Theory X** assumes that employees **dislike work, lack motivation, and require strict supervision**. Leaders who adopt a Theory X approach use **authoritarian, micromanaging, and control-based leadership** to enforce productivity.

- **Theory Y** assumes that employees **are self-motivated, enjoy their work, and seek responsibility**. Leaders who follow a Theory Y approach use **collaborative, empowering, and participative leadership** to encourage innovation and productivity.

Key characteristics of **Theory X Leadership**:

1. **Strict Supervision & Control** – Managers use **close monitoring and rigid policies**.

2. **Minimal Delegation** – Leaders **assign specific tasks with little autonomy**.

3. **Focus on Compliance & Discipline** – Employees are motivated by **fear of punishment or external rewards**.

Key characteristics of **Theory Y Leadership**:

1. **Trust & Empowerment** – Employees **are given autonomy and encouraged to take ownership**.

2. **Collaborative & Participative Management** – Leaders involve **teams in decision-making**.

3. **Intrinsic Motivation & Growth** – Employees **seek professional development and purpose**.

Unlike **transactional leadership, which focuses on rewards and punishments**, **Theory Y Leadership encourages creativity and innovation**.

Example

A strong example of **Theory X Leadership** is **Henry Ford, founder of Ford Motor Company**. In the early days of mass production, Ford implemented **strict work routines, tight supervision, and rigid discipline** to ensure efficiency. This structure worked well for assembly-line manufacturing but lacked flexibility.

A great example of **Theory Y Leadership** is **Richard Branson, founder of Virgin Group**. Branson promotes **employee empowerment, creative freedom, and a**

flexible work culture, encouraging employees to **innovate and take risks**. His leadership approach has contributed to Virgin's success across multiple industries.

Why It Works

- **Theory X Works in Structured, High-Control Environments** – Best for **manufacturing, military, and rule-driven industries**.

- **Theory Y Works in Dynamic, Innovation-Driven Fields** – Best for **technology, creative industries, and knowledge-based work**.

- **Adapting Both Models Creates Balance** – Leaders can **use Theory X when structure is needed and Theory Y when encouraging creativity**.

- **Employee Satisfaction Increases with Theory Y** – Employees **perform better when they feel trusted and engaged**.

Studies show that **organizations using Theory Y principles tend to have higher job satisfaction, lower turnover, and better innovation outcomes**.

How It Works

McGregor's model suggests leaders should:

1. **Assess Employee Motivation** – Determine whether employees need **strict guidance (Theory X) or autonomy (Theory Y)**.

2. **Adapt Leadership Style to the Workplace** – Structured jobs may require **Theory X**, while creative roles benefit from **Theory Y**.

3. **Balance Control & Empowerment** – Use a **hybrid approach** depending on team dynamics and company culture.

4. **Encourage Growth & Engagement** – Even in structured environments, **offering learning opportunities enhances employee motivation**.

Unlike **directive leadership, which is rigid, McGregor's model provides flexibility in leadership style**.

Application

McGregor's Theory X and Theory Y is widely applied in:

- **Manufacturing & Industrial Work (Theory X)** – Where strict procedures ensure **safety and efficiency**.

- **Tech & Innovation-Based Companies (Theory Y)** – Where autonomy and **collaboration drive breakthroughs**.

- **Education & Healthcare** – Where leaders **blend structure and empowerment**.

- **Startups & Entrepreneurial Ventures** – Using **Theory Y to foster creativity and employee ownership**.

Key Insights

1. **Leadership Style Depends on Employee Mindset** – Some teams require strict management, while others thrive on autonomy.

2. **Theory Y Encourages Innovation & Engagement** – Employees **perform better when they feel valued and trusted.**

3. **Theory X Works in Structured, Routine Tasks** – Not all jobs allow for flexibility; some require clear direction.

4. **Leaders Must Adapt, Not Rely on One Approach** – The best leaders know when to use elements of both theories.

McGregor's **Theory X and Theory Y Leadership Model** proves that **leaders who understand employee motivation can create better workplaces, leading to higher productivity and satisfaction.**

43. Herzberg's Two-Factor Theory

Herzberg's Two-Factor Leadership: A Breakdown

Theory

Herzberg's Two-Factor Theory, also known as the **Motivation-Hygiene Theory**, was developed by **Frederick Herzberg in 1959**. This leadership model suggests that two sets of factors influence employee motivation and job satisfaction: **hygiene factors** and **motivational factors**.

- **Hygiene Factors** – These are **extrinsic elements** that prevent dissatisfaction but do not necessarily motivate employees. They include **salary, job security, company policies, work conditions, and supervision**.

- **Motivational Factors** – These are **intrinsic elements** that drive employee satisfaction and high performance. They include **achievement, recognition, career growth, responsibility, and meaningful work**.

Herzberg's theory argues that **eliminating dissatisfaction (hygiene factors) is not enough to create motivation—** leaders must also enhance **motivational factors** to ensure high engagement and productivity.

Key characteristics of **Herzberg's Leadership Model**:

1. **Addressing Basic Needs First** – Ensuring fair **pay, job security, and a positive work environment.**

2. **Creating Meaningful Work** – Giving employees **challenging tasks and growth opportunities.**

3. **Encouraging Autonomy & Responsibility** – Empowering employees to **make decisions and take ownership.**

4. **Recognition & Career Progression** – Providing **consistent feedback, promotions, and personal development.**

5. **Balancing Extrinsic & Intrinsic Motivation** – **Fixing dissatisfiers while enhancing motivators.**

Unlike **Transactional Leadership, which relies on rewards and punishments, Herzberg's model focuses on creating long-term engagement through meaningful work.**

Example

A great example of **Herzberg's Two-Factor Leadership** is **Google's workplace culture.** Google ensures hygiene factors by offering **competitive salaries, great office environments, and job security.** However, what sets Google apart is its focus on **motivational factors— challenging work, autonomy, learning opportunities, and employee recognition.**

Another example is **Elon Musk's leadership at Tesla and SpaceX.** While Musk maintains **high expectations and demanding work conditions,** employees stay engaged because of **the exciting, mission-driven work and career growth opportunities**, which are strong **motivational factors**.

Why It Works

Herzberg's leadership model is effective because it:

- **Reduces Job Dissatisfaction** – Ensuring **fair pay, safe conditions, and clear policies**.

- **Drives Employee Engagement** – Employees are more motivated by **personal growth and meaningful work**.

- **Improves Retention & Loyalty** – Satisfied employees **stay longer and perform better**.

- **Encourages Creativity & Problem-Solving** – Motivated employees **contribute innovative ideas**.

- **Creates a Positive Workplace Culture** – A balance of hygiene and motivational factors **leads to long-term success**.

Research shows that **companies applying Herzberg's model have higher employee satisfaction, lower turnover, and better productivity**.

How It Works

Herzberg's Two-Factor Leadership follows a **dual-approach strategy**:

1. **Eliminate Dissatisfaction (Hygiene Factors)**

- o Offer **competitive salaries and job security.**

- o Improve **work conditions, policies, and management quality.**

- o Provide **fair treatment and workplace stability.**

2. **Enhance Motivation (Motivational Factors)**

   - o Assign **challenging, purpose-driven tasks.**

   - o Recognize and **reward achievements.**

   - o Offer **career advancement and learning opportunities.**

   - o Empower employees **with autonomy and decision-making authority.**

Unlike **Autocratic Leadership, which relies on control,** Herzberg's model fosters long-term intrinsic motivation.

Application

Herzberg's Two-Factor Leadership is widely applied in:

- **Corporate & Tech Industries** – Companies like **Google, Microsoft, and Amazon** use it to **motivate employees beyond salary.**

- **Healthcare & Education** – Creating environments where **teachers and medical staff feel valued and challenged.**

- **Startups & Innovation-Driven Companies** – Using challenging projects and autonomy to keep employees engaged.

- **Public & Nonprofit Sectors** – Ensuring **fair compensation while driving purpose-driven motivation**.

Key Insights

1. **Money & Benefits Prevent Dissatisfaction But Don't Motivate** – Hygiene factors must be addressed first, but **true motivation comes from meaningful work**.

2. **Career Growth & Recognition Drive Performance** – Employees work harder when they **see opportunities for advancement**.

3. **Fixing Workplace Problems Doesn't Inspire Excellence** – Simply removing dissatisfaction isn't **enough; leaders must actively engage employees**.

4. **Leaders Must Balance Structure & Motivation** – The best workplaces **support employees' basic needs while fostering passion and creativity**.

Herzberg's Two-Factor Leadership proves that **leaders must go beyond preventing dissatisfaction and actively create an environment that motivates employees to excel**.

44. Expectancy Theory (Vroom)

Expectancy Theory Leadership (Vroom): A Breakdown

Theory

Expectancy Theory, developed by Victor Vroom in 1964, is a leadership and motivation model that suggests employees are driven by the expected outcomes of their efforts. It proposes that people are motivated when they believe:

1. **Effort → Performance (Expectancy): If they put in effort, they will perform well.**

2. **Performance → Outcome (Instrumentality): If they perform well, they will receive rewards.**

3. **Outcome → Value (Valence): The reward or outcome must be meaningful to them.**

This means that leaders must ensure employees believe that their hard work will lead to tangible rewards that they value. Unlike fixed leadership models, Expectancy Theory Leadership is flexible and dependent on aligning employee effort with meaningful incentives.

Key characteristics of Expectancy Theory Leadership:

1. **Clear Goal Setting – Employees need to understand what is expected of them.**

2. Strong Reward Systems – Rewards must be fair, transparent, and desirable.

3. Direct Link Between Effort & Rewards – Employees must see a connection between their work and the benefits they receive.

4. Personalized Motivation Strategies – Leaders tailor rewards to match what employees value (money, promotions, recognition, etc.).

5. Eliminating Barriers to Success – Leaders remove obstacles that hinder performance and growth.

Unlike Autocratic Leadership, which enforces strict rules, Expectancy Theory Leadership focuses on individual motivation and personalized incentives.

Example

A great example of Expectancy Theory Leadership is Satya Nadella, CEO of Microsoft. Under his leadership, Microsoft shifted from a competitive culture to one that rewards innovation, collaboration, and employee growth. By aligning incentives with performance, Nadella boosted motivation, improved employee engagement, and increased productivity.

Another example is Google's performance-based compensation model, where employees are rewarded for contributions to innovation, problem-solving, and project success. Google ensures employees see a direct connection between effort, performance, and meaningful rewards like bonuses, promotions, and career development.

Why It Works

Expectancy Theory Leadership is effective because it:

- **Boosts Employee Engagement** – Employees work harder when they see real benefits from their efforts.

- **Encourages Productivity & Performance** – Clear performance-reward links drive employees to exceed expectations.

- **Increases Retention & Satisfaction** – Employees are more loyal when they feel valued and fairly rewarded.

- **Customizes Motivation Strategies** – Different employees are motivated by different incentives (salary, promotions, work-life balance, etc.).

- **Reduces Burnout & Frustration** – Employees stay engaged when they believe effort leads to success.

Studies show that companies using performance-linked rewards and individualized incentives have higher motivation and lower turnover.

How It Works

Expectancy Theory Leadership follows a three-step motivational process:

1. **Strengthen the Expectancy (Effort →
Performance):**

   o Provide training, tools, and support to
   improve skills.

   o Remove barriers that hinder performance.

   o Set realistic but challenging goals.

2. **Improve Instrumentality (Performance →
Rewards):**

   o Clearly define how success leads to specific
   rewards.

   o Ensure the process is transparent and fair.

   o Deliver consistent and timely rewards.

3. **Enhance Valence (Outcome → Value):**

   o Personalize rewards to match employee
   needs and values.

   o Offer both intrinsic (recognition,
   autonomy) and extrinsic (salary, bonuses)
   incentives.

   o Continuously assess whether rewards
   remain meaningful over time.

Unlike Directive Leadership, which dictates tasks,
Expectancy Theory Leadership allows employees to take
control of their motivation.

Application

Expectancy Theory Leadership is widely applied in:

- **Sales & Commission-Based Jobs** – Employees perform better when compensation is tied to measurable performance.

- **Technology & Innovation-Driven Companies** – Firms like Google and Amazon use incentive-based structures to drive innovation.

- **Corporate Leadership & Management** – Leaders set clear objectives with direct rewards for performance.

- **Education & Training** – Instructors reward student efforts with recognition, scholarships, and career growth opportunities.

Key Insights

1. **Motivation is Not One-Size-Fits-All** – Different employees require different rewards to stay engaged.

2. **Effort Must Be Linked to Performance** – Employees need to see that hard work leads to success.

3. **Performance Must Be Rewarded Fairly** – Leaders must ensure transparent, fair, and desirable incentives.

4. **Leaders Must Continuously Adapt** – Employee values change, so leaders must refine motivation strategies regularly.

Expectancy Theory Leadership proves that motivating employees requires aligning their efforts with valuable, achievable rewards, leading to higher engagement and productivity.

45. Self-Determination Theory

Self-Determination Theory (SDT) Leadership: A Breakdown

Theory

Self-Determination Theory (SDT), developed by **Edward Deci and Richard Ryan in the 1980s**, is a leadership and motivation model that focuses on **intrinsic motivation and personal growth**. It suggests that individuals perform at their best when their three core psychological needs are met:

1. **Autonomy** – The need to feel in control of one's actions and decisions.

2. **Competence** – The need to feel capable and effective in achieving tasks.

3. **Relatedness** – The need to feel connected to others and valued in a group.

In **SDT Leadership**, leaders create an environment that **supports these three psychological needs**, helping employees **become self-motivated, engaged, and highly productive**. Unlike traditional leadership models that rely on **external rewards and punishments**, SDT Leadership **fosters internal motivation, making employees feel fulfilled and empowered**.

Key characteristics of **SDT Leadership**:

1. **Empowering Employees with Autonomy** – Giving employees **freedom to make decisions and take ownership of their work**.

2. **Encouraging Growth & Mastery** – Providing **learning opportunities, constructive feedback, and challenges that build competence**.

3. **Fostering Meaningful Connections** – Creating **a supportive, inclusive, and collaborative workplace**.

4. **Focusing on Purpose Over Rewards** – Helping employees **find meaning in their work rather than just chasing incentives**.

5. **Reducing Controlling Behaviours** – Avoiding **micromanagement, excessive rules, and pressure-driven motivation**.

Unlike **Transactional Leadership, which relies on external motivation, SDT Leadership nurtures intrinsic motivation by fulfilling employees' core psychological needs**.

Example

A great example of **SDT Leadership** is **Satya Nadella, CEO of Microsoft**. Nadella transformed Microsoft's leadership culture by **empowering employees with autonomy, encouraging a growth mindset, and fostering collaboration**. His leadership has resulted in **higher employee engagement, innovation, and company-wide success**.

Another example is **Patagonia**, an outdoor clothing company that embraces **SDT principles by promoting work-life balance, environmental responsibility, and employee autonomy**. Employees are **motivated not just by financial incentives but by the meaningful impact of their work**.

Why It Works

SDT Leadership is effective because it:

- **Increases Employee Engagement & Retention** – People stay motivated **when their work is meaningful and fulfilling**.

- **Encourages Innovation & Creativity** – Employees are more **creative when they have the freedom to explore and solve problems**.

- **Boosts Productivity & Performance** – Self-determined employees **take initiative and go beyond basic expectations.**

- **Improves Workplace Morale & Well-Being** – Employees feel **happier and more connected in autonomy-supportive environments.**

- **Reduces Burnout & Stress** – Leaders who encourage **autonomy and competence help employees feel more in control and less pressured.**

Studies show that **employees who work in SDT-driven organizations perform better, experience less stress, and demonstrate higher long-term commitment.**

How It Works

SDT Leadership follows a **people-cantered, autonomy-supportive approach:**

1. **Encourage Autonomy –**

   o Provide employees with **choices and flexibility.**

   o Avoid **micromanaging and excessive control.**

2. **Develop Competence –**

   o Offer **training, mentorship, and meaningful challenges.**

- Give **constructive feedback that promotes growth**.

3. **Foster Relatedness** –

   - Create a **collaborative, trusting, and inclusive workplace**.

   - Show appreciation and **support employee well-being**.

4. **Shift Focus from Rewards to Purpose** –

   - Help employees **understand the impact of their work**.

   - Align company goals with **individual aspirations**.

Unlike **Directive Leadership, which enforces control**, SDT **Leadership thrives on trust, empowerment, and purpose-driven motivation**.

Application

Self-Determination Theory Leadership is widely applied in:

- **Tech & Innovation-Driven Companies** – Companies like **Google and Microsoft** use SDT principles to **empower creative problem-solving**.

- **Education & Learning Environments** – Teachers and mentors **encourage self-driven learning and student autonomy**.

- **Corporate & Startups** – Businesses foster **employee engagement and long-term commitment** by emphasizing **growth, autonomy, and purpose**.

- **Healthcare & Nonprofits** – Organizations ensure **workers remain motivated despite high-pressure environments**.

Key Insights

1. **Autonomy, Competence, and Relatedness Drive Motivation** – Employees perform best **when they feel empowered, skilled, and connected**.

2. **Internal Motivation is More Powerful Than External Rewards – Bonuses and perks alone do not sustain long-term engagement**.

3. **Leaders Should Enable, Not Control** – The best leaders **coach employees rather than micromanage them**.

4. **Purpose-Driven Work Boosts Performance** – Employees work harder **when they see meaning in their contributions**.

Self-Determination Theory Leadership proves that **leaders who nurture autonomy, mastery, and connection create highly engaged, motivated, and successful teams**.

46. Emotional Intelligence Leadership (Daniel Goleman)

Emotional Intelligence Leadership (Daniel Goleman): A Breakdown

Theory

Emotional Intelligence Leadership, developed by **Daniel Goleman**, is a leadership model that emphasizes the role of **emotional intelligence (EI) in effective leadership**. Unlike traditional leadership models that focus only on skills, knowledge, or strategy, **EI Leadership highlights self-awareness, empathy, and interpersonal relationships as key drivers of leadership success**.

Goleman identifies **five key components of emotional intelligence** that leaders must develop:

1. **Self-Awareness** – Understanding one's own emotions and how they impact decisions and behaviour.

2. **Self-Regulation** – Managing emotions effectively, staying calm under pressure, and avoiding impulsive actions.

3. **Motivation** – Having an internal drive for success beyond external rewards like money or status.

4. **Empathy** – Understanding and considering the emotions of others when making decisions.

5. **Social Skills** – Building strong relationships, influencing others, and managing conflict effectively.

Unlike **autocratic leadership, which relies on authority, Emotional Intelligence Leadership focuses on building trust, collaboration, and adaptability.**

Example

A great example of **EI Leadership** is **Oprah Winfrey**. She built a media empire not just through business acumen but by **demonstrating deep emotional intelligence— connecting with people, showing empathy, and inspiring millions through authentic leadership.**

Another example is **Satya Nadella, CEO of Microsoft**, who transformed the company's culture by **fostering collaboration, promoting a growth mindset, and emphasizing empathy in leadership**. His emotionally intelligent leadership has been instrumental in **Microsoft's resurgence in innovation and employee engagement.**

Why It Works

Emotional Intelligence Leadership is effective because it:

- **Improves Decision-Making** – Leaders **who understand their emotions and those of others make more thoughtful, balanced decisions.**

- **Builds Stronger Teams** – Employees feel **heard, valued, and motivated in an emotionally intelligent work environment**.

- **Enhances Communication & Conflict Resolution** – Leaders with high EI **navigate workplace challenges with diplomacy and tact**.

- **Boosts Employee Engagement & Morale** – Teams perform better when **leaders show empathy, motivation, and support**.

- **Increases Adaptability & Resilience** – Emotionally intelligent leaders **stay composed under pressure and guide teams through uncertainty**.

Studies show that **leaders with high emotional intelligence foster higher employee satisfaction, lower turnover, and stronger organizational performance**.

How It Works

EI Leadership follows a **relationship-driven, emotionally aware approach**:

1. **Develop Self-Awareness** – Leaders **reflect on their emotions, biases, and triggers**.

2. **Practice Self-Regulation** – Maintaining **composure in stressful situations and avoiding emotional outbursts**.

3. **Stay Internally Motivated** – Focusing on **long-term goals and intrinsic passion rather than external rewards.**

4. **Demonstrate Empathy** – Actively **listening to employees, understanding their concerns, and providing support.**

5. **Enhance Social Skills** – Building **collaborative relationships, resolving conflicts effectively, and inspiring teams.**

Unlike **directive leadership, which enforces compliance**, EI **Leadership builds trust and influence through emotional connection.**

Application

Emotional Intelligence Leadership is widely applied in:

- **Corporate & Executive Leadership** – Companies like **Google, Microsoft, and Apple prioritize emotionally intelligent leaders.**

- **Healthcare & Education** – Leaders use **empathy and self-awareness to manage teams effectively.**

- **Politics & Public Service** – Figures like **Barack Obama and Nelson Mandela use emotional intelligence to connect with people and lead with integrity.**

- **Startups & Entrepreneurial Ventures** – Founders with high EI **build strong, mission-driven cultures.**

Key Insights

1. **Leadership is About People, Not Just Strategy** – Emotionally intelligent leaders **inspire, motivate, and connect on a deeper level.**

2. **Empathy & Self-Awareness Enhance Decision-Making** – Leaders who **understand emotions make better business and interpersonal choices.**

3. **High EI Creates Resilient, Engaged Teams** – Employees **thrive in environments where leaders show emotional intelligence.**

4. **Emotionally Intelligent Leaders Adapt to Change** – They **stay composed under pressure and guide teams through challenges effectively.**

Emotional Intelligence Leadership proves that **leaders who cultivate self-awareness, empathy, and emotional regulation create stronger, more successful organizations built on trust, collaboration, and long-term vision.**

47. Neuroscience-Based Leadership

Neuroscience-Based Leadership: A Breakdown

Theory

Neuroscience-Based Leadership is a leadership model that applies **neuroscientific principles to enhance decision-**

making, motivation, emotional intelligence, and organizational performance. This model is based on research in cognitive science, brain function, and behavioural psychology, emphasizing how leaders can optimize brain processes to create more effective work environments.

Developed through insights from David Rock's SCARF Model (Status, Certainty, Autonomy, Relatedness, and Fairness) and advancements in neuroleadership, this approach helps leaders understand how the brain reacts to stress, rewards, learning, and social dynamics.

Key principles of Neuroscience-Based Leadership include:

1. Understanding the Brain's Response to Stress & Rewards – Leaders reduce fear-based reactions and enhance positive reinforcement.

2. Encouraging Neuroplasticity & Growth Mindset – Employees adapt and improve when given learning opportunities.

3. Using Emotional Regulation & Cognitive Control – Leaders make balanced, thoughtful decisions under pressure.

4. Enhancing Decision-Making & Focus – Understanding how attention, memory, and cognitive biases shape leadership choices.

5. **Building Trust & Psychological Safety** – Teams perform better when **leaders foster safe, inclusive work environments.**

Unlike **traditional leadership models that focus on experience-based strategies**, **Neuroscience-Based Leadership relies on brain science to improve motivation, engagement, and communication.**

Example

A great example of **Neuroscience-Based Leadership** is **Satya Nadella, CEO of Microsoft**. He transformed Microsoft's leadership culture by **applying insights from brain science to encourage curiosity, emotional intelligence, and a growth mindset**. By shifting from a **fixed, performance-driven approach to a learning-based leadership model**, he significantly improved **employee engagement and innovation.**

Another example is **Elon Musk**, who **leverages cognitive science principles to maintain focus, resilience, and adaptability** in his leadership at **Tesla and SpaceX**. His **ability to manage stress, think critically, and inspire teams aligns with neuroscience-based leadership strategies.**

Why It Works

Neuroscience-Based Leadership is effective because it:

- **Optimizes Employee Performance** – Leaders **align workplace strategies with brain function** to improve focus and productivity.

- **Reduces Stress & Burnout** – By understanding **how the brain processes stress,** leaders create **healthier work environments.**

- **Encourages Innovation & Learning** – Neuroplasticity research shows that **learning-focused environments improve adaptability.**

- **Improves Emotional Intelligence & Trust** – Leaders who understand **brain-based social behaviours build stronger team dynamics.**

- **Enhances Decision-Making & Leadership Agility** – Leaders use **cognitive science to make more rational, effective decisions.**

Studies show that **organizations applying neuroscience-based leadership principles have higher employee retention, engagement, and problem-solving capabilities.**

How It Works

Neuroscience-Based Leadership follows a **science-backed, behaviour-driven approach:**

1. **Minimizing Threat Responses** – Leaders reduce **fear-based reactions by fostering a psychologically safe workplace.**

2. **Strengthening Learning & Adaptability** – Encouraging **continuous learning enhances neuroplasticity and performance.**

3. **Applying Emotional Regulation Techniques** – Leaders **practice mindfulness and emotional control to manage stress effectively.**

4. **Optimizing Brain Function for Productivity** – Structuring **work environments to improve focus, motivation, and collaboration.**

5. **Encouraging Purpose & Autonomy** – Employees **perform better when they feel in control and have meaningful goals.**

Unlike **directive leadership, which relies on control,** **Neuroscience-Based Leadership promotes trust, learning, and cognitive efficiency.**

Application

Neuroscience-Based Leadership is widely applied in:

- **Corporate & Innovation-Driven Companies** – Tech firms like **Google and Microsoft use neuroleadership to optimize team performance.**

- **Healthcare & High-Stress Environments** – Hospitals and emergency services **apply neuroscience to improve decision-making under pressure.**

- **Education & Training** – Schools integrate **brain-based learning strategies for better student engagement.**

- **Executive Coaching & Leadership Development** – Organizations use neuroscience to **enhance emotional intelligence and cognitive agility**.

Key Insights

1. **The Brain Drives Leadership Effectiveness** – Understanding brain function **improves communication, decision-making, and motivation**.

2. **Psychological Safety & Emotional Intelligence Are Crucial** – Employees thrive in **trust-based environments that minimize stress responses**.

3. **Continuous Learning Enhances Performance** – Encouraging a **growth mindset rewires the brain for success**.

4. **Rational Decision-Making Comes from Cognitive Control** – Leaders must **train their brains to manage bias, stress, and emotions effectively**.

Neuroscience-Based Leadership proves that **leaders who understand brain function can create smarter, healthier, and more innovative organizations**.

48. Behavioural Economics Leadership

Behavioural Economics Leadership: A Breakdown

Theory

Behavioural Economics Leadership is a leadership model that integrates principles from **behavioural economics and psychology** to improve decision-making, motivation, and team performance. Unlike traditional economic theories that assume people act rationally, **behavioural economics recognizes that people often make decisions based on biases, emotions, and cognitive shortcuts.**

This leadership style applies **nudge theory, decision framing, and incentive structures** to guide employees toward better choices while minimizing irrational behaviours. **Leaders using behavioural economics principles create environments where employees make smarter decisions, stay motivated, and improve productivity without feeling pressured.**

Key principles of **Behavioural Economics Leadership**:

1. **Nudge Theory** – Leaders design environments that **subtly encourage better choices (e.g., default options, reminders, and framing messages positively).**

2. **Loss Aversion & Incentives** – Employees **respond more to avoiding losses than gaining rewards, so**

leaders use performance-based incentives strategically.

3. **Cognitive Bias Awareness** – Recognizing **common biases (e.g., overconfidence, anchoring, and social influence) helps leaders optimize decision-making**.

4. **Choice Architecture** – Structuring **decisions in a way that simplifies complex choices and reduces mental strain**.

5. **Social Proof & Influence** – People are influenced by what others do, so **leaders use peer behaviours to drive engagement**.

Unlike **traditional leadership models that assume rational decision-making, Behavioural Economics Leadership acknowledges human psychology and optimizes the work environment accordingly**.

Example

A great example of **Behavioural Economics Leadership** is **Richard Thaler's work with government and corporate leaders**. Thaler, a Nobel Prize-winning behavioural economist, helped implement **nudge-based policies** in organizations and governments to **increase savings, improve employee productivity, and encourage healthier choices**.

Another example is **Amazon's leadership in using behavioural economics**. Amazon optimizes **pricing, recommendations, and employee incentives** using behavioural insights. Their approach to **customer behaviour analysis and employee engagement techniques enhances decision-making and productivity.**

Why It Works

Behavioural Economics Leadership is effective because it:

- **Encourages Better Decision-Making** – Employees make **smarter, less biased choices with subtle guidance.**

- **Improves Motivation & Productivity** – Incentives **designed around loss aversion and social proof drive performance.**

- **Enhances Employee Engagement** – People are more engaged **when choices are framed positively and aligned with their goals.**

- **Reduces Decision Fatigue** – Leaders simplify decision processes, **reducing stress and improving efficiency.**

- **Optimizes Organizational Performance** – Behavioural insights **create more effective communication, strategy, and leadership.**

Studies show that **leaders who incorporate behavioural economics principles drive higher engagement, efficiency, and long-term success.**

How It Works

Behavioural Economics Leadership follows a **data-driven, psychology-based approach**:

1. **Identifying Cognitive Biases** – Leaders assess how **employees' mental shortcuts affect decision-making.**

2. **Applying Nudge Theory** – Subtly structuring **choices to encourage better behaviours without force.**

3. **Using Loss Aversion & Framing Techniques** – Motivating teams by **highlighting what's at stake rather than just rewards.**

4. **Creating Choice Architecture** – Simplifying **decision-making through clear, structured options.**

5. **Leveraging Social Influence** – Encouraging **desired behaviours through peer examples and group norms.**

Unlike **directive leadership, which enforces strict rules, Behavioural Economics Leadership subtly influences decisions for better outcomes.**

Application

Behavioural Economics Leadership is widely applied in:

- **Corporate & Sales Strategy** – Companies like **Amazon, Google, and Apple use behavioural insights to optimize customer experience and employee performance.**

- **Public Policy & Government Leadership** – Governments apply **nudge-based policies to encourage savings, healthcare enrolment, and tax compliance.**

- **Healthcare & Behavioural Change Programs** – Leaders **use choice framing to encourage better health and wellness behaviours.**

- **Tech & Product Design** – Behavioural principles help **design intuitive user experiences and decision-making processes.**

Key Insights

1. **People Are Not Rational Decision-Makers** – Leadership should **account for emotions, biases, and social influences.**

2. **Small Nudges Create Big Impact** – Simple changes **in decision framing and incentives drive major behavioural shifts.**

3. **Loss Aversion Is a Strong Motivator** – Employees **are more driven to avoid losses than to pursue equal gains.**

4. **Leaders Should Design Better Choices, Not Force Decisions** – Creating the right environment **naturally guides employees toward success.**

Behavioural Economics Leadership proves that **understanding human psychology and decision-making biases leads to smarter, more effective leadership** strategies that enhance motivation, performance, and engagement.

49. Social Learning Theory Leadership

Social Learning Theory Leadership: A Breakdown

Theory

Social Learning Theory Leadership is based on **Albert Bandura's Social Learning Theory (1977)**, which suggests that **people learn behaviours, attitudes, and skills by observing others, imitating their actions, and experiencing reinforcement or consequences**. This leadership model emphasizes **role modelling, mentorship, and observational learning** as key components of effective leadership.

Unlike traditional leadership models that focus on rules and instructions, **Social Learning Theory Leadership highlights the importance of learning through social interactions, observation, and feedback**. Leaders play an essential role by setting examples, **demonstrating desired behaviours, and reinforcing positive actions in their teams**.

Key principles of **Social Learning Theory Leadership**:

1. **Observational Learning (Modelling Behaviour)** – Employees **learn leadership styles, work ethics, and decision-making by watching leaders**.

2. **Vicarious Reinforcement** – People are **influenced by the rewards or consequences they see others experience**.

3. **Cognitive Processing & Retention** – Individuals **internalize observed behaviours and apply them in future situations**.

4. **Motivation Through Social Influence** – Leaders **encourage high performance by reinforcing positive role models**.

5. **Reciprocal Determinism** – Employee behaviour is shaped by **continuous interaction between individuals, their environment, and observed role models**.

Unlike **authoritative leadership, which enforces top-down control**, Social Learning Theory Leadership develops leaders by fostering an environment of mentorship, shared learning, and behavioural reinforcement.

Example

A great example of **Social Learning Theory Leadership** is **Howard Schultz, former CEO of Starbucks**. Schultz built a **strong workplace culture by modelling respect, customer service excellence, and ethical leadership**. By emphasizing **employee experience and leading by example, he created** a company where employees mirror his leadership approach.

Another example is **Nelson Mandela**, who demonstrated **peaceful leadership, reconciliation, and resilience**. His leadership style **inspired followers not through force, but through his behaviour, humility, and vision**, proving that leaders influence others by their actions.

Why It Works

Social Learning Theory Leadership is effective because it:

- **Creates a Strong Leadership Pipeline** – Employees **observe and internalize leadership behaviours, becoming future leaders.**

- **Improves Workplace Culture & Engagement** – Employees **mirror positive behaviours when leaders set strong examples.**

- **Encourages Ethical & Responsible Decision-Making** – Employees **learn ethical behaviour by watching integrity in leadership.**

- **Strengthens Employee Motivation & Performance** – When employees see **leaders rewarded for good practices, they are more likely to adopt them.**

- **Builds a Collaborative Learning Environment** – Organizations benefit from **knowledge sharing, mentorship, and peer learning.**

Studies show that **companies with strong role models and mentoring programs develop more effective, ethical, and engaged employees.**

How It Works

Social Learning Theory Leadership follows a **mentorship-driven, observational learning approach**:

1. **Modelling Positive Leadership Behaviour** – Leaders consistently **demonstrate professionalism, decision-making, and emotional intelligence.**

2. **Reinforcing & Rewarding Positive Behaviour** – Encouraging **team members who adopt strong leadership traits.**

3. **Creating Mentorship & Peer-Learning Systems** – **Pairing employees with experienced mentors** accelerates development.

4. **Providing Constructive Feedback & Reflection** – Helping employees **analyse their actions and improve through observation.**

5. **Fostering an Inclusive Learning Culture** – Promoting **collaboration and shared leadership development.**

Unlike **directive leadership, which focuses on commands, Social Learning Theory Leadership empowers employees by allowing them to develop through observation and experience.**

Application

Social Learning Theory Leadership is widely applied in:

- **Corporate & Business Leadership Development** – Companies like **Google and Amazon use mentorship programs and role modelling to develop future leaders.**

- **Education & Training Environments** – Teachers and coaches **lead by example, encouraging students to adopt best practices**.

- **Healthcare & Medical Training** – Physicians and nurses **learn procedures and ethical practices through observation and mentorship.**

- **Sports & Team Leadership** – Athletes **learn teamwork, discipline, and strategy by following experienced players and coaches.**

Key Insights

1. **Leaders Must Model the Behaviour They Want to See** – Employees **mirror leaders' actions more than their words.**

2. **Reinforcement & Recognition Strengthen Learning** – Employees adopt behaviours **when they see them rewarded or respected**.

3. **Mentorship Accelerates Leadership Development** – **Guidance from experienced leaders speeds up skill acquisition.**

4. **Culture Shapes Leadership Success** – A workplace that **values learning, collaboration, and role modelling builds stronger leaders over time**.

Social Learning Theory Leadership proves that **leaders are not just authority figures but role models who shape future leaders through their actions, values, and influence**.

50. Cognitive Load Leadership

Cognitive Load Leadership: A Breakdown

Theory

Cognitive Load Leadership is a leadership model that applies principles from **cognitive load theory (CLT)** to optimize decision-making, reduce mental fatigue, and improve productivity. **Cognitive Load Theory**, developed by **John Sweller (1988)**, explains how the human brain processes and retains information. It divides cognitive load into three types:

1. **Intrinsic Load** – The inherent difficulty of a task.

2. **Extraneous Load** – Unnecessary mental effort caused by distractions, poor communication, or inefficient systems.

3. **Germane Load** – The mental effort used for meaningful learning and problem-solving.

In **Cognitive Load Leadership**, leaders focus on **reducing extraneous load, managing intrinsic load, and optimizing germane load** to help teams function at their highest capacity. This model is crucial in today's fast-paced, information-heavy work environments where **leaders must prevent burnout, enhance focus, and streamline processes**.

Key principles of **Cognitive Load Leadership**:

1. **Simplifying Decision-Making** – Reducing **complexity in choices and information overload**.

2. **Prioritizing Mental Resources** – Helping employees **focus on high-value tasks instead of distractions**.

3. **Enhancing Learning & Retention** – Structuring **training and knowledge-sharing for maximum retention**.

4. **Improving Workflow Efficiency** – Eliminating **bureaucracy and redundant tasks** to optimize cognitive resources.

5. **Encouraging Mindfulness & Recovery** – Leaders **help teams manage mental fatigue and avoid burnout**.

Unlike **command-and-control leadership, which prioritizes strict oversight**, Cognitive Load Leadership **optimizes** brain function by managing information flow and mental energy.

Example

A great example of **Cognitive Load Leadership** is **Elon Musk at Tesla and SpaceX.** Musk **simplifies decision-making by enforcing clear priorities, reducing unnecessary meetings, and focusing on mission-critical tasks.** He encourages **first-principles thinking**, breaking down complex problems into simple, solvable components, which minimizes cognitive overload for his teams.

Another example is **Jeff Bezos at Amazon**, who **introduced the "Two-Pizza Rule" (teams should be small enough to be fed by two pizzas) to reduce complexity in communication and decision-making.** By limiting cognitive load, Amazon **maintains agility and innovation**.

Why It Works

Cognitive Load Leadership is effective because it:

- **Reduces Decision Fatigue** – Employees make **better choices when unnecessary complexity is removed**.

- **Enhances Productivity** – Teams **work more efficiently when their mental energy is focused on high-impact tasks**.

- **Prevents Burnout** – Leaders **balance workload and encourage cognitive recovery**.

- **Improves Learning & Retention** – Employees **grasp new information faster when it is structured effectively.**

- **Encourages Deep Work & Innovation** – Minimizing **distractions leads to better creativity and problem-solving.**

Studies show that **leaders who manage cognitive load effectively improve employee well-being, engagement, and organizational success.**

How It Works

Cognitive Load Leadership follows a **structured, efficiency-driven approach:**

1. **Minimizing Extraneous Load** – Leaders remove **unnecessary meetings, complex processes, and distractions.**

2. **Optimizing Intrinsic Load** – Breaking down **complex tasks into manageable steps.**

3. **Maximizing Germane Load** – Encouraging **problem-solving, mentorship, and meaningful learning.**

4. **Structuring Workflows for Cognitive Efficiency** – Using **automation, templates, and clear communication to simplify tasks.**

5. **Promoting Mental Recovery** – Leaders **encourage breaks, mindfulness, and work-life balance.**

Unlike **directive leadership, which often overwhelms employees with strict oversight**, **Cognitive Load Leadership optimizes mental resources for high performance**.

Application

Cognitive Load Leadership is widely applied in:

- **Tech & Innovation-Driven Companies** – Firms like **Google and Tesla minimize cognitive overload to enhance problem-solving.**

- **Healthcare & High-Stress Professions** – Hospitals use **structured workflows to reduce decision fatigue among doctors and nurses.**

- **Corporate Leadership & Startups** – Leaders **streamline operations to prevent information overload and burnout.**

- **Education & Training** – Schools and e-learning platforms **use cognitive load principles to improve knowledge retention.**

Key Insights

1. **Mental Energy is a Limited Resource** – Leaders must **reduce cognitive strain to improve focus and efficiency.**

2. **Simplification Boosts Productivity** – Clear, structured workflows **help employees perform better and learn faster.**

3. **Eliminating Distractions Increases Innovation –** **Cognitive efficiency allows for deep thinking and creativity.**

4. **Burnout Prevention is Leadership's Responsibility** – Leaders must **balance workloads and encourage mental recovery.**

Cognitive Load Leadership proves that **leaders who manage cognitive resources effectively create smarter, healthier, and more productive teams.**

Leadership in Crisis & Change Management

51. Crisis Leadership

Crisis Leadership: A Breakdown

Theory

Crisis Leadership is a leadership model that focuses on **guiding organizations, teams, and individuals through unexpected, high-pressure situations**. It requires leaders to **make fast, strategic decisions, maintain stability, and inspire confidence while navigating uncertainty**.

Crisis Leadership integrates elements of **Adaptive Leadership, Transformational Leadership, and Situational Leadership**, ensuring that leaders remain **resilient, decisive, and communicative during crises**. The ability to **anticipate, respond, and recover effectively** defines successful crisis leadership.

Key characteristics of **Crisis Leadership** include:

1. **Decisiveness & Rapid Decision-Making** – Leaders analyse risks quickly and act with confidence.

2. **Clear & Transparent Communication** – Providing accurate, timely, and reassuring information to stakeholders.

3. **Resilience & Emotional Stability** – Managing **stress and uncertainty without spreading panic.**

4. **Flexibility & Adaptability** – Adjusting **strategies in real-time as new information emerges.**

5. **Empathy & Team Support** – Maintaining **trust and morale by prioritizing people's well-being.**

Unlike **traditional leadership models that operate under stable conditions, Crisis Leadership thrives in volatile, high-risk situations where uncertainty and time constraints dominate.**

Example

A great example of **Crisis Leadership** is **Winston Churchill's leadership during World War II**. Churchill's **decisive actions, inspiring speeches, and ability to maintain national morale** helped Britain navigate extreme adversity. His ability to **remain composed, communicate effectively, and adapt to rapidly changing war conditions** showcases strong crisis leadership.

Another example is **Jacinda Ardern, former Prime Minister of New Zealand**, who demonstrated **empathy, decisiveness, and transparency** during the COVID-19 pandemic. Her leadership style focused on **clear communication, science-driven decision-making, and public reassurance**, making New Zealand's response one of the most effective globally.

Why It Works

Crisis Leadership is effective because it:

- **Restores Stability & Confidence** – Employees and the public **trust leaders who act decisively and communicate clearly.**

- **Reduces Panic & Chaos** – Leaders **provide structure and direction amid uncertainty.**

- **Accelerates Problem-Solving & Recovery** – Adaptive leaders **identify solutions quickly and mobilize resources.**

- **Maintains Morale & Engagement** – Strong leadership **keeps teams motivated despite difficult circumstances.**

- **Enhances Organizational Resilience** – Companies with strong crisis leadership **recover faster and stronger from setbacks.**

Studies show that **organizations with effective crisis leaders experience lower turnover, higher trust levels, and faster recovery post-crisis.**

How It Works

Crisis Leadership follows a **strategic, action-oriented approach:**

1. **Assess & Analyse the Situation Quickly** – Leaders **gather facts, identify risks, and anticipate challenges.**

2. **Communicate Clearly & Consistently** – Providing **timely updates, reassurance, and transparency.**

3. **Take Decisive Action** – Leaders **execute solutions efficiently while remaining adaptable to change.**

4. **Support & Empower Teams** – Prioritizing **employee well-being and enabling decentralized decision-making.**

5. **Reflect & Learn Post-Crisis** – Evaluating **what worked, what failed, and how to improve future crisis responses.**

Unlike **directive leadership, which focuses on rigid control**, Crisis Leadership requires **adaptability, rapid learning, and strategic risk management.**

Application

Crisis Leadership is widely applied in:

- **Public Health & Emergency Management** – Leaders respond to **pandemics, natural disasters, and global crises.**

- **Corporate Crisis Management** – Companies handle **financial downturns, cybersecurity breaches, and PR crises.**

- **Government & Political Leadership** – Officials manage **national security threats and economic instability.**

- **Military & High-Stakes Industries** – Leaders navigate **combat, rescue missions, and extreme pressure environments**.

Key Insights

1. **Preparedness & Agility Are Critical** – Crisis leaders must **anticipate risks and be ready to act immediately**.

2. **Trust & Communication Drive Stability** – Teams and the public **follow leaders who provide clarity and transparency**.

3. **Emotional Intelligence & Composure Matter** – Leaders who **remain calm and empathetic reduce panic and inspire confidence**.

4. **Post-Crisis Reflection Strengthens Future Responses** – The best leaders **analyse past crises to improve long-term resilience**.

Crisis Leadership proves that **leaders who remain decisive, transparent, and adaptable in high-pressure situations can guide teams and organizations through uncertainty and toward recovery**.

52. Change Management Leadership (Kotter's 8 Steps)

Change Management Leadership (Kotter's 8 Steps): A Breakdown

Theory

Change Management Leadership, based on **John Kotter's 8-Step Change Model**, is a leadership approach designed to guide organizations through transformation successfully. Change is often met with **resistance, uncertainty, and fear**, and Kotter's model provides a structured process to help leaders implement and sustain change effectively.

Kotter's 8 steps for successful change management are:

1. **Create a Sense of Urgency** – Communicate **why change is necessary and inspire action.**

2. **Build a Guiding Coalition** – Assemble **a strong leadership team to drive change.**

3. **Develop a Vision & Strategy** – Define **a clear direction and roadmap for the change process.**

4. **Communicate the Vision** – Use **consistent messaging to align employees with the change goals.**

5. **Empower Employees for Action** – Remove **barriers and give employees the tools they need to succeed**.

6. **Generate Short-Term Wins** – Create **quick, visible successes to build momentum and credibility**.

7. **Sustain Acceleration** – Use **early wins to drive continued progress and prevent stagnation**.

8. **Anchor the Change in Culture** – Embed **new behaviours into the organization's culture for long-term success**.

Unlike **directive leadership, which forces compliance, Change Management Leadership fosters engagement, collaboration, and adaptability** to make transitions smoother.

Example

A great example of **Change Management Leadership** is **Satya Nadella's transformation of Microsoft**. When he became CEO, Microsoft faced **cultural stagnation and declining innovation**. By applying Kotter's principles, Nadella:

- **Created urgency** by emphasizing the need for cultural and digital transformation.

- **Built a coalition** by bringing in new leadership with a shared vision.

- **Developed a clear strategy** around cloud computing and AI.

- **Communicated consistently**, ensuring all employees understood the vision.

- **Empowered teams** with a "growth mindset" philosophy.

- **Achieved quick wins**, such as expanding Microsoft's cloud services.

- **Sustained momentum**, driving continued product innovation.

- **Embedded change in Microsoft's culture**, making it more collaborative and adaptive.

His leadership resulted in **Microsoft's revival as an industry leader in AI, cloud computing, and workplace innovation**.

Why It Works

Kotter's Change Management Leadership is effective because it:

- **Reduces Resistance** – Employees are more willing to change when they understand the **"why" and "how."**

- **Builds Commitment & Engagement** – Teams feel **included in the change process, increasing motivation**.

- **Ensures a Structured, Sustainable Approach** – The 8-step model **prevents disorganized change efforts**.

- **Maintains Momentum & Prevents Regression** – Leaders use **short-term wins to drive long-term adoption**.

- **Integrates Change into Culture** – Change is embedded into the organization's DNA, ensuring lasting impact.

Studies show that **organizations using Kotter's model experience higher success rates in transformation efforts compared to those without structured leadership**.

How It Works

Change Management Leadership follows a **phased, engagement-driven approach**:

1. **Identify the Need for Change & Build Support** – Establish **urgency and form coalitions**.

2. **Develop & Communicate a Clear Vision** – Ensure everyone understands the change strategy.

3. **Remove Barriers & Empower Action** – Give employees **the tools, authority, and resources to adapt**.

4. **Create Quick Wins & Reinforce Success** – Show visible progress to maintain motivation.

5. **Anchor Change Through Culture & Leadership** – Reinforce **new behaviours with strong role models and systems.**

Unlike **transactional leadership, which focuses on routine efficiency, Change Management Leadership navigates complex transformations with adaptability and clarity.**

Application

Change Management Leadership is widely applied in:

- **Corporate Transformations** – Companies like **Microsoft, IBM, and Apple use structured change management to adapt to market shifts.**

- **Mergers & Acquisitions** – Leaders integrate **new teams, cultures, and processes smoothly.**

- **Digital Transformations** – Organizations transition to **AI, cloud computing, and automation.**

- **Public Sector & Policy Changes** – Governments implement **new policies, regulations, and reforms effectively.**

Key Insights

1. **Successful Change Requires a Clear Vision & Communication** – Employees need **clarity and direction** to embrace change.

2. **Momentum is Critical for Long-Term Success** – **Quick wins keep teams motivated and prevent regression.**

3. **Change is Not Just Structural, But Cultural** – Leaders must **embed change into company values and behaviours**.

4. **Employee Buy-In Determines the Success of Change** – The more **people feel involved, the more they commit to change**.

Change Management Leadership proves that **leaders who follow a structured, people-focused approach can drive transformation, reduce resistance, and ensure long-term success**.

53. VUCA Leadership

VUCA Leadership: A Breakdown

Theory

VUCA Leadership is a leadership model designed to navigate **Volatility, Uncertainty, Complexity, and Ambiguity (VUCA)** in rapidly changing environments. The VUCA framework, originally developed by the **U.S. Army War College**, highlights the challenges modern leaders face in dynamic, unpredictable conditions.

VUCA Leadership focuses on developing **agility, resilience, and strategic foresight** to help organizations thrive amid uncertainty. Leaders must be **adaptive, visionary, and emotionally intelligent** to manage change effectively.

The four components of **VUCA and Leadership Responses**:

1. **Volatility (V)** – Rapid and unpredictable changes.

   o **Leadership Response:** Vision – Setting a clear direction to guide teams through instability.

2. **Uncertainty (U)** – Lack of clarity about the future.

   o **Leadership Response:** Understanding – Gathering information and fostering adaptability.

3. **Complexity (C)** – Multiple interconnected factors influencing decisions.

   o **Leadership Response:** Clarity – Simplifying problems and prioritizing key actions.

4. **Ambiguity (A)** – Unclear cause-and-effect relationships.

   o **Leadership Response:** Agility – Remaining flexible and experimenting with solutions.

Unlike **traditional leadership models that focus on stability, VUCA Leadership embraces uncertainty and equips leaders to manage change dynamically**.

Example

A great example of **VUCA Leadership** is **Jeff Bezos, founder of Amazon**. Bezos built Amazon by **embracing uncertainty, experimenting with innovations, and adapting to market disruptions**. His leadership principles, such as **customer obsession, long-term thinking, and rapid decision-making**, align with the VUCA model, allowing Amazon to **pivot quickly and dominate multiple industries**.

Another example is **Elon Musk**, who applies **VUCA principles in Tesla and SpaceX** by **navigating technological, economic, and geopolitical uncertainties**. His ability to **set a compelling vision, adapt to challenges, and make bold decisions** demonstrates strong VUCA leadership.

Why It Works

VUCA Leadership is effective because it:

- **Prepares Organizations for Rapid Change** – Leaders anticipate and respond proactively.

- **Encourages Adaptability & Innovation** – Teams embrace change rather than resist it.

- **Improves Decision-Making in Uncertainty** – Leaders **analyse data, assess risks, and take calculated actions.**

- **Strengthens Resilience & Agility** – Organizations remain competitive despite external disruptions.

- **Enhances Employee Confidence & Morale** – Leaders **create stability even in uncertain times.**

Studies show that **companies with VUCA-ready leaders outperform competitors by fostering adaptability and strategic foresight.**

How It Works

VUCA Leadership follows a **future-focused, agile approach:**

1. **Develop a Clear Vision** – Establish **long-term objectives to guide the team through volatility.**

2. **Build Situational Awareness** – Continuously **scan the environment for risks and opportunities.**

3. **Enhance Decision-Making Agility** – Encourage **rapid experimentation and adaptive learning.**

4. **Communicate with Transparency** – Keep teams informed **to reduce uncertainty and confusion**.

5. **Foster Innovation & Collaboration** – Create **a culture where teams are empowered to problem-solve dynamically**.

Unlike **bureaucratic leadership, which relies on rigid structures**, **VUCA Leadership thrives on flexibility, learning, and proactive decision-making**.

Application

VUCA Leadership is widely applied in:

*   **Technology & Digital Transformation** – Companies like **Google and Tesla embrace uncertainty and innovation**.

*   **Crisis & Emergency Response** – Governments and organizations manage **pandemics, cybersecurity threats, and global crises**.

*   **Entrepreneurship & Startups** – Founders adapt **to shifting market trends and customer demands**.

*   **Corporate Strategy & Leadership Development** – Executives **train teams to navigate uncertainty with agility**.

Key Insights

1. **Uncertainty is Inevitable—Adaptability is Essential** – Leaders **must prepare for change rather than resist it**.

2. **Vision & Clarity Reduce Chaos** – Even in volatile environments, **leaders who communicate a clear direction keep teams focused**.

3. **Agility & Learning Drive Competitive Advantage** – Organizations that **experiment, iterate, and pivot outperform rigid competitors**.

4. **Emotional Intelligence & Resilience Matter** – Leaders must **stay calm, decisive, and empathetic under pressure**.

VUCA Leadership proves that **leaders who embrace uncertainty, prioritize agility, and inspire resilience create organizations that thrive in unpredictable environments**.

54. Antifragile Leadership (Nassim Taleb)

Antifragile Leadership (Nassim Taleb): A Breakdown

Theory

Antifragile Leadership, inspired by **Nassim Nicholas Taleb's concept of antifragility**, is a leadership model that **not only withstands uncertainty and stress but thrives and improves from it**. Unlike traditional leadership models that focus on resilience (withstanding pressure) or robustness (resisting change), **Antifragile Leadership**

leverages volatility, uncertainty, and adversity to become stronger.

Taleb defines antifragility as the opposite of fragility:

- **Fragile** systems break under stress.

- **Robust** systems withstand stress but do not improve.

- **Antifragile** systems grow stronger and improve through stress and uncertainty.

In leadership, this means **developing a mindset and organizational culture that welcomes challenges, embraces uncertainty, and uses disruptions as catalysts for growth**. Leaders practicing antifragility **experiment, adapt, decentralize decision-making, and continuously evolve in response to external shocks**.

Key characteristics of **Antifragile Leadership**:

1. **Embracing Volatility & Uncertainty** – Leaders **see change as an opportunity, not a threat**.

2. **Encouraging Decentralization** – Empowering **teams to make decisions enhances adaptability**.

3. **Building Optionality** – Having **multiple strategies and backup plans to pivot quickly**.

4. **Learning Through Experimentation** – Encouraging **trial, failure, and iteration to drive innovation**.

5. **Removing Over-Reliance on Predictability** – Leaders **prepare for the unexpected rather than assuming stability**.

Unlike **rigid leadership models that seek control, Antifragile Leadership thrives in chaos and change**.

Example

A great example of **Antifragile Leadership** is **Elon Musk and his approach at Tesla and SpaceX**. Musk's leadership embraces **risk, experimentation, and decentralized problem-solving**. SpaceX, for example, **improves rocket designs by learning from rapid iterations and failures**— instead of avoiding failures, they use them as fuel for innovation.

Another example is **Amazon's business model under Jeff Bezos**, which **embraces uncertainty by continuously testing new ideas, rapidly scaling successful ones, and eliminating failures quickly**. Amazon Web Services (AWS) was an unexpected innovation that emerged from Amazon's willingness to experiment and adapt to market needs.

Why It Works

Antifragile Leadership is effective because it:

- **Turns Challenges into Strengths** – Organizations become stronger after setbacks.

- **Encourages Innovation & Agility** – Leaders experiment and pivot quickly to stay competitive.

- **Reduces Risk Through Decentralization** – Teams solve problems independently, increasing adaptability.

- **Enhances Long-Term Success** – Organizations **that adapt and learn from volatility outperform competitors who resist change**.

- **Prepares for the Unknown** – Leaders **design systems that benefit from uncertainty rather than collapse under it**.

Studies show that **companies with antifragile strategies outperform those relying on rigid, risk-averse approaches in uncertain environments**.

How It Works

Antifragile Leadership follows a **decentralized, adaptive approach**:

1. **Encourage Decentralization & Autonomy** – Allowing **small teams to make independent decisions increases adaptability**.

2. **Promote Experimentation & Fast Failure** – Leaders **run multiple small tests, learn from failures, and scale what works**.

3. **Create Redundancy & Optionality** – Organizations maintain **backup strategies and diversified revenue streams to reduce fragility**.

4. **Embrace Stress as a Catalyst for Growth** – Leaders see volatility as a competitive advantage, not a weakness.

5. **Remove Bureaucratic Constraints** – Reducing **over-reliance on fixed plans and embracing agility ensures continuous evolution.**

Unlike **hierarchical leadership models that rely on strict control, Antifragile Leadership thrives on adaptability, innovation, and decentralized decision-making.**

Application

Antifragile Leadership is widely applied in:

- **Startups & High-Growth Companies** – Companies **experiment, iterate quickly, and scale successful ideas.**

- **Technology & Innovation Sectors** – Organizations like **Tesla and Google foster antifragile cultures.**

- **Investment & Financial Markets** – Leaders in **venture capital and hedge funds use antifragility to capitalize on volatility.**

- **Crisis Management & Disaster Response** – Governments and NGOs apply **antifragile principles in emergency preparedness.**

Key Insights

1. **Uncertainty & Chaos Can Be an Advantage** – Leaders who **leverage change instead of fearing it create stronger organizations**.

2. **Failure is a Learning Tool, Not a Setback** – Experimentation and small failures **lead to breakthrough innovations**.

3. **Rigid Structures Collapse Under Pressure** – Decentralization and adaptability **enable resilience in unpredictable environments**.

4. **The Best Leaders Prepare for the Unknown** – Instead of trying to predict the future, **they create systems that thrive in uncertainty**.

Antifragile Leadership proves that **leaders who embrace uncertainty, empower decentralized teams, and foster continuous learning build organizations that grow stronger from disruption and change**.

55. Post-Heroic Leadership

Post-Heroic Leadership: A Breakdown

Theory

Post-Heroic Leadership is a leadership model that **moves away from the traditional "heroic" leader archetype**, where a single leader makes all decisions, takes control, and solves problems alone. Instead, it promotes **collaborative, shared, and servant-based leadership**, emphasizing team empowerment, inclusivity, and collective intelligence.

Unlike **heroic leadership models that focus on individual charisma, authority, and command, Post-Heroic Leadership sees leadership as a shared responsibility**, encouraging **distributed decision-making, employee autonomy, and mutual accountability**. This model is particularly relevant in today's complex, knowledge-driven work environments.

Key characteristics of **Post-Heroic Leadership**:

1. **Decentralization & Shared Power** – Leadership is **distributed across teams, rather than concentrated in one figure**.

2. **Collaboration & Team Empowerment** – Employees are **given autonomy, trust, and a voice in decision-making**.

3. **Servant Leadership Mindset** – Leaders **support, mentor, and develop their teams rather than command them**.

4. **Emphasis on Learning & Adaptability** – Encouraging **continuous growth, feedback, and shared learning**.

5. **Collective Success Over Individual Recognition** –
   The focus is on **organizational and team
   achievements, not leader-cantered accolades.**

Unlike **Autocratic Leadership, which relies on top-down
control**, Post-Heroic Leadership thrives on collaboration,
trust, and shared accountability.

Example

A strong example of **Post-Heroic Leadership** is **Satya
Nadella's leadership at Microsoft**. When Nadella became
CEO, he **shifted Microsoft's leadership culture from a
competitive, top-down structure to a collaborative,
growth-focused environment.** He encouraged **open
communication, team-driven decision-making, and
servant leadership principles**, resulting in **higher
employee engagement and company-wide innovation.**

Another example is **Southwest Airlines' leadership model**,
which **prioritizes employee empowerment, decentralized
decision-making, and customer-focused collaboration.** By
treating employees as partners rather than subordinates,
Southwest **maintains a strong workplace culture, high job
satisfaction, and excellent customer service.**

Why It Works

Post-Heroic Leadership is effective because it:

- **Encourages Team Buy-In & Commitment** –
  Employees feel **more valued and motivated when
  they have a say in decisions.**

- **Enhances Problem-Solving & Innovation** – Teams generate better solutions when diverse perspectives are involved.

- **Improves Employee Satisfaction & Retention** – Workers **are more engaged and less likely to leave in collaborative cultures.**

- **Builds Resilient & Adaptive Organizations** – Decentralized leadership **allows companies to adapt to change more effectively.**

- **Reduces Burnout & Leadership Pressure** – Responsibility **is distributed, reducing the burden on any one leader.**

Studies show that **companies practicing Post-Heroic Leadership experience higher team performance, improved collaboration, and more sustainable long-term growth.**

How It Works

Post-Heroic Leadership follows a **people-cantered, empowerment-driven approach:**

1. **Distribute Leadership Responsibilities** – Encourage **team leaders, managers, and employees to take ownership.**

2. **Develop & Coach Instead of Command** – Leaders **act as mentors, guiding teams rather than controlling them.**

3. **Encourage Open Communication & Feedback** – Create **a culture where employees feel safe to share ideas and challenges.**

4. **Foster a Growth-Oriented Mindset** – Support **learning, adaptability, and continuous improvement.**

5. **Celebrate Team Success Over Individual Recognition** – Shift the focus from **leader-centric achievements to collective wins.**

Unlike **Transactional Leadership, which relies on strict oversight and rewards, Post-Heroic Leadership builds long-term engagement and shared accountability.**

Application

Post-Heroic Leadership is widely applied in:

- **Corporate Leadership Development** – Organizations **replace hierarchical leadership with collaborative models.**

- **Startups & Innovation-Driven Companies** – Tech companies **empower teams to drive creativity and rapid problem-solving.**

- **Healthcare & Nonprofits** – Hospitals and social organizations **focus on servant leadership and team-based decision-making.**

- **Education & Academic Institutions** – Schools and universities **use shared leadership to improve learning outcomes.**

Key Insights

1. **Leadership is Not About One Person—It's a Shared Responsibility** – Organizations thrive **when leadership is distributed across teams.**

2. **Trust & Empowerment Increase Engagement** – Employees perform best **when they feel valued, autonomous, and involved.**

3. **Collaboration Fuels Innovation** – The best solutions **emerge from diverse perspectives, not from a single leader.**

4. **Long-Term Success Requires Adaptability & Shared Growth** – Teams that **learn together and share leadership become more resilient.**

Post-Heroic Leadership proves that **leaders who empower, trust, and develop their teams create stronger, more innovative, and sustainable organizations.**

56. Distributed Leadership

Distributed Leadership: A Breakdown

Theory

Distributed Leadership is a leadership model that moves away from a **single, top-down leader making all the decisions** and instead **spreads leadership responsibilities across multiple individuals within an organization**. This model recognizes that leadership is **not confined to one person but can emerge from different people at different levels, depending on expertise, context, and need**.

Unlike traditional hierarchical leadership models, **Distributed Leadership promotes collective decision-making, shared accountability, and collaboration**. It is based on the idea that **leadership is an organizational function rather than an individual trait**, allowing teams to be **more agile, adaptive, and innovative**.

Key characteristics of **Distributed Leadership**:

1. **Shared Decision-Making** – Authority is **spread across a team rather than centralized in a single leader**.

2. **Collaboration & Interdependence** – Leaders **work together across departments, roles, and expertise**.

3. **Empowerment & Trust** – Employees **are encouraged to take ownership of initiatives**.

4. **Situational Leadership Emergence** – Leadership shifts depending on expertise and the situation.

5. **Decentralized Power Structure** – Organizations function through networks rather than rigid hierarchies.

Unlike **Autocratic Leadership, which relies on one leader's control, Distributed Leadership creates a culture where leadership is a shared responsibility.**

Example

A great example of **Distributed Leadership** is **Google's approach to innovation.** Google fosters **a flat, decentralized structure where employees are empowered to lead projects and make decisions.** Teams operate **with autonomy, collaborating across functions without waiting for approval from senior leadership.** This distributed leadership model has led to innovations like **Google Search, Gmail, and Google Maps, which originated from employee-driven initiatives.**

Another example is **the Mayo Clinic**, a world-renowned healthcare institution that **distributes leadership across medical professionals, administrators, and research teams.** Instead of relying solely on hospital executives, **doctors, nurses, and specialists actively contribute to decision-making,** ensuring **patient-cantered care and continuous innovation.**

Why It Works

Distributed Leadership is effective because it:

- **Encourages Agility & Innovation** – Organizations **respond faster to challenges when leadership is decentralized.**

- **Reduces Bottlenecks & Improves Efficiency** – Teams **don't have to wait for top leaders to make every decision.**

- **Enhances Employee Engagement & Accountability** – Employees **take ownership of projects and are more invested in outcomes.**

- **Promotes Collaboration & Knowledge Sharing** – Different expertise **contributes to well-rounded, informed decisions.**

- **Builds Resilient & Adaptable Organizations** – Leadership **isn't dependent on one person but is embedded throughout the organization.**

Studies show that **companies with distributed leadership structures are more innovative, have higher employee satisfaction, and adapt better to market changes.**

How It Works

Distributed Leadership follows a **collaborative, empowerment-driven approach**:

1. **Identify & Develop Leaders at All Levels** – Organizations **train and recognize leadership potential across teams.**

2. **Encourage Collaborative Decision-Making** – Teams are **given autonomy to solve problems and drive initiatives.**

3. **Foster a Culture of Trust & Accountability** – Employees **are empowered but also responsible for their decisions.**

4. **Use Technology & Networks for Coordination** – Digital tools **enhance communication and support decentralized decision-making.**

5. **Adapt Leadership to Situations & Expertise** – The right leaders **step forward based on knowledge, not job titles.**

Unlike **Transactional Leadership, which relies on strict roles and rewards, Distributed Leadership allows for flexible, situational leadership.**

Application

Distributed Leadership is widely applied in:

*   **Technology & Innovation Sectors** – Companies like **Google and Spotify use decentralized teams for agility.**

*   **Healthcare & Public Services** – Hospitals and research institutions **use team-based decision-making for better patient care.**

- **Education & Academic Institutions** – Schools and universities **encourage faculty leadership beyond administrators.**

- **Corporate & Large Organizations** – Businesses **decentralize leadership to improve efficiency and engagement.**

Key Insights

1. **Leadership is a Function, Not a Title** – Anyone with **expertise and vision can lead when needed.**

2. **Decentralized Decision-Making Enhances Efficiency** – Organizations operate **faster and more effectively when leadership is distributed.**

3. **Collaboration Strengthens Innovation** – Multiple **leaders bring diverse insights, leading to better problem-solving.**

4. **Organizations Become More Resilient & Adaptive** – When leadership is spread across teams, **companies are less vulnerable to leadership turnover or crises.**

Distributed Leadership proves that **organizations thrive when leadership is shared, collaborative, and situational, rather than concentrated in a single figurehead.**

57. Lean Leadership

Lean Leadership: A Breakdown

Theory

Lean Leadership is a leadership model derived from **Lean Thinking**, which originated from the **Toyota Production System (TPS)**. It focuses on **continuous improvement (Kaizen), eliminating waste, empowering employees, and fostering a culture of problem-solving**. Unlike traditional leadership models that emphasize top-down decision-making, **Lean Leadership prioritizes collaboration, efficiency, and value creation for customers.**

At its core, **Lean Leadership** follows these principles:

1. **Lead with Respect** – Leaders **engage with employees, listen actively, and foster trust.**

2. **Develop & Coach People** – Employees **are continuously trained, mentored, and empowered.**

3. **Go to the Source (Gemba Walks)** – Leaders **observe work directly to understand processes and challenges.**

4. **Encourage Continuous Improvement (Kaizen)** – Small, ongoing improvements **enhance efficiency and eliminate waste.**

5. **Focus on Value & Waste Reduction** – Every action should **maximize value and minimize inefficiencies**.

Unlike **command-and-control leadership, which enforces strict oversight**, **Lean Leadership creates a learning-driven, problem-solving workplace**.

Example

A great example of **Lean Leadership** is **Toyota's leadership culture**. Toyota's **leaders are trained to be mentors rather than traditional managers**, focusing on **coaching employees, improving workflows, and reducing inefficiencies**. Toyota's commitment to **continuous improvement, employee engagement, and waste reduction** has made it one of the most efficient and successful automotive manufacturers in the world.

Another example is **Jeff Bezos' leadership at Amazon**. Amazon applies **Lean principles in operations, customer service, and innovation**, ensuring **efficiency, streamlined logistics, and rapid process improvement**. Amazon's **obsession with customer value and operational excellence** reflects Lean Leadership principles.

Why It Works

Lean Leadership is effective because it:

- **Improves Efficiency & Reduces Waste** – Organizations **identify and eliminate unnecessary steps, reducing costs and increasing speed**.

- **Empowers Employees** – Teams **are given ownership of their work, increasing engagement and accountability**.

- **Encourages Continuous Learning** – A culture of **experimentation and improvement drives long-term success**.

- **Strengthens Customer Value** – Lean thinking ensures **products and services deliver maximum value to customers**.

- **Builds a Problem-Solving Culture** – Employees and leaders **work together to solve inefficiencies and optimize workflows**.

Studies show that **companies using Lean Leadership experience higher productivity, stronger employee satisfaction, and faster problem resolution**.

How It Works

Lean Leadership follows a **structured, improvement-driven approach**:

1. **Engage Employees & Foster Ownership** – Leaders **empower employees to take initiative in problem-solving**.

2. **Observe Work Directly (Gemba Walks)** – Leaders **visit workplaces to understand challenges firsthand**.

3. **Encourage Incremental Improvements (Kaizen)** – Teams **implement small, ongoing improvements** rather than large, disruptive changes.

4. **Simplify & Standardize Processes** – Eliminating unnecessary complexity **ensures consistency and efficiency**.

5. **Develop Leaders at All Levels** – Lean leadership **creates a pipeline of problem-solving, adaptable leaders.**

Unlike **Transactional Leadership, which relies on structured rewards and punishments, Lean Leadership builds a culture of intrinsic motivation and self-improvement**.

Application

Lean Leadership is widely applied in:

- **Manufacturing & Production** – Companies like **Toyota and Tesla optimize operations for efficiency**.

- **Healthcare & Public Services** – Hospitals **reduce patient wait times and improve service delivery**.

- **Corporate & Tech Sectors** – Companies like **Amazon and Intel use Lean principles for process optimization.**

- **Startups & Entrepreneurship** – Lean thinking **helps new businesses minimize waste and iterate quickly.**

Key Insights

1. **Efficiency & Waste Reduction Drive Success** – Lean leaders **focus on optimizing processes and removing inefficiencies.**

2. **Leadership is About Coaching, Not Controlling** – Employees perform best when **leaders support, mentor, and trust them.**

3. **Continuous Improvement Creates Long-Term Growth** – Kaizen ensures that **organizations evolve and stay competitive.**

4. **Customer Value is the Ultimate Goal** – Every decision should **enhance customer experience and product quality.**

Lean Leadership proves that **leaders who focus on efficiency, continuous learning, and empowering employees build sustainable, high-performing organizations.**

58. Fractal Leadership

Fractal Leadership: A Breakdown

Theory

Fractal Leadership is a leadership model based on **self-similarity, decentralization, and adaptability**, inspired by **fractals in nature and mathematics**. Just as fractals repeat patterns at different scales, **Fractal Leadership creates self-replicating leadership structures within an organization**. This means that leadership principles are **embedded at every level, ensuring consistency, autonomy, and efficiency**.

Unlike hierarchical leadership, which relies on **centralized decision-making**, Fractal Leadership allows for **distributed authority and adaptive problem-solving**. Each unit within an organization operates with a degree of independence while still following the overall vision and values. This structure makes organizations more **agile, scalable, and resilient to change**.

Key characteristics of **Fractal Leadership**:

1. **Self-Similarity Across Levels** – Leadership values and behaviours **are mirrored at every level of the organization**.

2. **Decentralized & Autonomous Teams** – Small teams
   operate independently while maintaining
   alignment with the organization's mission.

3. **Adaptability & Resilience** – Organizations **adjust**
   easily to challenges, much like fractals evolve in
   nature.

4. **Empowered Decision-Making** – Employees at all
   levels **are encouraged to take initiative and lead.**

5. **Scalable Leadership Development** – New leaders
   emerge naturally, creating a continuous leadership
   pipeline.

Unlike **traditional hierarchical leadership, which enforces**
control from the top, Fractal Leadership fosters
distributed leadership and flexibility.

Example

A great example of **Fractal Leadership** is **the management**
structure at Haier, a multinational appliance company.
Haier operates through **autonomous micro-enterprises,**
where small teams function independently, making their
own decisions while still aligning with the company's larger
goals. This decentralized, self-replicating leadership model
enables agility, innovation, and efficiency.

Another example is **Spotify's squad-based model,** where
small, self-organizing teams ("squads") operate like
independent startups while aligning with Spotify's broader

vision. This **fractal approach to leadership enables rapid innovation, adaptability, and responsiveness to change**.

Why It Works

Fractal Leadership is effective because it:

- **Creates Scalable, Resilient Organizations** – Leadership **naturally emerges at all levels**.

- **Encourages Agility & Innovation** – Teams **can respond quickly to challenges and opportunities**.

- **Strengthens Decision-Making & Accountability** – Employees **take ownership of their work and outcomes**.

- **Reduces Bureaucracy & Improves Efficiency** – Decentralized decision-making **eliminates slow, top-down processes**.

- **Builds a Leadership Pipeline** – Organizations **develop leaders organically, ensuring long-term sustainability**.

Studies show that **companies using fractal leadership structures outperform rigid hierarchies in dynamic, fast-changing industries**.

How It Works

Fractal Leadership follows a **networked, empowerment-driven approach**:

1. **Define Core Leadership Values & Vision** – Ensure that **leadership principles are clear and scalable**.

2. **Empower Teams with Autonomy & Accountability** – Each team **acts as a self-sufficient unit, aligned with the larger mission**.

3. **Encourage Distributed Decision-Making** – Leaders **trust teams to make local decisions without micromanagement**.

4. **Develop Self-Sustaining Leadership Networks** – Leadership is **not a position but a behaviour encouraged at every level**.

5. **Adapt & Evolve Based on Feedback** – Like fractals in nature, **organizations continuously refine their structures to stay competitive**.

Unlike **Directive Leadership, which centralizes control**, **Fractal Leadership creates self-organizing teams that maintain alignment and agility**.

Application

Fractal Leadership is widely applied in:

- **Tech & Agile Organizations** – Companies like **Spotify and Haier use decentralized leadership for innovation**.

- **Startups & High-Growth Companies** – Entrepreneurs **use fractal structures to scale quickly while maintaining flexibility**.

- **Nonprofits & Community Organizations** – Leadership is **shared among grassroots teams for greater impact**.

- **Government & Military Strategy** – Military units **adopt decentralized command structures for adaptability**.

Key Insights

1. **Leadership Should Be Embedded at Every Level** – The best organizations **allow leadership to emerge naturally**.

2. **Decentralization Increases Agility & Resilience** – Teams **that operate independently can respond faster to change**.

3. **Scalability Comes from Repeating Patterns of Leadership** – Organizations thrive when **leadership is self-replicating across all levels**.

4. **Trust & Autonomy Strengthen Performance** – Employees perform best when **given responsibility and decision-making power**.

Fractal Leadership proves that **organizations that distribute leadership and encourage autonomy build more adaptive, scalable, and innovative structures that can evolve with change**.

59. Holacracy Leadership

Holacracy Leadership: A Breakdown

Theory

Holacracy Leadership is a **decentralized leadership model** that replaces traditional hierarchical structures with **self-organizing teams, distributed decision-making, and adaptive governance**. Developed by **Brian Robertson**, Holacracy is based on the idea that **authority and leadership should be embedded within roles rather than individuals**, allowing organizations to be more **agile, efficient, and responsive to change**.

In contrast to traditional leadership models where power is concentrated at the top, **Holacracy distributes authority across self-managed teams** (often called **circles**). Each circle has **specific roles and responsibilities**, and decisions are made **collaboratively rather than through top-down control**.

Key characteristics of **Holacracy Leadership**:

1. **Decentralized Decision-Making** – Power is **spread across teams instead of resting with executives**.

2. **Self-Organizing Teams (Circles)** – Each team (circle) **operates independently while aligning with the organization's purpose**.

3. **Role-Based Structure Instead of Job Titles** – Individuals **hold multiple roles based on their skills rather than fixed positions.**

4. **Adaptive Governance** – Decision-making is **flexible and adjusts to changing circumstances.**

5. **Emphasis on Transparency & Accountability** – Every team member **has clear responsibilities and ownership of tasks.**

Unlike **Autocratic Leadership, which centralizes power,** Holacracy fosters shared leadership and autonomy.**

Example

A well-known example of **Holacracy Leadership** is **Zappos, the online retailer.** In 2013, CEO **Tony Hsieh implemented Holacracy** to create a **more adaptable and empowered workforce.** Instead of managers directing employees, Zappos employees work within **self-managed circles,** where **decisions are made collectively.** This has led to **greater innovation, flexibility, and employee engagement.**

Another example is **Buurtzorg**, a Dutch home healthcare company that operates without traditional managers. Nurses **self-organize into teams, decide on patient care, and manage their own schedules.** This **autonomous, decentralized model has led to higher patient satisfaction and better healthcare outcomes.**

Why It Works

Holacracy Leadership is effective because it:

- **Eliminates Bureaucracy & Increases Efficiency** – Decisions **are made faster without hierarchical bottlenecks.**

- **Enhances Employee Engagement & Autonomy** – Workers **feel more empowered and motivated when they have decision-making power.**

- **Encourages Innovation & Adaptability** – Self-managed teams **respond quickly to challenges and opportunities.**

- **Improves Transparency & Accountability** – Each role has **clear responsibilities, reducing confusion.**

- **Builds a Scalable & Resilient Organization** – Holacratic structures **adjust easily as the company grows.**

Studies show that **organizations using Holacracy experience increased agility, faster decision-making, and stronger employee satisfaction.**

How It Works

Holacracy Leadership follows a **structured yet decentralized approach:**

1. **Define Organizational Purpose & Roles** – Instead of job titles, **each person has multiple roles based on skills.**

2. **Establish Circles for Self-Management** – Teams operate **autonomously with aligned goals.**

3. **Implement Governance Meetings** – Regular meetings ensure **roles and processes stay relevant and efficient.**

4. **Use a Transparent Decision-Making Process** – Policies and structures **are updated based on team feedback.**

5. **Encourage Continuous Learning & Adaptation** – Organizations evolve **as challenges and opportunities emerge.**

Unlike **Hierarchical Leadership, which relies on strict control**, **Holacracy Leadership fosters flexibility and shared responsibility.**

Application

Holacracy Leadership is widely applied in:

- **Tech & Innovation Companies** – Organizations like **Zappos and Medium use Holacracy for flexibility and creativity.**

- **Healthcare & Nonprofits** – Buurtzorg's **self-managed teams deliver more personalized patient care.**

- **Corporate & Large Enterprises** – Some divisions of **Google and other progressive firms experiment with Holacratic structures.**

- **Startups & Entrepreneurial Ventures** – Small companies **use Holacracy to scale without excessive bureaucracy**.

Key Insights

1. **Leadership is Distributed, Not Hierarchical** – Power shifts **from individual leaders to team-driven decision-making**.

2. **Employee Autonomy Drives Performance** – Teams **work more efficiently when they have ownership over their work**.

3. **Eliminating Bureaucracy Increases Agility** – Organizations **respond faster to market changes and challenges**.

4. **Role-Based Structures Allow Flexibility** – People **contribute based on skills rather than rigid job descriptions**.

Holacracy Leadership proves that **organizations thrive when leadership is decentralized, adaptable, and focused on empowering teams rather than enforcing hierarchy**.

60. Situational Crisis Communication Theory (SCCT)

Situational Crisis Communication Theory (SCCT): A Breakdown

Theory

Situational Crisis Communication Theory (SCCT), developed by **W. Timothy Coombs**, is a leadership and communication framework that helps organizations effectively manage crises by choosing the right communication strategy based on the **type of crisis, perceived responsibility, and reputational threat**.

SCCT is built on the idea that **leaders must adapt their crisis response based on public perception and the degree of responsibility attributed to the organization**. The model identifies **three types of crises** and suggests appropriate response strategies:

1. **Victim Crises** (low responsibility) – The organization is **a victim of external factors** (e.g., natural disasters, terrorism, rumours).

    - **Recommended Response:** Express **sympathy, provide information, and take corrective action if needed**.

2. **Accidental Crises** (moderate responsibility) – The crisis is **unintentional** (e.g., technical errors, product defects).

   o **Recommended Response: Apologize, offer corrective action, and show commitment to fixing the issue.**

3. **Preventable Crises** (high responsibility) – The organization is **directly responsible due to negligence or unethical behaviour** (e.g., fraud, misconduct).

   o **Recommended Response:** Take **full responsibility, issue a strong apology, compensate victims, and implement major reforms.**

Unlike **generic crisis communication strategies, SCCT tailors responses to minimize reputational damage and rebuild public trust.**

Example

A well-known example of **SCCT in action** is **Johnson & Johnson's response to the 1982 Tylenol poisoning crisis.** When cyanide-laced Tylenol capsules led to deaths, the company **quickly recalled all products, communicated transparently, and introduced tamper-proof packaging.** Because Johnson & Johnson was **a victim of an external attack (Victim Crisis), they focused on public safety and responsibility without taking blame.** This response **preserved their reputation and restored consumer trust.**

In contrast, **Volkswagen's 2015 emissions scandal** (a **Preventable Crisis**) required **stronger crisis communication**. Initially, Volkswagen **downplayed the issue**, which worsened public backlash. Only after admitting fault, apologizing, and implementing reforms did the company begin **rebuilding trust**.

Why It Works

SCCT is effective because it:

- **Reduces Reputational Damage** – Matching crisis response to **public perception prevents further backlash**.

- **Restores Stakeholder Trust** – Transparent and responsible communication **reassures customers, investors, and the public**.

- **Encourages Crisis Preparedness** – Organizations **proactively plan response strategies for different crisis scenarios**.

- **Minimizes Financial & Legal Risks** – The right response **prevents lawsuits, boycotts, and long-term losses**.

- **Ensures Ethical & Responsible Leadership** – Leaders **acknowledge responsibility and take corrective action**.

Studies show that **organizations using SCCT recover faster from crises and maintain stronger long-term reputations**.

How It Works

SCCT follows a **structured, response-driven approach**:

1. **Assess the Crisis Type** – Determine whether the crisis is **a Victim, Accidental, or Preventable situation**.

2. **Evaluate Organizational Responsibility** – Understand how **stakeholders perceive the company's role in the crisis**.

3. **Select the Appropriate Communication Strategy** – Choose the right **response based on the crisis type** (e.g., apology, corrective action, denial).

4. **Engage in Transparent & Timely Communication** – Provide **consistent updates and avoid misleading statements**.

5. **Monitor Public Response & Adjust Strategy** – Address **ongoing concerns and reinforce positive messaging**.

Unlike **Directive Leadership, which enforces control, SCCT relies on strategic, adaptive crisis communication** to manage public perception.

Application

SCCT is widely applied in:

- **Corporate Crisis Management** – Companies handle **product recalls, PR crises, and ethical scandals**.

- **Government & Political Communication** – Governments manage **public health emergencies, national security threats, and misinformation.**

- **Nonprofits & Humanitarian Organizations** – NGOs respond to **allegations, donor concerns, and mission challenges.**

- **Technology & Cybersecurity** – Organizations address **data breaches, system failures, and cyberattacks.**

Key Insights

1. **Crisis Response Must Match Public Perception** – Organizations should **adjust communication strategies based on stakeholder expectations.**

2. **Taking Responsibility Strengthens Long-Term Trust – Denying blame in a preventable crisis worsens reputational damage.**

3. **Transparency & Speed Are Crucial** – Delayed or misleading responses **increase public scepticism and backlash.**

4. **Corrective Actions Matter More Than Words** – Organizations **must follow up with concrete solutions, not just apologies.**

Situational Crisis Communication Theory proves that **leaders who tailor crisis responses to the nature of the crisis, stakeholder expectations, and reputational risks can effectively mitigate damage and restore public trust.**

Leadership Based on Corporate Culture & Team Dynamics

61. Culture-Driven Leadership

Culture-Driven Leadership: A Breakdown

Theory

Culture-Driven Leadership is a leadership model that emphasizes **organizational culture as the foundation for decision-making, strategy, and employee engagement**. It is based on the idea that **a strong, values-based culture guides behaviour, fosters collaboration, and enhances performance**. Unlike leadership styles that focus solely on structure or results, **Culture-Driven Leadership integrates shared values, beliefs, and mission into daily operations**.

This model aligns closely with **Edgar Schein's Organizational Culture Theory**, which defines culture as a combination of:

1. **Artifacts** – Visible structures, symbols, and behaviours.

2. **Espoused Values** – Stated beliefs and norms.

3. **Underlying Assumptions** – Deep, unconscious beliefs that drive organizational behaviour.

Key characteristics of **Culture-Driven Leadership**:

1. **Vision & Core Values Alignment** – Leaders **embed the company's mission into everyday decisions.**

2. **People-Centric Approach** – Employees **are empowered to align personal and organizational values.**

3. **Consistency Between Actions & Values** – Leadership **models behaviours that reflect company culture.**

4. **Long-Term Thinking & Sustainability** – Decisions **prioritize purpose over short-term gains.**

5. **High Trust & Engagement** – Employees **feel more committed when they share a common cultural foundation.**

Unlike **authoritarian leadership, which enforces rules from the top, Culture-Driven Leadership shapes behaviour through shared values and inspiration.**

Example

A great example of **Culture-Driven Leadership** is **Patagonia**, the outdoor apparel company. Founder **Yvon Chouinard built Patagonia's culture around environmental sustainability and ethical business practices**. The company integrates these values into everything from **product design to employee benefits (e.g., on-site childcare, paid activism leave)**. Because leadership consistently reinforces these values, employees and customers **deeply connect with the company's mission**, leading to **strong loyalty and brand trust.**

Another example is **Netflix**, where the culture is built on **freedom and responsibility.** Netflix fosters **a high-performance culture with minimal bureaucracy**, allowing employees to make independent decisions aligned with company values. This trust-based leadership approach has **enabled Netflix to remain innovative and adaptive in a highly competitive industry.**

Why It Works

Culture-Driven Leadership is effective because it:

- **Increases Employee Engagement & Retention** – Employees **stay longer and perform better when they resonate with company values.**

- **Strengthens Decision-Making** – A strong culture **guides consistent, ethical choices.**

- **Enhances Customer Loyalty** – Consumers **trust and support brands with authentic, mission-driven leadership**.

- **Encourages Innovation & Collaboration** – Teams **feel psychologically safe to take risks and contribute ideas.**

- **Builds Long-Term Organizational Success** – Companies with **clear cultural foundations navigate change more effectively.**

Research shows that **companies with strong cultures outperform competitors in profitability, innovation, and employee satisfaction.**

How It Works

Culture-Driven Leadership follows a **values-based, people-focused approach**:

1. **Define & Communicate Core Values** – Leadership clearly articulates **mission, vision, and principles.**

2. **Lead by Example** – Leaders **consistently demonstrate cultural values through their actions.**

3. **Empower Employees to Uphold Culture** – Teams are encouraged to make culture-aligned decisions independently.

4. **Integrate Culture into Policies & Systems** – Hiring, training, and performance evaluation **align with cultural values.**

5. **Continuously Reinforce & Adapt** – Leadership regularly evaluates cultural alignment and adjusts as needed.

Unlike **transactional leadership, which focuses on rules and rewards, Culture-Driven Leadership fosters intrinsic motivation and long-term purpose.**

Application

Culture-Driven Leadership is widely applied in:

- **Corporate & Brand-Driven Companies** – Companies like **Patagonia and Zappos build cultures that align with customer expectations.**

- **Startups & Entrepreneurial Ventures** – Young companies **embed values from the start to shape long-term culture.**

- **Healthcare & Nonprofits** – Organizations **prioritize mission-driven leadership to enhance service delivery.**

- **Education & Public Institutions** – Schools and governments **develop strong cultures to guide ethical leadership.**

Key Insights

1. **Culture is the Foundation of Leadership** – Strong cultures **guide decision-making and build long-term success.**

2. **Values Drive Employee Engagement** – When employees **identify with company values, they perform better and stay longer.**

3. **Authenticity & Consistency Build Trust** – Leadership must **live the culture, not just talk about it.**

4. **Culture Evolves, But Core Values Stay Constant** – Organizations **must adapt while maintaining their foundational principles.**

Culture-Driven Leadership proves that **organizations led by shared values, rather than rigid authority, create more engaged teams, loyal customers, and long-term success.**

62. Toxic Leadership

Toxic Leadership: A Breakdown

Theory

Toxic Leadership is a leadership model characterized by **destructive behaviours, manipulation, and a negative work environment** that undermines team morale, productivity, and overall organizational health. Unlike leadership models that focus on **inspiring, empowering, and guiding employees**, Toxic Leadership often results in **fear, mistrust, high turnover, and reduced efficiency.**

Jean Lipman-Blumen (2005) identified **Toxic Leadership as a leadership style that prioritizes personal gain over team well-being**, often involving:

1. **Abuse of Power** – Using authority to **intimidate, manipulate, or control employees.**

2. **Microaggression & Bullying** – Creating a **hostile or demoralizing work culture.**

3. **Narcissistic & Self-Cantered Behaviour** – Focusing on **personal success over collective goals.**

4. **Inconsistent & Unethical Decision-Making** – Encouraging **dishonesty or favouritism**.

5. **Blame-Shifting & Lack of Accountability** – Refusing to **accept responsibility for failures**.

Unlike **Transformational Leadership, which uplifts employees, Toxic Leadership damages team cohesion, mental health, and long-term performance.**

Example

A well-known example of **Toxic Leadership** is **Elizabeth Holmes, former CEO of Theranos**. Holmes created a **toxic work environment driven by secrecy, unrealistic expectations, and deception.** Employees were **fearful of speaking out, faced retaliation for questioning leadership, and operated under extreme pressure**, leading to **the company's collapse due to fraudulent claims.**

Another example is **Travis Kalanick, former CEO of Uber.** Under his leadership, Uber developed a **culture of aggression, sexism, and ethical misconduct**, leading to **a toxic workplace that resulted in lawsuits and reputational damage.** His leadership ultimately led to his forced resignation.

Why It Works (Temporarily)

Toxic Leadership can sometimes **produce short-term results**, but it is **unsustainable** because:

- **Fear-Based Management Increases Compliance** – Employees **may follow orders to avoid retaliation.**

- **High Pressure Can Drive Short-Term Performance** – Some leaders create **urgency through intimidation**.

- **Authoritarian Control Can Create Efficiency** – Centralized decision-making **removes bureaucracy but stifles creativity**.

However, long-term success is **unsustainable** due to **high turnover, burnout, reputational damage, and eventual collapse**.

How It Works

Toxic Leadership follows a **fear-driven, authoritarian approach**:

1. **Manipulation & Control** – Leaders **use threats, favouritism, or false promises to maintain power**.

2. **Intimidation & Public Criticism** – Employees **are publicly humiliated or unfairly reprimanded**.

3. **Suppressing Dissent & Feedback** – Toxic leaders **discourage transparency and silence opposing views**.

4. **Excessive Workloads & Unrealistic Expectations** – Employees **are pushed beyond reasonable limits without support**.

5. **Prioritizing Ego Over Ethics** – Leadership **engages in dishonest or unethical behaviour for personal gain**.

Unlike **Servant Leadership, which prioritizes team well-being, Toxic Leadership prioritizes personal ambition at the expense of others.**

Application

Toxic Leadership is unfortunately **common in high-pressure industries,** including:

- **Corporate Environments** – Leaders **obsessed with short-term profits often foster toxic cultures.**

- **Politics & Government** – Authoritarian figures **use manipulation and intimidation to maintain power.**

- **Startups & Tech Firms** – High-growth companies **sometimes promote aggressive, cutthroat cultures.**

- **Military & High-Stress Professions** – Some leaders **adopt rigid, demeaning leadership styles under the guise of discipline.**

Key Insights

1. **Short-Term Success Does Not Equal Good Leadership** – Toxic leaders may drive results initially but damage long-term success.

2. **Fear-Based Cultures Create Dysfunction** – When employees fear retaliation, innovation and trust disappear.

3. **Toxic Leadership Breeds High Turnover & Low Morale – Organizations with toxic cultures face high resignation rates.**

4. **Leaders Must Be Accountable for Workplace Culture – Ignoring toxicity enables destructive behaviour.**

Toxic Leadership proves that **leadership without integrity, empathy, and ethical responsibility leads to organizational failure, burnout, and reputational harm.**

63. Shared Leadership

Shared Leadership: A Breakdown

Theory

Shared Leadership is a leadership model where **responsibility, influence, and decision-making are distributed across multiple individuals rather than centralized in a single leader**. Unlike traditional hierarchical leadership, **Shared Leadership fosters collaboration, accountability, and collective problem-solving** by leveraging the strengths of an entire team.

This model is based on the idea that **leadership is not tied to a position but emerges through expertise, contribution, and influence**. Researchers like **Pearce & Conger (2003)** define Shared Leadership as a **dynamic, interactive process where leadership shifts depending on the situation and team needs**.

Key characteristics of **Shared Leadership**:

1. **Decentralized Authority** – Leadership responsibilities **are spread across multiple individuals**.

2. **Collaborative Decision-Making** – Teams **share input and contribute to leadership tasks**.

3. **Trust & Mutual Accountability** – Members **support each other and take ownership of results**.

4. **Flexibility & Adaptability** – Leadership **emerges organically based on expertise and context.**

5. **Collective Vision & Purpose** – Teams **align around shared goals rather than following a single leader's direction.**

Unlike **Autocratic Leadership, which relies on top-down control, Shared Leadership distributes power to create a more engaged and innovative workforce.**

Example

A well-known example of **Shared Leadership** is **the healthcare industry,** particularly in **surgical and emergency response teams.** These teams operate in high-stakes environments where **leadership shifts dynamically based on expertise and the demands of the situation.** A senior surgeon may lead during surgery, but a nurse or anaesthesiologist may take charge in critical moments based on their specialized knowledge.

Another example is **Google's project teams,** where employees work in **cross-functional groups with decentralized decision-making.** Rather than relying on a single manager, team members **collaborate, share leadership responsibilities, and contribute based on their strengths,** fostering **greater innovation and efficiency.**

Why It Works

Shared Leadership is effective because it:

- **Enhances Innovation & Problem-Solving** – Diverse perspectives **lead to better decisions and creative solutions.**

- **Increases Employee Engagement & Empowerment** – Teams **feel valued and motivated when they have leadership opportunities.**

- **Improves Adaptability in Complex Situations** – Organizations **respond more quickly to challenges when leadership is flexible.**

- **Encourages a High-Trust, Inclusive Culture** – Employees **collaborate more effectively when leadership is a shared responsibility.**

- **Reduces Leadership Overload & Burnout** – Responsibility is **distributed, preventing a single leader from being overwhelmed.**

Studies show that **organizations with Shared Leadership models experience higher team performance, job satisfaction, and long-term success.**

How It Works

Shared Leadership follows a **team-driven, participatory approach:**

1. **Develop a Culture of Trust & Collaboration** – Leaders **foster an environment where employees feel safe to lead.**

2. **Encourage Skill-Based Leadership Roles** – Leadership **shifts based on expertise rather than hierarchy.**

3. **Create a Supportive Decision-Making Structure** – Teams **have clear processes for sharing authority and resolving conflicts.**

4. **Empower & Train Employees** – Leadership **development is embedded at all levels, ensuring teams can step up when needed.**

5. **Continuously Adapt & Improve** – Organizations **refine leadership distribution based on feedback and evolving goals.**

Unlike **Transactional Leadership, which relies on formal authority, Shared Leadership thrives on collaboration and collective ownership.**

Application

Shared Leadership is widely applied in:

- **Corporate & Cross-Functional Teams** – Companies like **Google and Microsoft encourage decentralized leadership for innovation.**

- **Healthcare & Emergency Response** – Teams **shift leadership based on real-time expertise and situational demands.**

- **Education & Research Institutions** – Schools **use shared governance models to empower teachers and administrators.**

- **Nonprofits & Social Movements** – Organizations **leverage community-driven leadership for social impact.**

Key Insights

1. **Leadership is a Shared Responsibility, Not a Title – Anyone can lead based on expertise and team needs.**

2. **Collaboration Strengthens Decision-Making – Shared input leads to better, more informed choices.**

3. **Employee Empowerment Drives Engagement & Innovation – Teams perform better when leadership is distributed.**

4. **Shared Leadership Requires Trust & Clear Communication – Without coordination, decentralization can lead to confusion.**

Shared Leadership proves that **when leadership is distributed, teams become more engaged, adaptable, and effective in achieving organizational success.**

64. Flat Hierarchy Leadership

Flat Hierarchy Leadership: A Breakdown

Theory

Flat Hierarchy Leadership is a leadership model that **reduces or eliminates traditional hierarchical layers in an organization**, fostering a **more open, decentralized, and collaborative work environment**. Unlike traditional leadership structures that rely on **a clear chain of command, flat organizations encourage autonomy, direct communication, and shared decision-making**.

This model is based on the belief that **fewer management layers improve efficiency, employee empowerment, and innovation**. **Frederick Laloux's Reinventing Organizations (2014)** and concepts from **Holacracy and Agile Management** support this leadership approach, arguing that organizations function better when **employees have the freedom to self-manage and make decisions without excessive managerial oversight**.

Key characteristics of **Flat Hierarchy Leadership**:

1. **Minimal or No Middle Management** – Decision-making **is shared across employees rather than flowing through multiple managerial levels**.

2. **Open Communication & Transparency** – Employees **interact directly with leadership rather than going through intermediaries.**

3. **Autonomy & Self-Management** – Teams **make independent decisions based on trust and accountability.**

4. **Collaborative Decision-Making** – Employees **have a voice in shaping policies, strategies, and innovations.**

5. **Fast-Paced & Agile Work Environment** – Organizations **adapt quickly because there are fewer bureaucratic delays.**

Unlike **Traditional Bureaucratic Leadership, which relies on rigid structures and hierarchy, Flat Hierarchy Leadership fosters empowerment, speed, and collaboration.**

Example

A well-known example of **Flat Hierarchy Leadership** is **Valve, the video game company behind Half-Life and Steam.** Valve **eliminated traditional management roles, allowing employees to self-organize and choose projects.** Employees **move freely between teams based on interests and skills, driving innovation and creativity.**

Another example is **Gore-Tex (W.L. Gore & Associates),** which operates on a **flat leadership model**. Gore's **teams manage themselves, and leadership emerges naturally**

rather than being assigned. Employees **collaborate across functions without a rigid hierarchy**, leading to **continuous product innovation and strong employee engagement**.

Why It Works

Flat Hierarchy Leadership is effective because it:

- **Enhances Employee Engagement & Ownership** – Workers **feel more invested in decisions when they have autonomy**.

- **Encourages Innovation & Agility** – Fewer bureaucratic barriers **allow teams to pivot and innovate faster**.

- **Reduces Communication Bottlenecks** – Employees **get direct access to leadership, speeding up problem-solving**.

- **Builds a Culture of Trust & Responsibility** – Employees **are accountable for their work rather than relying on micromanagement**.

- **Eliminates Unnecessary Management Costs** – Companies **save resources by reducing excessive layers of leadership**.

Studies show that **organizations with flat structures often experience higher employee satisfaction, increased creativity, and faster decision-making**.

How It Works

Flat Hierarchy Leadership follows a **decentralized, self-management approach**:

1. **Empower Employees with Decision-Making Authority** – Workers **are given autonomy to make strategic decisions.**

2. **Encourage Direct, Open Communication** – Employees interact **without navigating rigid managerial layers.**

3. **Foster a Culture of Self-Accountability** – Employees **own their work and take responsibility for success and failures.**

4. **Support Agile & Flexible Team Structures** – Teams **form and dissolve dynamically based on needs and skills.**

5. **Minimize Bureaucracy & Optimize Efficiency** – Leaders **remove unnecessary policies and layers of approval.**

Unlike **Command-and-Control Leadership, which enforces strict supervision, Flat Hierarchy Leadership thrives on employee autonomy and decentralized decision-making.**

Application

Flat Hierarchy Leadership is widely applied in:

- **Tech & Innovation-Driven Companies** – Companies like **Valve, Zappos, and Gore-Tex use flat structures to drive creativity.**

- **Startups & Entrepreneurial Ventures** – Small businesses **operate more efficiently without unnecessary management layers**.

- **Agile & Remote Work Environments** – Remote-first companies **use flat models to empower distributed teams**.

- **Nonprofits & Mission-Driven Organizations** – Decentralized leadership **allows grassroots teams to lead initiatives independently**.

Key Insights

1. **Less Hierarchy = More Engagement** – Employees **perform better when they have ownership over decisions**.

2. **Direct Communication Speeds Up Problem-Solving** – Flat organizations **eliminate unnecessary bureaucracy**.

3. **Self-Management Increases Accountability** – Employees **thrive when given trust and responsibility**.

4. **Flat Hierarchies Require Strong Cultures** – Without a **clear culture of accountability and collaboration, flat structures can lead to chaos**.

Flat Hierarchy Leadership proves that **removing excessive layers of management fosters innovation, agility, and stronger employee ownership, but it requires a culture of trust and accountability to succeed.**

65. Team-Oriented Leadership

Team-Oriented Leadership: A Breakdown

Theory

Team-Oriented Leadership is a leadership model that prioritizes **collaboration, shared goals, and collective success over individual authority.** Leaders in this model **focus on building strong, cohesive teams where members work together effectively to achieve common objectives.**

Unlike **authoritarian or hierarchical leadership,** which places power in the hands of a single leader, **Team-Oriented Leadership fosters mutual respect, trust, and interdependence.** It aligns closely with theories like **Servant Leadership, Transformational Leadership, and Shared Leadership,** which emphasize the importance of **empowering and developing team members.**

Key characteristics of **Team-Oriented Leadership:**

1. **Shared Vision & Goals** – Leaders **ensure that all team members align with a common purpose.**

2. **Collaboration Over Individual Authority** – Success is **measured by team performance rather than individual achievements.**

3. **Trust & Psychological Safety** – Teams **function best when members feel safe to express ideas and take risks.**

4. **Empowerment & Distributed Leadership** – Leadership **is shared, and decisions are made collectively**.

5. **Focus on Communication & Conflict Resolution** – Effective **dialogue and conflict management strengthen team cohesion**.

Unlike **Transactional Leadership, which relies on rewards and punishments, Team-Oriented Leadership is built on motivation, shared purpose, and collective effort**.

Example

A great example of **Team-Oriented Leadership** is **Satya Nadella's leadership at Microsoft**. When Nadella became CEO, he shifted Microsoft's **competitive and hierarchical culture toward a more collaborative and team-oriented approach**. He **encouraged cross-functional teamwork, open communication, and a growth mindset**, resulting in a **more innovative and engaged workforce**.

Another example is **the 2008 U.S. Olympic Basketball "Redeem Team," coached by Mike Krzyzewski**. Instead of relying on individual superstars, Coach K **instilled a team-first mentality, emphasizing unselfish play, shared leadership, and trust**, which ultimately led to **gold medal success**.

Why It Works

Team-Oriented Leadership is effective because it:

- **Improves Team Performance** – Collaborative environments **drive better problem-solving and decision-making**.

- **Boosts Employee Engagement & Satisfaction** – Team members **feel valued and motivated when working in a supportive group**.

- **Encourages Innovation & Creativity** – Teams **generate diverse ideas and challenge each other constructively**.

- **Reduces Workplace Conflicts** – Strong teamwork **enhances communication and minimizes misunderstandings**.

- **Builds Long-Term Organizational Success** – Organizations with **highly engaged teams outperform competitors**.

Research shows that **team-oriented workplaces experience higher employee retention, improved productivity, and stronger adaptability to change**.

How It Works

Team-Oriented Leadership follows a **collaborative, engagement-driven approach**:

1. **Set a Clear Team Vision & Purpose** – Leaders **define collective goals that align with organizational objectives**.

2. **Encourage Open Communication** – Teams **regularly discuss ideas, progress, and challenges openly**.

3. **Develop Team Skills & Trust** – Leaders **invest in training, mentorship, and relationship-building**.

4. **Share Leadership Responsibilities** – Decision-making is **distributed, ensuring collective ownership**.

5. **Foster Accountability & Recognition** – Teams **celebrate wins together and support each other through challenges**.

Unlike **Top-Down Leadership, which centralizes power**, **Team-Oriented Leadership decentralizes influence and fosters unity**.

Application

Team-Oriented Leadership is widely applied in:

- **Corporate & Business Teams** – Companies like **Google and Microsoft promote team collaboration for innovation**.

- **Sports & Coaching** – Successful teams **prioritize collective effort over individual stardom**.

- **Healthcare & Emergency Response** – Medical teams **rely on teamwork to provide efficient patient care**.

- **Military & Crisis Management** – Units **operate through shared responsibility and trust**.

Key Insights

1. **Teams Outperform Individuals in Complex Environments** – Collaborative leadership enables better adaptability and problem-solving.

2. **Trust & Communication Are the Foundation of Team Success** – Without trust, teamwork breaks down.

3. **Leaders Must Prioritize Collective Success Over Personal Recognition** – The best leaders elevate their teams, not themselves.

4. **A Strong Team Culture Drives Long-Term Performance** – High-functioning teams consistently deliver better results.

Team-Oriented Leadership proves that **leaders who prioritize collaboration, shared accountability, and collective success build stronger, more engaged, and higher-performing organizations**.

66. Customer-Centric Leadership

Customer-Centric Leadership: A Breakdown

Theory

Customer-Centric Leadership is a leadership model that places **customer needs, experiences, and satisfaction at the core of decision-making and organizational strategy**. Unlike traditional leadership models that focus primarily on **profit, efficiency, or internal processes**, this approach **aligns business objectives with customer expectations to drive long-term success**.

This model is rooted in **Customer Experience (CX) Theory, Servant Leadership, and Value-Based Leadership**, emphasizing that **leaders should serve customers by creating products, services, and cultures that prioritize their needs and expectations**.

Key characteristics of **Customer-Centric Leadership**:

1. **Customer-First Mindset** – Every decision, from product development to marketing, **centres around customer impact**.

2. **Empowering Employees to Enhance Customer Experience** – Employees **are trained and encouraged to prioritize customer satisfaction**.

3. **Data-Driven Customer Insights** – Leaders **use feedback, analytics, and market trends to improve service and innovation**.

4. **Building Long-Term Relationships Over Short-Term Gains** – Focuses on **loyalty, retention, and delivering long-term value to customers**.

5. **Company-Wide Alignment Around Customer Goals** – All departments, from sales to IT, **work together to enhance the customer journey**.

Unlike **profit-driven leadership, which prioritizes revenue at all costs, Customer-Centric Leadership ensures sustainable growth by fostering strong customer loyalty and trust**.

Example

A great example of **Customer-Centric Leadership** is **Jeff Bezos and Amazon**. From the start, Bezos built Amazon with a **customer-first philosophy**, ensuring that **every innovation, from one-click shopping to Prime delivery, was designed to enhance convenience and experience**. Amazon's customer-centric strategy **drives its success, loyalty, and competitive edge in e-commerce**.

Another example is **Apple under Steve Jobs and Tim Cook**, where **customer experience and intuitive product design are central to business decisions**. Apple's **seamless integration of hardware, software, and services** ensures that **customer needs and usability guide innovation,** resulting in **high brand loyalty and premium market positioning**.

Why It Works

Customer-Centric Leadership is effective because it:

- **Drives Customer Loyalty & Retention** – Businesses that **prioritize customers retain them longer**.

- **Encourages Innovation Based on Real Needs** – Products and services **evolve based on customer insights, not assumptions**.

- **Improves Brand Reputation & Trust** – Customers **trust companies that consistently meet their needs**.

- **Increases Revenue Through Customer Satisfaction** – Happy customers **spend more, return, and refer others**.

- **Enhances Employee Engagement** – Teams **feel motivated when they understand their impact on customers**.

Studies show that **customer-centric companies outperform competitors in profitability, growth, and brand trust**.

How It Works

Customer-Centric Leadership follows a **customer-driven, data-informed approach**:

1. **Develop a Customer-Obsessed Culture** – Train and empower employees **to prioritize customer satisfaction**.

2. **Gather & Act on Customer Feedback** – Use surveys, reviews, and analytics **to refine products and services**.

3. **Innovate with the Customer in Mind** – Product development **starts with solving customer pain points**.

4. **Align Internal Processes Around Customer Success** – Every department **focuses on delivering value to customers**.

5. **Continuously Improve Customer Experience** – Leaders **adapt based on changing customer expectations**.

Unlike **Transactional Leadership, which focuses on efficiency and control, Customer-Centric Leadership builds loyalty, trust, and sustainable growth through meaningful engagement**.

Application

Customer-Centric Leadership is widely applied in:

- **Retail & E-Commerce** – Companies like **Amazon, Apple, and Zappos prioritize seamless customer experiences**.

- **Technology & SaaS** – Firms like **Salesforce and Adobe align product development with customer needs**.

- **Healthcare & Services** – Hospitals and service providers **enhance patient and client experiences for better outcomes**.

- **Hospitality & Tourism** – Hotels and airlines **focus on personalized customer service to improve satisfaction**.

Key Insights

1. **Customer-Centric Companies Win in the Long Run** – Businesses **that prioritize customers outperform competitors in retention and revenue**.

2. **Innovation Should Solve Real Customer Problems** – **Companies succeed when products and services address actual customer needs**.

3. **Customer Experience is Everyone's Responsibility** – **From frontline employees to executives, customer satisfaction should be a shared goal**.

4. **Trust & Loyalty Are Built Through Consistency** – **Customer relationships thrive when organizations consistently deliver value**.

Customer-Centric Leadership proves that **leaders who focus on delivering exceptional customer experiences drive loyalty, growth, and long-term success in any industry**.

67. Purpose-Driven Leadership

Purpose-Driven Leadership: A Breakdown

Theory

Purpose-Driven Leadership is a leadership model where **leaders and organizations operate with a clear mission beyond profits, focusing on values, impact, and long-term societal contributions.** This model is rooted in the idea that **leaders who align their vision with a strong purpose inspire employees, attract loyal customers, and create sustainable success.**

Inspired by theories such as **Simon Sinek's "Start with Why" and Viktor Frankl's ideas on purpose and meaning,** Purpose-Driven Leadership emphasizes:

1. **Clarity of Purpose** – Leaders **define and communicate a strong "why" that guides the organization.**

2. **Mission Over Profit** – Success is **measured not just by revenue but by the positive impact on people and society.**

3. **Employee Engagement & Motivation** – Purpose **creates meaning, fostering deeper commitment from employees.**

4. **Authentic & Ethical Leadership** – Leaders **act with integrity and align actions with values.**

5. **Long-Term Vision & Sustainable Growth** –
   Decisions **are made with future impact in mind,
   not just short-term gains.**

Unlike **transactional leadership, which focuses on
efficiency and rewards, Purpose-Driven Leadership**
creates meaning and long-term value for employees,
customers, and stakeholders.

Example

A well-known example of **Purpose-Driven Leadership** is
Patagonia, led by Yvon Chouinard. The outdoor apparel
brand has built its business around **environmental
sustainability, ethical production, and activism**. Instead of
prioritizing short-term profits, Patagonia **invests in eco-
friendly materials, donates profits to conservation efforts,
and encourages responsible consumerism**. This strong
purpose **attracts loyal customers, engaged employees,
and long-term success**.

Another example is **Microsoft under Satya Nadella**, who
reshaped the company's culture with a **growth mindset
and a focus on empowering individuals and organizations
through technology**. His purpose-driven approach
**enhanced innovation, inclusivity, and long-term
sustainability**, reviving Microsoft's competitive edge.

Why It Works

Purpose-Driven Leadership is effective because it:

- **Inspires Employee Engagement & Retention** – Employees **feel connected to a larger mission, increasing motivation and job satisfaction.**

- **Builds Customer Loyalty & Trust** – Consumers **support brands that align with their values.**

- **Encourages Ethical Decision-Making** – Leaders **prioritize integrity, sustainability, and long-term impact.**

- **Drives Innovation & Resilience** – Organizations **pursuing a clear purpose adapt better to change and challenges.**

- **Creates a Positive Social & Environmental Impact** – Purpose-driven companies **improve communities while maintaining profitability.**

Studies show that **companies with a strong purpose outperform competitors in customer loyalty, employee engagement, and long-term profitability.**

How It Works

Purpose-Driven Leadership follows a **mission-focused, values-driven approach:**

1. **Define & Communicate a Clear Purpose** – Leaders articulate a strong vision that aligns with values and goals.

2. **Lead by Example** – Leaders **demonstrate purpose-driven actions in daily decisions.**

3. **Align Culture & Strategy with Purpose** – The mission is **integrated into hiring, marketing, and business operations.**

4. **Empower Employees to Contribute to the Purpose** – Teams **are encouraged to innovate and make purpose-driven decisions.**

5. **Measure Success Beyond Profit** – Organizations **track social, environmental, and long-term impact alongside financial performance.**

Unlike **authoritarian leadership, which enforces control**, **Purpose-Driven Leadership inspires through vision and shared values.**

Application

Purpose-Driven Leadership is widely applied in:

- **Sustainable & Ethical Businesses** – Companies like **Patagonia, Tesla, and Ben & Jerry's prioritize social impact.**

- **Nonprofits & Social Enterprises** – Organizations **focus on mission-driven initiatives to create positive change.**

- **Corporate Culture Transformations** – Leaders reshape **companies around meaningful missions, as seen in Microsoft and Unilever.**

- **Education & Healthcare** – Institutions **align their services with a deeper sense of community impact.**

Key Insights

1. **A Strong "Why" Inspires People More Than Profits** – Employees and customers **are drawn to organizations with a meaningful mission.**

2. **Purpose Creates a Competitive Advantage** – Companies with a strong purpose **differentiate themselves and build lasting loyalty.**

3. **Leaders Must Embody the Purpose** – Authenticity **is key—leaders must walk the talk.**

4. **Measuring Success Goes Beyond Financial Metrics** – **Impact, sustainability, and cultural influence matter in the long run.**

Purpose-Driven Leadership proves that **leaders who prioritize mission, values, and social impact build stronger, more sustainable, and more influential organizations.**

68. Adaptive Team Leadership

Adaptive Team Leadership: A Breakdown

Theory

Adaptive Team Leadership is a leadership model that emphasizes **flexibility, responsiveness, and continuous learning** to help teams navigate dynamic and complex environments. This model is based on the idea that **effective leaders do not rely on a single leadership style but instead adjust their approach based on team needs, external conditions, and challenges faced**.

Rooted in **Adaptive Leadership (Ronald Heifetz) and Team Effectiveness Theory**, Adaptive Team Leadership incorporates:

1. **Situational Awareness** – Leaders **analyse the environment and adjust their leadership style accordingly**.

2. **Empowering Teams** – Decision-making **is distributed, allowing teams to take ownership of tasks and challenges**.

3. **Encouraging Agility & Experimentation** – Teams **are encouraged to try new approaches and learn from feedback**.

4. **Balancing Stability & Change** – Leaders **maintain a clear vision while being open to pivoting strategies.**

5. **Fostering Psychological Safety** – Teams **feel safe to voice concerns, propose ideas, and take calculated risks.**

Unlike **Directive Leadership, which follows rigid structures, Adaptive Team Leadership thrives in uncertain and evolving environments by encouraging flexibility and innovation.**

Example

A strong example of **Adaptive Team Leadership** is **NASA's Apollo 13 mission.** When a life-threatening malfunction occurred in space, the mission control team had to **rapidly adapt, collaborate, and innovate under extreme pressure.** Instead of following a fixed plan, the leadership team **shifted strategies, empowered experts, and relied on rapid experimentation** to bring the astronauts home safely.

Another example is **Spotify's Squad Model**, where small, self-organizing teams (**"squads"**) work on different aspects of the product. Instead of rigid hierarchies, teams **adapt their leadership based on project demands, expertise, and evolving goals,** ensuring that **Spotify remains agile in the fast-paced tech industry.**

Why It Works

Adaptive Team Leadership is effective because it:

- **Enhances Team Resilience & Agility** – Teams respond effectively to change rather than resisting it.

- **Improves Decision-Making Under Uncertainty** – Leaders **gather insights from different perspectives and adjust accordingly.**

- **Boosts Employee Engagement & Innovation** – Employees **are empowered to contribute solutions and adapt to challenges.**

- **Encourages Collaboration & Learning** – Teams **continuously evolve and refine their approaches based on real-time feedback.**

- **Prepares Organizations for Future Challenges** – Companies with **adaptive teams navigate disruptions more effectively.**

Studies show that **adaptive teams are more successful in fast-changing industries like technology, healthcare, and crisis management.**

How It Works

Adaptive Team Leadership follows a **fluid, situational approach**:

1. **Assess Team & Environmental Needs** – Leaders **observe and analyse changing dynamics.**

2. **Adjust Leadership Style as Needed** – Depending on the situation, leaders may **be directive, collaborative, or hands-off.**

3. **Empower Team Members to Lead** – Leadership **is distributed, allowing the best-qualified individuals to take charge.**

4. **Encourage Experimentation & Learning** – Teams **test new ideas, iterate quickly, and learn from feedback.**

5. **Foster a Culture of Psychological Safety** – Ensuring that **employees feel safe to take risks and express concerns.**

Unlike **Traditional Leadership, which relies on static strategies, Adaptive Team Leadership evolves continuously** to match changing demands.

Application

Adaptive Team Leadership is widely applied in:

- **Crisis Management & Emergency Response** – Teams **must quickly shift strategies under high-pressure situations.**

- **Technology & Agile Organizations** – Companies like **Google and Spotify embrace adaptive leadership to drive innovation.**

- **Startups & High-Growth Companies** – Entrepreneurs **adjust leadership styles based on growth stages and challenges**.

- **Military & Tactical Teams** – Special forces **train in adaptability to handle unpredictable missions**.

Key Insights

1. **Leadership is Not One-Size-Fits-All** – The best leaders **adjust their style based on the situation**.

2. **Teams Thrive When They Are Empowered to Adapt** – Giving teams autonomy enables faster, better decision-making.

3. **Flexibility & Agility Drive Innovation** – Adaptive teams solve problems creatively and efficiently.

4. **Psychological Safety Enables Risk-Taking & Learning** – A safe environment fosters continuous improvement and experimentation.

Adaptive Team Leadership proves that **leaders who embrace flexibility, empower teams, and encourage continuous learning create resilient, high-performing organizations capable of thriving in uncertainty.**

69. Workplace Diversity Leadership

Workplace Diversity Leadership: A Breakdown

Theory

Workplace Diversity Leadership is a leadership model that prioritizes **inclusion, equity, and the value of diverse perspectives** in organizational decision-making and culture. It is based on the belief that **diverse teams perform better, foster innovation, and create a more inclusive work environment**.

This leadership model integrates principles from **Inclusive Leadership, Transformational Leadership, and Equity & Inclusion Frameworks**, ensuring that leaders **actively promote diversity across race, gender, age, abilities, cultural backgrounds, and thought perspectives**.

Key characteristics of **Workplace Diversity Leadership**:

1. **Commitment to Inclusion** – Leaders **actively create a work environment where everyone feels valued and heard**.

2. **Equitable Opportunities** – Ensuring **fair hiring, promotion, and professional growth for all employees**.

3. **Diverse Decision-Making** – Encouraging **input from varied backgrounds to enhance creativity and problem-solving**.

4. **Addressing Unconscious Bias** – Leaders **train themselves and their teams to recognize and counteract bias**.

5. **Cultural Competency** – Developing **an understanding of different perspectives and fostering respect among team members**.

Unlike **traditional leadership models that focus solely on hierarchy or efficiency, Workplace Diversity Leadership emphasizes equity, representation, and inclusion as key drivers of success**.

Example

A well-known example of **Workplace Diversity Leadership** is **Microsoft under Satya Nadella**. Nadella made **diversity, equity, and inclusion (DEI) a strategic priority**, implementing initiatives that **increased female representation in leadership, improved accessibility for disabled employees, and fostered an inclusive culture**. His leadership has helped Microsoft become one of the **most diverse and inclusive tech companies globally**.

Another example is **Airbnb**, which has implemented **DEI programs aimed at reducing bias in hiring and ensuring inclusivity in its global workforce**. Airbnb's leadership **focuses on diverse perspectives to improve customer experiences across different cultures**.

Why It Works

Workplace Diversity Leadership is effective because it:

- **Enhances Creativity & Innovation** – Diverse teams bring different perspectives, leading to more innovative solutions.

- **Improves Employee Engagement & Retention** – Inclusive workplaces **create a sense of belonging, reducing turnover.**

- **Expands Market Reach** – Companies with diverse leadership **better understand global customers and cultural nuances.**

- **Strengthens Decision-Making** – Diverse perspectives **help avoid groupthink and improve strategic problem-solving.**

- **Promotes Fairness & Equity** – Organizations **become more ethical and socially responsible.**

Studies show that **companies with diverse leadership teams outperform those without in terms of profitability, employee satisfaction, and brand reputation.**

How It Works

Workplace Diversity Leadership follows a **structured, inclusive approach:**

1. **Develop & Implement DEI Policies** – Leaders **ensure diversity and inclusion are part of company strategy.**

2. **Foster an Inclusive Culture** – Organizations **train employees on bias, inclusivity, and cultural awareness.**

3. **Encourage Diverse Hiring & Promotion Practices** – Creating **opportunities for underrepresented groups.**

4. **Establish Employee Resource Groups (ERGs)** – Supporting **diverse voices within the organization.**

5. **Measure & Track Diversity Progress** – Companies **regularly assess diversity initiatives and improve strategies.**

Unlike **Authoritarian Leadership, which enforces control from the top, Workplace Diversity Leadership is collaborative, open, and focused on equitable participation.**

Application

Workplace Diversity Leadership is widely applied in:

- **Corporate & Tech Companies** – Firms like **Google, Microsoft, and Airbnb integrate DEI into their strategies.**

- **Public & Government Organizations** – Promoting **diverse representation in policy-making and leadership.**

- **Nonprofits & Social Enterprises** – Ensuring **fair representation and inclusion in mission-driven organizations**.

- **Educational Institutions** – Universities and schools **adopt diversity initiatives to foster inclusive learning environments**.

Key Insights

1. **Diversity Strengthens Business Performance – Inclusive teams drive better innovation, decision-making, and financial success.**

2. **Leaders Must Actively Champion Diversity – It's not enough to support diversity passively— leaders must embed it into strategy and culture.**

3. **Equity & Inclusion Matter as Much as Representation – A diverse workforce without inclusion does not lead to success.**

4. **Measuring Progress Ensures Accountability – Companies that track DEI efforts see better long-term results.**

Workplace Diversity Leadership proves that **leaders who embrace inclusion, fairness, and diverse perspectives create stronger, more innovative, and successful organizations.**

70. Psychological Safety Leadership

Psychological Safety Leadership: A Breakdown

Theory

Psychological Safety Leadership is a leadership model that focuses on **creating an environment where employees feel safe to speak up, take risks, and express ideas without fear of punishment or humiliation**. Coined by **Dr. Amy Edmondson**, psychological safety is essential for **innovation, collaboration, and high-performing teams**.

This leadership approach is based on the idea that **when employees feel psychologically safe, they are more engaged, contribute ideas freely, and take initiative without fear of negative consequences**. Leaders in this model foster **trust, open communication, and inclusivity**.

Key characteristics of **Psychological Safety Leadership**:

1. **Encouraging Open Dialogue** – Employees **are free to voice opinions, ask questions, and challenge ideas without fear**.

2. **Removing Fear of Failure** – Mistakes **are seen as learning opportunities rather than punishable offenses**.

3. **Creating an Inclusive Environment** – Everyone **feels respected, valued, and heard**.

4. **Providing Constructive Feedback** – Leaders **offer guidance in a supportive, non-punitive way**.

5. **Modelling Vulnerability & Humility** – Leaders **admit mistakes and encourage learning from failures**.

Unlike **authoritarian leadership, which relies on fear and control, Psychological Safety Leadership builds trust, innovation, and resilience within teams.**

Example

A strong example of **Psychological Safety Leadership** is **Google's Project Aristotle**, a study that found the highest-performing teams had one key trait: psychological safety. Google implemented **team norms encouraging open dialogue, risk-taking, and mutual respect**, which led to **higher engagement, better problem-solving, and improved productivity.**

Another example is **Ed Catmull at Pixar**, who encouraged **employees to challenge leadership, provide feedback, and openly discuss failures**. This approach **created a culture of creativity and collaboration**, leading to **groundbreaking animated films like Toy Story and Inside Out**.

Why It Works

Psychological Safety Leadership is effective because it:

- **Encourages Innovation & Creativity** – Employees freely share ideas and take risks without fear of failure.

- **Improves Team Collaboration** – Open communication **reduces misunderstandings and enhances teamwork.**

- **Increases Employee Engagement & Retention** – Employees **feel valued, leading to stronger commitment and loyalty.**

- **Enhances Learning & Growth** – Teams **focus on continuous improvement rather than avoiding mistakes.**

- **Reduces Workplace Stress & Anxiety** – A safe environment **prevents fear-based decision-making and burnout.**

Studies show that **psychologically safe teams consistently outperform those operating under fear-based cultures.**

How It Works

Psychological Safety Leadership follows a **trust-driven, inclusion-based approach:**

1. **Establish Open Communication Norms** – Leaders **encourage honest feedback and dialogue.**

2. **Emphasize Learning Over Blame** – Mistakes **are treated as learning opportunities, not failures.**

3. **Model Vulnerability & Transparency** – Leaders admit when they are wrong and share their learning experiences.

4. **Encourage Team Collaboration** – Teams **work together to solve problems, ensuring all voices are heard.**

5. **Provide Supportive & Constructive Feedback** – Feedback **is framed as a tool for improvement, not punishment.**

Unlike **fear-based leadership, which discourages dissent, Psychological Safety Leadership fosters an open and growth-oriented work culture.**

Application

Psychological Safety Leadership is widely applied in:

- **Tech & Innovation Companies** – Firms like **Google, Microsoft, and Pixar use it to drive creativity and problem-solving.**

- **Healthcare & High-Stakes Environments** – Hospitals **adopt it to improve teamwork and prevent errors.**

- **Education & Learning Institutions** – Schools **encourage open discussion to foster critical thinking.**

- **Corporate Leadership & Startups** – Organizations **use it to boost engagement and team cohesion.**

Key Insights

1. **Fear Stifles Growth—Safety Fosters Innovation** – Employees perform better **when they feel safe to express themselves.**

2. **Leaders Must Model Vulnerability & Openness** – **Admitting mistakes and welcoming feedback creates a culture of trust.**

3. **Psychological Safety Strengthens Teamwork** – Teams work best **when all members feel respected and included.**

4. **A Safe Work Culture Drives Long-Term Success** – Organizations **with psychological safety retain top talent and outperform competitors.**

Psychological Safety Leadership proves that **leaders who create a culture of trust, inclusivity, and learning enable teams to reach their highest potential**.

Future & Innovative Leadership Models

71. AI-Integrated Leadership

AI-Integrated Leadership: A Breakdown

Theory

AI-Integrated Leadership is a leadership model that incorporates **artificial intelligence (AI) into decision-making, strategy, and team management** to enhance efficiency, innovation, and problem-solving. This model recognizes that **leaders must leverage AI as a tool rather than view it as a replacement for human leadership.**

The foundation of AI-Integrated Leadership is built on:

1. **Augmented Decision-Making** – AI **analyses data to help leaders make informed and strategic choices.**

2. **Process Automation & Efficiency** – AI **automates repetitive tasks, allowing leaders to focus on higher-value activities.**

3. **Enhanced Predictive Analytics** – AI **identifies patterns and forecasts trends, improving proactive leadership.**

4. **Personalized Leadership Approaches** – AI **assists in understanding employee behaviours, engagement, and productivity needs.**

5. **Ethical & Responsible AI Usage** – Leaders **ensure transparency, fairness, and unbiased AI applications in organizations**.

Unlike **traditional leadership models that rely solely on human intuition and experience, AI-Integrated Leadership leverages technology to enhance, rather than replace, human decision-making and leadership effectiveness.**

Example

A strong example of **AI-Integrated Leadership** is **Satya Nadella's leadership at Microsoft**, where AI plays a key role in product innovation, operational efficiency, and customer engagement. Microsoft integrates **AI into business intelligence, cybersecurity, and cloud computing**, allowing data-driven decision-making at all levels.

Another example is **Elon Musk's leadership at Tesla**, where AI is central to **autonomous driving technology, manufacturing optimization, and predictive maintenance**. Musk's leadership leverages AI to **enhance operational efficiency while maintaining a human-driven company vision**.

Why It Works

AI-Integrated Leadership is effective because it:

- **Enhances Decision Accuracy** – AI processes large datasets to provide insights that humans might overlook.

- **Increases Operational Efficiency** – AI automates routine and repetitive tasks, freeing leaders for strategic thinking.

- **Boosts Innovation & Problem-Solving** – AI assists in discovering new market opportunities and optimizing workflows.

- **Improves Employee & Customer Experience** – AI personalizes interactions, improving engagement and satisfaction.

- **Reduces Human Bias in Decision-Making** – AI-driven analytics **help leaders make more objective, data-backed decisions.**

Studies show that **companies integrating AI into leadership experience faster decision-making, reduced inefficiencies, and better scalability.**

How It Works

AI-Integrated Leadership follows a **tech-enabled, data-driven approach**:

1. **Implement AI for Data-Driven Decision-Making** – Leaders use **AI-powered analytics to enhance forecasting and business intelligence.**

2. **Automate & Optimize Repetitive Processes** – AI is used to **handle administrative tasks, freeing leaders for strategic initiatives**.

3. **Leverage AI for Talent Management** – AI helps **identify employee strengths, predict attrition, and personalize training**.

4. **Ensure Ethical AI Use & Bias Mitigation** – Leaders **monitor AI models for fairness, transparency, and accountability**.

5. **Maintain a Human-Centric AI Approach** – Leaders **use AI as a tool to complement human intuition, not replace it**.

Unlike **directive leadership, which relies on hierarchical decision-making**, **AI-Integrated Leadership decentralizes intelligence and enhances leadership capabilities**.

Application

AI-Integrated Leadership is widely applied in:

- **Corporate & Business Strategy** – AI enhances **decision-making, risk management, and operational efficiency**.

- **Healthcare & Medical Research** – AI assists **in diagnostics, treatment recommendations, and patient care analytics**.

- **Technology & Innovation** – Companies like **Google, Amazon, and Microsoft use AI to drive business transformation.**

- **Retail & Customer Service** – AI-powered chatbots and analytics **optimize customer engagement and personalization.**

Key Insights

1. **AI is a Leadership Tool, Not a Replacement – Successful leaders use AI to enhance, not replace, human intuition and decision-making.**

2. **Data-Driven Leadership Enhances Strategic Thinking – AI provides insights that improve long-term decision-making and risk assessment.**

3. **AI-Integrated Leadership Requires Ethical Oversight – Leaders must ensure AI is used responsibly and fairly.**

4. **AI-Enhanced Teams Operate More Efficiently – AI improves productivity, allowing employees to focus on higher-value tasks.**

AI-Integrated Leadership proves that **leaders who embrace AI as a strategic asset can drive efficiency, innovation, and smarter decision-making while maintaining human oversight and ethical responsibility.**

72. Hybrid Work Leadership

Hybrid Work Leadership: A Breakdown

Theory

Hybrid Work Leadership is a leadership model designed to effectively manage teams in a **hybrid work environment**, where employees split their time between remote and in-office work. This model prioritizes **flexibility, digital collaboration, trust, and inclusion**, ensuring that both remote and in-person employees remain equally engaged and productive.

This leadership approach integrates concepts from **Situational Leadership, Digital Transformation Leadership, and Employee-Centric Leadership**, recognizing that leaders must **adapt their management style to different work settings while fostering team cohesion and efficiency.**

Key characteristics of **Hybrid Work Leadership**:

1. **Flexible & Adaptive Leadership Style** – Leaders **balance remote and in-office needs, adjusting strategies accordingly.**

2. **Technology-Driven Collaboration** – Digital tools **ensure seamless communication and workflow integration.**

3. **Results-Oriented Performance Management** – Focus shifts **from hours worked to outcomes delivered.**

4. **Building Trust & Psychological Safety** – Employees **feel valued, supported, and included, regardless of location.**

5. **Equal Access to Opportunities** – Remote employees **receive the same career growth, mentorship, and recognition as in-office workers.**

Unlike **traditional office-based leadership models, Hybrid Work Leadership is designed for flexibility, inclusivity, and digital efficiency.**

Example

A great example of **Hybrid Work Leadership** is **Microsoft under Satya Nadella.** Microsoft embraced **a flexible work culture, investing in digital collaboration tools (Microsoft Teams, Azure, and AI-driven productivity insights).** Nadella's leadership **ensured employees had the tools, support, and flexibility to succeed in a hybrid environment while maintaining a strong corporate culture.**

Another example is **Spotify's "Work From Anywhere" policy**, where employees **choose their work environment while staying connected through digital collaboration strategies.** This approach has resulted in **higher employee satisfaction, productivity, and retention.**

Why It Works

Hybrid Work Leadership is effective because it:

- **Enhances Employee Productivity & Satisfaction** – Employees **work in environments where they perform best**.

- **Attracts & Retains Top Talent** – Flexibility **is a key factor in job satisfaction and employee retention**.

- **Encourages Work-Life Balance** – Employees **achieve better balance, reducing burnout and increasing engagement**.

- **Drives Innovation & Collaboration** – Digital tools **enable remote and in-office employees to collaborate effectively**.

- **Reduces Operational Costs** – Companies **save on office space while maintaining efficiency**.

Studies show that **companies with strong hybrid leadership models experience higher productivity, improved employee morale, and stronger business continuity**.

How It Works

Hybrid Work Leadership follows a **digital-first, employee-focused approach**:

1. **Establish Clear Communication Channels** – Leaders **use digital tools to ensure transparency and inclusivity**.

2. **Prioritize Results Over Presence** – Performance is measured by outcomes rather than hours worked.

3. **Ensure Equal Access to Career Growth** – Hybrid employees **receive mentorship, promotions, and leadership opportunities.**

4. **Foster a Strong Hybrid Team Culture** – Leaders **create engagement through virtual check-ins, team-building, and recognition programs.**

5. **Leverage Technology for Seamless Collaboration** – Companies **adopt AI, cloud-based platforms, and hybrid meeting solutions.**

Unlike **hierarchical leadership, which emphasizes physical presence, Hybrid Work Leadership embraces flexibility and digital transformation.**

Application

Hybrid Work Leadership is widely applied in:

- **Technology & Remote-First Companies** – Organizations like **Microsoft, Google, and Spotify optimize hybrid work strategies.**

- **Corporate & Professional Services** – Firms **balance in-office collaboration with remote productivity.**

- **Education & Learning Institutions** – Universities **adopt hybrid teaching models to enhance accessibility.**

- **Healthcare & Consulting** – Professionals **integrate remote and in-person client engagement**.

Key Insights

1. **Flexibility is the Future of Work** – Hybrid models increase employee satisfaction, retention, and productivity.

2. **Leaders Must Balance Digital & Human Connection** – Technology should enhance, not replace, human collaboration.

3. **Work Performance Should Be Measured by Results, Not Location** – Leaders must focus on outcomes rather than office attendance.

4. **Inclusivity & Equal Opportunities Are Essential** – Remote employees should have the same growth and visibility as in-office workers.

Hybrid Work Leadership proves that **leaders who embrace flexibility, digital collaboration, and inclusive strategies create engaged, high-performing, and future-ready teams**.

73. Data-Driven Leadership

Data-Driven Leadership: A Breakdown

Theory

Data-Driven Leadership is a leadership model that **leverages analytics, insights, and metrics to guide decision-making, optimize performance, and drive innovation.** Unlike traditional leadership models that rely primarily on **intuition, experience, or hierarchy**, this model integrates **quantifiable data to enhance strategic decisions and organizational success.**

Rooted in **Evidence-Based Decision-Making, Business Intelligence, and Digital Transformation Leadership**, Data-Driven Leadership ensures that **leaders use factual insights rather than assumptions to guide their teams and businesses.**

Key characteristics of **Data-Driven Leadership**:

1. **Fact-Based Decision-Making** – Leaders **use data to validate strategies, reducing bias and guesswork.**

2. **Real-Time Performance Monitoring** – AI and analytics **help leaders track and optimize operational efficiency.**

3. **Predictive & Prescriptive Analytics** – Data **identifies trends, anticipates risks, and suggests solutions.**

4. **Transparency & Accountability** – Decisions **are justified through evidence, fostering trust and credibility.**

5. **Continuous Learning & Adaptation** – Organizations **refine strategies based on evolving data insights.**

Unlike **traditional leadership that relies on instinct and experience**, **Data-Driven Leadership prioritizes analytics, performance metrics, and predictive insights for smarter, more agile decision-making.**

Example

A strong example of **Data-Driven Leadership** is **Netflix's leadership under Reed Hastings.** Netflix **uses data analytics to determine content production, personalize user recommendations, and optimize pricing strategies.** The company's data-driven approach **has allowed it to predict user preferences, improve customer retention, and remain the leading streaming service globally.**

Another example is **Amazon, led by Jeff Bezos**, where data influences **everything from inventory management to customer experience personalization.** Amazon's use of AI-driven insights **enhances product recommendations, streamlines logistics, and improves overall efficiency,** making it a pioneer in data-driven decision-making.

Why It Works

Data-Driven Leadership is effective because it:

- **Reduces Decision-Making Errors** – Leaders **rely on data rather than assumptions, improving accuracy**.

- **Enhances Efficiency & Productivity** – AI-driven insights **optimize operations, reducing waste and inefficiencies.**

- **Improves Customer Experience** – Data enables **personalized, customer-centric decision-making.**

- **Strengthens Competitive Advantage** – Companies **stay ahead by using predictive analytics to anticipate trends.**

- **Encourages Accountability & Objectivity** – Data-backed decisions **reduce bias and ensure transparency.**

Studies show that **organizations using data-driven leadership outperform competitors in revenue growth, customer satisfaction, and operational efficiency.**

How It Works

Data-Driven Leadership follows a **structured, analytics-based approach**:

1. **Collect & Analyse Relevant Data** – Leaders **gather insights from multiple sources (customer feedback, market trends, internal metrics).**

2. **Leverage AI & Predictive Analytics** – Data tools **identify trends, risks, and opportunities before they become critical.**

3. **Integrate Data into Decision-Making** – Business strategies **are shaped by evidence rather than intuition**.

4. **Foster a Data-Driven Culture** – Employees **are trained to use data in their roles, promoting informed decision-making.**

5. **Monitor & Adapt Based on Insights** – Leaders **continuously refine strategies based on updated analytics**.

Unlike **hierarchical leadership, which relies on top-down decision-making**, **Data-Driven Leadership decentralizes insights and empowers all levels of an organization to make informed choices.**

Application

Data-Driven Leadership is widely applied in:

- **Tech & Digital Companies** – Firms like **Google, Amazon, and Netflix use AI and analytics for competitive advantage.**

- **Finance & Investment Sectors** – Data **optimizes risk management, fraud detection, and investment strategies.**

- **Healthcare & Pharmaceuticals** – AI-driven analytics **improve diagnostics, treatment plans, and patient care.**

- **Retail & E-Commerce** – Businesses **use customer data to enhance personalization and inventory management.**

Key Insights

1. **Data is a Strategic Asset** – Organizations that use data effectively outperform competitors in agility and decision-making.

2. **Leadership Must Be Both Data-Driven & Human-Centric** – While data guides strategy, human insight ensures ethical and empathetic leadership.

3. **Predictive Analytics Create a Competitive Edge** – Organizations that anticipate trends and risks can pivot faster than those that react late.

4. **A Data-Driven Culture Fosters Continuous Improvement** – Companies must embed data literacy across all levels to maximize benefits.

Data-Driven Leadership proves that **leaders who leverage analytics, AI, and evidence-based decision-making drive smarter, faster, and more effective business outcomes.**

74. Metaverse Leadership

Metaverse Leadership: A Breakdown

Theory

Metaverse Leadership is a leadership model that focuses on **managing teams, fostering collaboration, and driving innovation within virtual, immersive, and decentralized digital environments**. With the rise of the **metaverse, virtual reality (VR), augmented reality (AR), and Web3 technologies**, leaders must adapt to **new ways of engaging with employees, customers, and stakeholders in virtual spaces**.

This model integrates elements of **Digital Leadership, Remote Leadership, and AI-Integrated Leadership**, emphasizing **flexibility, digital fluency, and virtual engagement**. Metaverse Leadership is particularly important for **organizations operating in digital-first environments, decentralized businesses, and global remote teams**.

Key characteristics of **Metaverse Leadership**:

1. **Immersive Virtual Collaboration** – Leaders facilitate meetings, training, and teamwork in 3D virtual spaces.

2. **Decentralized & Hybrid Work Environments** – Teams **operate across physical and digital realities, requiring new engagement strategies.**

3. **Use of AI & Digital Avatars** – Leaders **leverage AI-driven insights and virtual avatars for communication.**

4. **Web3 & Blockchain Integration** – Organizations **adopt decentralized governance and smart contracts for decision-making.**

5. **Digital Inclusion & Ethical Considerations** – Leaders **ensure equitable access, data privacy, and ethical AI usage in virtual environments.**

Unlike **traditional leadership, which relies on in-person interactions, Metaverse Leadership adapts to a digital-first reality where presence, engagement, and influence transcend physical limitations.**

Example

A strong example of **Metaverse Leadership** is **Meta (formerly Facebook) under Mark Zuckerberg**, where leadership focuses on **creating an immersive digital ecosystem for work, social interaction, and commerce.** Meta's **Horizon Workrooms allows teams to collaborate using VR avatars, bridging the gap between remote and in-office teams.**

Another example is **Decentraland, a virtual world governed through decentralized leadership structures.**

Organizations operating in Decentraland **use blockchain-based decision-making and tokenized economies to empower community-driven leadership.**

Why It Works

Metaverse Leadership is effective because it:

- **Enhances Remote Collaboration** – Teams **interact in more engaging ways than traditional video conferencing.**

- **Expands Global Talent & Accessibility** – Companies **hire and collaborate with top talent without geographical constraints.**

- **Encourages Innovation & Digital Transformation** – The metaverse **creates new opportunities for business growth and creativity.**

- **Redefines Employee & Customer Experience** – Organizations **offer immersive experiences that go beyond conventional interactions.**

- **Improves Engagement & Productivity** – Virtual environments **reduce meeting fatigue and enhance interactivity.**

Studies show that **virtual and immersive workspaces increase employee satisfaction, learning retention, and creativity compared to traditional digital tools.**

How It Works

Metaverse Leadership follows a **virtual-first, tech-enabled approach**:

1. **Build Digital-First Workspaces** – Leaders **adopt VR, AR, and AI tools to enhance communication and workflow**.

2. **Create a Decentralized & Inclusive Culture** – Web3 technologies **support transparent decision-making and community-driven leadership**.

3. **Develop Digital Avatars & Virtual Identities** – Employees and leaders **engage in digital environments with personalized avatars**.

4. **Use AI & Big Data for Insights** – AI-powered analytics **help leaders track productivity, engagement, and team dynamics in virtual spaces**.

5. **Ensure Digital Ethics & Security** – Leaders **establish guidelines for data privacy, cybersecurity, and ethical metaverse interactions**.

Unlike **Hybrid Work Leadership, which balances remote and in-office work, Metaverse Leadership fully integrates immersive digital environments for collaboration and operations**.

Application

Metaverse Leadership is widely applied in:

- **Technology & Innovation Companies** – Firms like **Meta, Microsoft, and Nvidia invest in metaverse-based workspaces.**

- **Remote & Global Organizations** – Companies leverage **virtual offices to bridge geographical gaps.**

- **Education & Corporate Training** – Universities and businesses **use VR for immersive learning experiences.**

- **Retail & Customer Experience** – Brands **create virtual stores and experiences to engage consumers in the metaverse.**

Key Insights

1. **The Future of Leadership is Virtual & Immersive – As metaverse adoption grows, leaders must develop digital fluency.**

2. **Decentralized Decision-Making Empowers Teams – Blockchain and Web3 technologies enable new leadership structures.**

3. **AI & VR Enhance Engagement & Productivity – Metaverse workspaces increase collaboration beyond traditional digital tools.**

4. **Ethical Leadership is Crucial in Digital Worlds – Privacy, accessibility, and inclusivity must be prioritized in metaverse leadership.**

Metaverse Leadership proves that **leaders who embrace immersive technologies, digital collaboration, and decentralized decision-making will drive the future of work and organizational innovation**.

75. Generational Leadership

Generational Leadership: A Breakdown

Theory

Generational Leadership is a leadership model that **adapts leadership styles, communication strategies, and workplace policies to effectively manage and engage a multigenerational workforce**. This model recognizes that different generations—**Baby Boomers, Generation X, Millennials, and Generation Z—have unique work values, expectations, and technological proficiencies**.

Rooted in **Situational Leadership and Diversity & Inclusion Leadership**, Generational Leadership aims to **bridge generational gaps, foster collaboration, and leverage the strengths of a diverse workforce**. Leaders must **adapt their approach to motivate, engage, and align employees of different age groups toward a common vision**.

Key characteristics of **Generational Leadership**:

1. **Flexible Leadership Approach** – Leaders **adjust strategies to meet the expectations of different generations**.

2. **Effective Multigenerational Communication** – Tailoring **communication styles to resonate with digital-first Gen Z or traditionalist Boomers**.

3. **Balancing Experience & Innovation** – Leveraging the wisdom of older employees and the tech-savviness of younger ones.

4. **Encouraging Cross-Generational Collaboration** – Teams **work together to share knowledge and skills across generations.**

5. **Fostering Inclusion & Adaptability** – Creating **a workplace culture where all age groups feel valued and respected.**

Unlike **rigid leadership models that apply a one-size-fits-all approach, Generational Leadership recognizes the unique motivations and expectations of different age groups, ensuring a more engaged and productive workforce.**

Example

A great example of **Generational Leadership** is **IBM's multigenerational workforce strategy.** IBM integrates **mentorship programs where Baby Boomers and Gen X mentor younger employees while also learning from Millennials and Gen Z about digital transformation.** This reciprocal knowledge-sharing approach **preserves institutional knowledge while driving innovation and technological adoption.**

Another example is **Deloitte**, which has implemented **generationally inclusive workplace policies** such as **flexible work arrangements for Millennials and Gen Z, while offering leadership development and phased**

retirement programs for older employees. This strategy has **enhanced employee retention and engagement across all age groups.**

Why It Works

Generational Leadership is effective because it:

- **Enhances Team Performance – Different generations bring diverse perspectives and skills, leading to better problem-solving.**

- **Increases Employee Engagement & Retention – Employees feel valued when leadership acknowledges their unique needs.**

- **Encourages Knowledge Transfer – Cross-generational mentorship helps retain institutional knowledge while integrating new ideas.**

- **Bridges Communication Gaps – Tailored communication styles ensure clarity and inclusivity.**

- **Fosters Workplace Innovation – Leveraging generational strengths drives technological and cultural advancements.**

Studies show that **companies with strong generational leadership strategies experience higher collaboration, productivity, and employee satisfaction.**

How It Works

Generational Leadership follows an **adaptive, people-cantered approach**:

1. **Understand Generational Differences** – Leaders educate themselves on the values, expectations, and work styles of each generation.

2. **Implement Flexible Leadership Styles** – Adjusting leadership approaches to align with different age groups.

3. **Encourage Reverse Mentorship** – Older employees learn from younger colleagues and vice versa.

4. **Personalize Communication & Feedback** – Using different formats (e.g., in-person meetings for Boomers, instant messaging for Gen Z).

5. **Create Inclusive Policies & Workspaces** – Ensuring all generations feel supported through flexible benefits, learning programs, and technology integration.

Unlike **hierarchical leadership models that impose a single management style**, **Generational Leadership is adaptable, inclusive, and responsive to workforce diversity**.

Application

Generational Leadership is widely applied in:

- **Corporate & Multinational Companies** – Organizations like **IBM, Google, and Deloitte** promote generationally inclusive strategies.

- **Government & Public Services** – Agencies **adapt policies to engage a multigenerational workforce**.

- **Healthcare & Education** – Hospitals and universities **bridge generational knowledge gaps through mentorship programs**.

- **Startups & Tech Companies** – Companies **leverage the innovation of younger employees while integrating the experience of senior professionals**.

Key Insights

1. **Workforces Are More Diverse Than Ever – Leadership must be flexible to manage generational differences effectively**.

2. **Different Generations Have Unique Strengths – Combining experience with innovation leads to better outcomes**.

3. **Personalized Communication Enhances Engagement – Leaders should adapt their approach to each generation's preferred style**.

4. **Cross-Generational Collaboration Is Essential for Growth – Successful organizations foster teamwork between older and younger employees**.

Generational Leadership proves that **leaders who understand and adapt to generational differences create more engaged, collaborative, and high-performing teams.**

76. Sustainable Leadership

Sustainable Leadership: A Breakdown

Theory

Sustainable Leadership is a leadership model that focuses on **long-term success, environmental and social responsibility, and ethical decision-making**. Unlike traditional leadership models that prioritize short-term gains and profit maximization, **Sustainable Leadership integrates economic, environmental, and social considerations into organizational strategy**.

This model is built on principles from **Triple Bottom Line Leadership (People, Planet, Profit), Corporate Social Responsibility (CSR), and Ethical Leadership**, ensuring that **leaders create value for future generations while maintaining financial stability**. Sustainable Leadership also emphasizes **stakeholder engagement, resilience, and the well-being of employees and communities**.

Key characteristics of **Sustainable Leadership**:

1. **Long-Term Vision & Impact** – Decisions **prioritize sustainability over immediate financial returns**.

2. **Environmental & Social Responsibility** – Leaders **incorporate eco-friendly and ethical business practices**.

3. **Stakeholder-Centric Approach** – Organizations **balance the needs of employees, communities, and investors**.

4. **Resilience & Adaptability** – Leaders **build organizations that can thrive despite economic or environmental challenges**.

5. **Ethical & Transparent Leadership** – Decision-making **is based on integrity, fairness, and sustainability principles**.

Unlike **profit-driven leadership models that focus on shareholder returns, Sustainable Leadership balances business success with social and environmental impact**.

Example

A strong example of **Sustainable Leadership** is **Paul Polman's leadership at Unilever**. Under his leadership, Unilever launched the **Sustainable Living Plan, focusing on reducing environmental impact, improving health and well-being, and enhancing livelihoods**. By integrating sustainability into core business operations, Unilever **reduced waste, increased energy efficiency, and maintained profitability while making a positive social impact**.

Another example is **Tesla, led by Elon Musk**, which champions **sustainable energy and electric vehicles as a business strategy**. By promoting clean energy solutions, Tesla **aligns business growth with environmental** sustainability, proving that **profit and sustainability can coexist**.

Why It Works

Sustainable Leadership is effective because it:

- **Builds Long-Term Business Success** – Organizations **reduce risks by focusing on sustainability and ethical governance.**

- **Enhances Brand Trust & Reputation** – Consumers and investors **support businesses that prioritize sustainability.**

- **Drives Innovation & Efficiency** – Sustainable practices **often lead to cost savings and new business opportunities.**

- **Engages & Retains Employees** – People prefer **to work for organizations with a strong ethical and sustainability mission.**

- **Ensures Regulatory Compliance** – Companies avoid **legal and reputational risks by adhering to sustainability policies.**

Studies show that **companies with strong sustainability initiatives outperform competitors in long-term financial performance and brand loyalty.**

How It Works

Sustainable Leadership follows a **responsible, future-focused approach**:

1. **Develop a Clear Sustainability Vision** – Leaders define long-term goals for environmental and social impact.

2. **Embed Sustainability into Business Strategy** – Sustainability **is integrated into operations, supply chains, and product development**.

3. **Engage Stakeholders & Employees** – Organizations involve employees, customers, and investors in sustainability efforts.

4. **Measure & Report Sustainability Impact** – Leaders track carbon footprint, resource usage, and social contributions.

5. **Adapt & Innovate for Long-Term Growth** – Sustainable organizations **continuously evolve to meet environmental and social demands**.

Unlike **Transactional Leadership, which prioritizes immediate performance metrics, Sustainable Leadership ensures that business success aligns with social and environmental well-being.**

Application

Sustainable Leadership is widely applied in:

- **Corporate & Multinational Companies** – Firms like **Unilever, Tesla, and Patagonia embed sustainability into their business models.**

- **Government & Public Policy** – Policymakers **promote sustainable initiatives for long-term economic stability.**

- **Nonprofits & Social Enterprises** – Organizations **focus on social responsibility and environmental impact.**

- **Technology & Innovation** – Companies **develop green technologies and ethical business solutions.**

Key Insights

1. **Sustainability is a Competitive Advantage – Companies that integrate sustainability into their strategy build stronger brands and customer loyalty.**

2. **Long-Term Thinking Drives Business Resilience – Sustainable leadership helps organizations navigate economic and environmental challenges.**

3. **Stakeholder Engagement is Crucial – Success depends on balancing business goals with social and environmental responsibilities.**

4. **Ethical Leadership Builds a Stronger Workforce – Employees are more engaged and committed when working for purpose-driven organizations.**

Sustainable Leadership proves that **leaders who prioritize ethical, environmental, and long-term business strategies create organizations that thrive financially while making a positive impact on society and the planet.**

77. Human-Cantered Leadership

Human-Cantered Leadership: A Breakdown

Theory

Human-Cantered Leadership is a leadership model that **prioritizes the well-being, development, and empowerment of individuals within an organization**. Instead of focusing solely on efficiency, profit, or rigid structures, this approach emphasizes **empathy, emotional intelligence, and people-first decision-making**.

Rooted in **Humanistic Psychology, Servant Leadership, and Transformational Leadership**, Human-Cantered Leadership ensures that **leaders create environments where employees feel valued, respected, and motivated to reach their full potential**. This model aligns with modern leadership trends that recognize **people as the most important asset of any organization**.

Key characteristics of **Human-Cantered Leadership**:

1. **Empathy & Emotional Intelligence** – Leaders **actively listen, understand, and address the needs of employees.**

2. **Employee Well-Being & Mental Health** – Organizations **prioritize work-life balance, mental health, and job satisfaction.**

3. **Trust & Psychological Safety** – Employees **feel safe to express ideas, take risks, and innovate.**

4. **Collaborative & Inclusive Leadership** – Decision-making **is participatory, ensuring all voices are heard.**

5. **Personal & Professional Growth Focus** – Leaders **invest in employees' skill development, career growth, and personal fulfilment.**

Unlike **authoritarian or transactional leadership, which focuses on control and efficiency, Human-Cantered Leadership builds engagement, trust, and long-term organizational success.**

Example

A great example of **Human-Cantered Leadership** is **Satya Nadella's transformation of Microsoft.** When Nadella became CEO, he shifted Microsoft's culture from **competitive and rigid to one based on empathy, collaboration, and a growth mindset. By focusing on employees' well-being, fostering psychological safety, and promoting continuous learning,** he revitalized Microsoft, leading to **greater innovation and company growth.**

Another example is **Patagonia, led by Yvon Chouinard,** which implements **people-first policies such as on-site childcare, flexible work schedules, and strong environmental values.** Employees feel a deep connection to the company's mission, **resulting in high job satisfaction, loyalty, and strong financial performance.**

Why It Works

Human-Cantered Leadership is effective because it:

- **Boosts Employee Engagement & Productivity** – Employees **perform better when they feel valued and supported.**

- **Increases Retention & Reduces Burnout** – A positive work culture **reduces turnover and enhances job satisfaction.**

- **Fosters Creativity & Innovation** – Employees **are more willing to take risks and contribute new ideas.**

- **Strengthens Organizational Reputation** – Companies **attract top talent by demonstrating a commitment to employee well-being.**

- **Builds Long-Term Business Success** – Organizations **focused on people see higher loyalty, collaboration, and growth.**

Studies show that **companies with human-cantered leadership experience better financial performance, stronger workplace culture, and higher levels of employee trust and satisfaction**.

How It Works

Human-Cantered Leadership follows a **people-first, empathy-driven approach**:

1. **Cultivate a Culture of Trust & Inclusion** – Leaders foster a safe, open, and inclusive work environment.

2. **Prioritize Employee Well-Being** – Work policies support mental health, flexibility, and work-life balance.

3. **Encourage Open Communication & Feedback** – Leaders **listen to employees and integrate their insights into decision-making.**

4. **Invest in Employee Growth & Development** – Organizations **offer training, mentorship, and opportunities for career progression.**

5. **Lead with Empathy & Authenticity** – Leaders demonstrate vulnerability, emotional intelligence, and personal connection with employees.

Unlike **traditional leadership models focused on authority and control, Human-Cantered Leadership fosters connection, collaboration, and well-being as a pathway to business success.**

Application

Human-Cantered Leadership is widely applied in:

- **Corporate & Tech Companies** – Organizations like **Microsoft, Salesforce, and Google implement employee-first cultures.**

- **Nonprofits & Mission-Driven Organizations** – NGOs **focus on people-centric leadership for community impact**.

- **Healthcare & Education** – Hospitals and schools **prioritize well-being and employee engagement to improve service delivery**.

- **Startups & Innovation Sectors** – Fast-growing companies **use human-cantered approaches to attract and retain top talent**.

Key Insights

1. **People Are the Core of Any Organization** – **Companies thrive when employees are engaged, valued, and empowered**.

2. **Empathy is a Leadership Superpower** – **Emotionally intelligent leaders build trust, loyalty, and innovation**.

3. **Psychological Safety Drives Performance** – **Employees perform best when they feel safe to express ideas and take risks**.

4. **Human-Cantered Leadership Leads to Business Success** – **Organizations that prioritize employee well-being outperform those that don't**.

Human-Cantered Leadership proves that **leaders who focus on people—not just profits—create sustainable, high-performing, and engaged organizations**.

78. Open-Source Leadership

Open-Source Leadership: A Breakdown

Theory

Open-Source Leadership is a leadership model that emphasizes **collaboration, transparency, and decentralized decision-making**. Inspired by the **open-source movement in software development**, this model applies the same principles to leadership—**empowering employees, encouraging innovation through collective intelligence, and fostering a culture of shared knowledge.**

Rooted in **Democratic Leadership, Distributed Leadership, and Agile Leadership**, Open-Source Leadership believes that **leadership is not confined to a single person or hierarchy but is instead a shared function within an organization**. Leaders act as **facilitators rather than controllers**, guiding teams by providing access to information, removing barriers, and encouraging participation from all levels.

Key characteristics of **Open-Source Leadership**:

1. **Decentralized Decision-Making** – Power is **shared across teams rather than concentrated in a few individuals.**

2. **Radical Transparency** – Information and strategies are openly shared to enable collaboration and innovation.

3. **Crowdsourced Problem-Solving** – Employees and stakeholders **contribute ideas, leading to faster and more creative solutions.**

4. **Agility & Adaptability** – The organization **evolves based on real-time feedback and open participation.**

5. **Empowered Employees** – Leadership **trusts employees to take initiative, self-organize, and make decisions.**

Unlike **authoritarian leadership, which relies on top-down directives**, **Open-Source Leadership thrives on decentralization, autonomy, and shared knowledge.**

Example

A strong example of **Open-Source Leadership** is **Linux, the open-source operating system**. Unlike traditional tech companies that closely guard proprietary software, Linux's development is **community-driven, with contributions from developers worldwide**. Leadership is distributed, and **decisions about the software's evolution are made collaboratively, fostering innovation and rapid improvement**.

Another example is **Haier, the multinational appliance company** that adopted a **decentralized, self-managed**

leadership model. Haier broke its organization into **autonomous micro-enterprises, allowing employees to act as entrepreneurs.** This open-source approach **led to increased agility, innovation, and employee engagement.**

Why It Works

Open-Source Leadership is effective because it:

- **Increases Innovation & Agility** – Organizations **leverage collective intelligence for faster, more creative solutions.**

- **Enhances Employee Engagement & Ownership** – Employees **feel valued when they have autonomy and decision-making power.**

- **Improves Problem-Solving** – A decentralized structure **allows faster responses to challenges with diverse input.**

- **Encourages Transparency & Trust** – Open information sharing **fosters credibility and collaboration.**

- **Drives Continuous Learning & Improvement** – Organizations **evolve rapidly based on community-driven feedback.**

Studies show that **businesses that embrace decentralized decision-making and open collaboration tend to outperform traditional hierarchical organizations in innovation and adaptability.**

How It Works

Open-Source Leadership follows a **collaborative, decentralized approach**:

1. **Establish a Transparent Communication Culture** – Leaders **ensure information is accessible to all employees**.

2. **Empower Teams with Autonomy** – Employees **are encouraged to take initiative and self-manage**.

3. **Leverage Crowdsourced Innovation** – Organizations **gather input from employees, customers, and stakeholders**.

4. **Implement Agile & Iterative Processes** – Companies **continuously adapt based on open feedback loops**.

5. **Foster a Learning & Knowledge-Sharing Environment** – Employees **contribute to collective learning and skill development**.

Unlike **Command-and-Control Leadership, which limits decision-making to executives, Open-Source Leadership democratizes leadership and innovation across the organization**.

Application

Open-Source Leadership is widely applied in:

- **Technology & Software Development** – Companies like **GitHub, Linux, and Mozilla rely on open-source collaboration.**

- **Corporate & Agile Workplaces** – Organizations **implement decentralized leadership models for innovation.**

- **Startups & Entrepreneurial Ventures** – Small teams **operate with flexibility and shared leadership.**

- **Nonprofits & Community-Driven Initiatives** – Open-source models **engage stakeholders in decision-making.**

Key Insights

1. **Leadership is a Shared Responsibility** – **Organizations thrive when leadership is distributed and participatory.**

2. **Transparency Builds Trust & Innovation** – **Open access to information fosters creativity and collaboration.**

3. **Decentralized Decision-Making Enhances Agility** – **Organizations that empower employees respond faster to change.**

4. **Continuous Learning Drives Long-Term Success** – **Knowledge-sharing cultures create more adaptable and innovative teams.**

Open-Source Leadership proves that **leaders who embrace transparency, decentralization, and collaborative decision-making can build more innovative, agile, and engaged organizations**.

79. Influencer Leadership

Influencer Leadership: A Breakdown

Theory

Influencer Leadership is a leadership model that focuses on **inspiring, persuading, and mobilizing people through influence rather than authority**. Unlike traditional leadership, which relies on hierarchical power, **Influencer Leadership leverages credibility, emotional connection, and social influence to drive change**.

Rooted in **Charismatic Leadership, Social Influence Theory, and Digital Leadership**, this model recognizes that in today's digital age, **leaders must engage audiences through authenticity, storytelling, and community-building**. Influencer leaders are often seen as **thought leaders, visionaries, or trusted figures who shape opinions and inspire action**.

Key characteristics of **Influencer Leadership**:

1. **Authenticity & Credibility** – Leaders **gain trust by being transparent, relatable, and genuine**.

2. **Emotional Intelligence & Connection** – Leadership is **built on empathy, storytelling, and personal engagement**.

3. **Leveraging Digital & Social Platforms** – Influencer leaders **use media, social networks, and content to reach audiences**.

4. **Community Building & Engagement** – Success is **measured by engagement, loyalty, and shared purpose**.

5. **Persuasion Over Authority** – Instead of issuing commands, leaders **motivate action through influence and inspiration**.

Unlike **Transactional Leadership, which focuses on structure and incentives, Influencer Leadership thrives on emotional connection, trust, and personal brand power**.

Example

A strong example of **Influencer Leadership** is **Elon Musk**, whose social media presence and visionary leadership have **mobilized investors, employees, and customers without relying solely on traditional authority**. His ability to **shape public perception, engage communities, and inspire action has played a crucial role in Tesla and SpaceX's success**.

Another example is **Oprah Winfrey**, who built a global brand through **authentic storytelling, emotional connection, and thought leadership**. Oprah's influence extends beyond media, as she has shaped social conversations, consumer behaviour, and philanthropic efforts through **trust and credibility**.

Why It Works

Influencer Leadership is effective because it:

- **Builds Trust & Authenticity** – People **follow leaders they believe in, not just those in authority**.

- **Encourages Grassroots Engagement** – Influence **mobilizes action from communities and audiences organically**.

- **Inspires & Motivates Without Force** – Leaders **persuade and inspire rather than mandate**.

- **Leverages Digital & Social Platforms for Reach** – Modern leaders **extend influence beyond physical boundaries**.

- **Creates a Strong Personal Brand & Legacy** – Influencer leaders **build lasting impact through trust and reputation**.

Studies show that **leaders with high influence drive stronger engagement, brand loyalty, and long-term success compared to traditional authoritative leaders**.

How It Works

Influencer Leadership follows a **relationship-driven, credibility-based approach**:

1. **Establish a Personal Brand & Clear Message** – Leaders **define their vision, values, and expertise to build trust**.

2. **Engage & Communicate Authentically** – Connection is **built through honest storytelling and genuine engagement**.

3. **Leverage Digital & Social Platforms** – Leaders **use content, media, and networking to amplify influence**.

4. **Build a Loyal Community** – Influence **grows through strong audience relationships and shared values**.

5. **Lead Through Persuasion & Inspiration** – Instead of authority, leaders **mobilize action through emotional impact and credibility**.

Unlike **Directive Leadership, which enforces control**, **Influencer Leadership inspires voluntary commitment and participation**.

Application

Influencer Leadership is widely applied in:

- **Entrepreneurship & Personal Branding** – Leaders like **Gary Vaynerchuk and Richard Branson use influence to drive business growth**.

- **Social Media & Digital Platforms** – Influencers shape public opinion, marketing, and brand engagement.

- **Corporate & Organizational Leadership** – Leaders engage employees and stakeholders through trust and inspiration.

- **Politics & Social Movements** – Figures like **Greta Thunberg and Malala Yousafzai mobilize global communities through influence.**

Key Insights

1. **Trust & Authenticity Are the Core of Influence – People follow leaders they trust, not just those in power.**

2. **Emotion Drives Action More Than Authority – Persuasion through storytelling and connection is more effective than command-based leadership.**

3. **Influence Scales Through Digital & Social Media – Modern leaders expand their impact through digital presence.**

4. **Sustained Influence Requires Community Engagement – Loyal communities drive long-term leadership success.**

Influencer Leadership proves that **leaders who inspire, connect, and engage through trust and influence—not authority—create lasting impact and movements that drive change.**

80. Neurodiversity Leadership

Neurodiversity Leadership: A Breakdown

Theory

Neurodiversity Leadership is a leadership model that **recognizes, supports, and leverages the unique strengths of neurodivergent individuals** in the workplace. It is based on the understanding that **conditions like autism, ADHD, dyslexia, and other cognitive differences are not deficits but variations of human cognition that bring distinct strengths, creativity, and problem-solving abilities.**

Rooted in **Inclusive Leadership, Strength-Based Leadership, and Workplace Diversity Leadership**, this model ensures that **organizations foster an inclusive environment where neurodivergent employees can thrive.** Neurodiversity Leadership **moves away from a one-size-fits-all approach to leadership and instead tailors management strategies to different cognitive styles.**

Key characteristics of **Neurodiversity Leadership**:

1. **Recognition of Cognitive Diversity** – Leaders **understand that neurodivergent individuals contribute unique skills and perspectives.**

2. **Creating Inclusive & Adaptive Work Environments** – Organizations **adjust communication styles,**

workflows, and expectations to accommodate neurodiverse employees.

3. **Strength-Based Leadership Approach** – Instead of focusing on perceived weaknesses, leaders **capitalize on the strengths of neurodivergent individuals.**

4. **Psychological Safety & Flexibility** – Neurodiverse-friendly workplaces **reduce stigma and create a culture where employees feel safe and valued.**

5. **Training & Awareness for Teams** – Leaders and colleagues **are educated on neurodiversity to promote understanding and inclusion.**

Unlike **traditional leadership models that assume a uniform approach to management, Neurodiversity Leadership personalizes leadership to unlock the potential of cognitively diverse employees.**

Example

A strong example of **Neurodiversity Leadership** is **Microsoft's Autism Hiring Program**, which **recruits and supports neurodivergent talent by adapting interview processes and providing tailored workplace accommodations.** This initiative has led to **higher retention, greater innovation, and improved job performance among neurodiverse employees.**

Another example is **SAP's Autism at Work program**, which has successfully **integrated neurodiverse employees into**

teams, leveraging their skills in pattern recognition, problem-solving, and data analysis. By adopting a neurodiversity-friendly leadership approach, SAP has **increased team performance and innovation while fostering an inclusive workplace culture.**

Why It Works

Neurodiversity Leadership is effective because it:

- **Harnesses Unique Cognitive Strengths** – Neurodivergent employees **excel in pattern recognition, logical thinking, and creativity.**

- **Improves Team Innovation & Problem-Solving** – Diverse cognitive perspectives **enhance strategic thinking and innovation.**

- **Increases Employee Retention & Satisfaction** – Inclusive environments **reduce burnout and improve engagement for neurodivergent workers.**

- **Enhances Organizational Reputation** – Companies **leading in neurodiversity attract top talent and socially conscious investors.**

- **Creates More Effective & Adaptable Teams** – Understanding cognitive diversity **strengthens collaboration and adaptability.**

Studies show that **workplaces that embrace neurodiversity experience increased productivity, innovation, and employee loyalty.**

How It Works

Neurodiversity Leadership follows a **strength-based, inclusion-driven approach**:

1. **Redesign Hiring & Onboarding Processes** – Implement **alternative interview methods and flexible onboarding strategies**.

2. **Create Neurodiverse-Friendly Workspaces** – Adjust sensory environments, communication methods, and task structures.

3. **Encourage Flexible Work & Management Styles** – Offer **customized work schedules, quiet spaces, and alternative task management approaches**.

4. **Provide Neurodiversity Awareness Training** – Educate **leaders and teams on neurodiversity to reduce stigma and improve collaboration**.

5. **Foster Mentorship & Support Systems** – Implement **mentorship programs and employee resource groups for neurodivergent employees**.

Unlike **Rigid Leadership Models, which enforce standardized processes, Neurodiversity Leadership adapts structures to individual cognitive needs, unlocking greater team potential**.

Application

Neurodiversity Leadership is widely applied in:

- **Technology & Data-Driven Industries** – Companies like **Microsoft, SAP, and EY integrate neurodivergent employees into data and AI-driven roles.**

- **Creative & Design Fields** – Neurodiverse individuals **excel in graphic design, architecture, and creative problem-solving.**

- **Education & Research Institutions** – Schools and universities **adopt neurodiverse-friendly teaching and work environments.**

- **Healthcare & Social Services** – Organizations **develop specialized programs to support neurodivergent professionals and clients.**

Key Insights

1. **Cognitive Diversity is a Competitive Advantage** – **Leveraging neurodivergent strengths leads to higher innovation and efficiency.**

2. **Workplace Flexibility Unlocks Potential** – **Providing alternative work environments increases productivity and satisfaction.**

3. **Neurodivergent Employees Need Psychological Safety** – **A supportive culture allows employees to thrive without fear of stigma.**

4. **Organizations Must Educate Leaders & Teams** – **Training improves collaboration and breaks down misconceptions about neurodiversity.**

Neurodiversity Leadership proves that **leaders who embrace cognitive diversity, adapt management strategies, and foster inclusion create stronger, more innovative, and high-performing organizations**.

Niche & Philosophical Leadership Approaches

81. Stoic Leadership

Stoic Leadership: A Breakdown

Theory

Stoic Leadership is a leadership model based on **the principles of Stoicism, an ancient philosophy that emphasizes rationality, resilience, self-discipline, and virtue in decision-making**. Stoic leaders **remain calm under pressure, focus on what they can control, and lead with integrity, wisdom, and emotional discipline**.

Rooted in **Stoic Philosophy (Marcus Aurelius, Seneca, Epictetus)** and **Resilient Leadership**, Stoic Leadership teaches that **leaders should focus on their character, make decisions based on reason rather than emotion, and lead by example rather than authority**. The model is particularly effective in **high-pressure, uncertain, or crisis-driven environments**.

Key characteristics of **Stoic Leadership**:

1. **Emotional Control & Rational Thinking** – Leaders **do not react impulsively but remain composed and logical**.

2. **Resilience & Adaptability** – Challenges and failures **are seen as opportunities for growth rather than setbacks**.

3. **Integrity & Ethical Leadership** – Decisions **are made based on virtue and long-term principles, not short-term gains**.

4. **Focus on What Can Be Controlled** – Leaders **accept what they cannot change and channel energy into productive action**.

5. **Lead by Example** – Stoic leaders **embody the values they wish to instil in others, fostering trust and respect**.

Unlike **charismatic or emotionally-driven leadership styles, Stoic Leadership values calm, thoughtful, and consistent leadership even in times of uncertainty or crisis**.

Example

A great example of **Stoic Leadership** is **Marcus Aurelius, the Roman Emperor and Stoic philosopher**, who led during war, plague, and economic crises. Despite challenges, he remained **calm, strategic, and committed to his principles**, as recorded in his personal writings, *Meditations*.

In modern times, **Angela Merkel**, the former Chancellor of Germany, displayed Stoic Leadership during crises such as the European financial crisis and the COVID-19 pandemic. She **remained composed, made rational decisions based on facts, and avoided emotional rhetoric**, earning global respect.

Why It Works

Stoic Leadership is effective because it:

- **Enhances Decision-Making Under Pressure** – Leaders **stay rational and composed, avoiding reactionary mistakes.**

- **Builds Resilient & Trustworthy Teams** – Employees **follow leaders who remain steady in uncertainty.**

- **Encourages Long-Term Thinking & Ethical Choices** – Leaders **prioritize sustainable success over short-term gains.**

- **Reduces Workplace Stress & Conflict** – A stoic approach **creates stability and clarity in teams.**

- **Improves Leadership Credibility & Respect** – People **trust leaders who lead by example and remain unwavering in principles.**

Studies show that **leaders who practice emotional control, ethical consistency, and resilience are more effective in long-term leadership roles.**

How It Works

Stoic Leadership follows a **principle-driven, self-disciplined approach:**

1. **Practice Self-Awareness & Emotional Control** – Leaders **train themselves to respond with logic, not emotion.**

2. **Adopt a Growth Mindset Toward Challenges –** Obstacles **are seen as lessons that strengthen leadership skills.**

3. **Focus on What Can Be Controlled –** Energy is **spent on actions within one's influence, not external events.**

4. **Lead with Integrity & Rationality –** Leaders **act ethically and make decisions based on reason, not impulse.**

5. **Cultivate Resilience & Long-Term Thinking –** Leadership **is a steady commitment to principles, not momentary reactions.**

Unlike **ego-driven leadership models, Stoic Leadership minimizes personal biases and emotions to focus on rational, ethical decision-making.**

Application

Stoic Leadership is widely applied in:

- **Business & Corporate Leadership –** CEOs like **Warren Buffett exhibit Stoic principles in rational decision-making.**

- **Military & Crisis Leadership –** Leaders in **the military and emergency response remain calm and strategic under pressure.**

- **Politics & Government Leadership** – Figures like Angela Merkel lead with composure and ethical clarity.

- **Entrepreneurship & Startups** – Founders **navigate uncertainty and setbacks with a Stoic mindset.**

Key Insights

1. **Resilient Leaders Create Stable Organizations – A calm, rational leader builds confidence in teams.**

2. **Focus on Virtue, Not Popularity** – Stoic leaders prioritize ethical decisions over emotional or crowd-driven reactions.

3. **Challenges Are Opportunities for Growth – Hardships shape better, stronger, and more rational leaders.**

4. **Control Your Response, Not the Situation – Leadership is about managing one's reaction to events, not controlling every outcome.**

Stoic Leadership proves that **leaders who remain calm, ethical, and focused on long-term principles inspire trust, resilience, and sustainable success in their teams and organizations.**

82. Zen Leadership

Zen Leadership: A Breakdown

Theory

Zen Leadership is a leadership model rooted in **Zen Buddhist philosophy, mindfulness, and self-awareness**, emphasizing **clarity, presence, and non-attachment** in decision-making and leadership. This approach encourages **leaders to cultivate inner peace, emotional intelligence, and deep awareness**, leading to **calm, focused, and compassionate leadership**.

Zen Leadership integrates principles from **Mindfulness Leadership, Servant Leadership, and Transformational Leadership**, teaching that **true leadership arises from a place of stillness and deep self-understanding rather than force or control**. Leaders who embody Zen principles **remain adaptable, make decisions with clarity, and lead without ego**.

Key characteristics of **Zen Leadership**:

1. **Presence & Mindfulness** – Leaders **stay fully present, responding to situations with clarity and calmness**.

2. **Non-Attachment & Ego-Free Leadership** – Decisions **are made based on wisdom, not personal desires or emotions**.

3. **Deep Self-Awareness** – Leaders **understand their emotions, thoughts, and biases, leading with authenticity.**

4. **Compassion & Empathy** – Leadership **prioritizes well-being, harmony, and understanding over competition.**

5. **Simplicity & Focus** – Leaders **eliminate distractions, focusing on what truly matters.**

Unlike **hierarchical or control-based leadership models, Zen Leadership fosters adaptability, self-reflection, and clarity, ensuring sustainable success through conscious decision-making.**

Example

A great example of **Zen Leadership** is **Steve Jobs** during his later years at Apple. Deeply influenced by **Zen Buddhism,** Jobs practiced **meditation, mindfulness, and minimalism,** which shaped his leadership style. His ability to **cut through distractions, focus on simplicity, and make clear, intuitive decisions led to Apple's groundbreaking innovations.**

Another example is **Jon Kabat-Zinn**, the founder of **Mindfulness-Based Stress Reduction (MBSR),** who introduced **Zen principles into corporate leadership and healthcare, helping leaders cultivate mindfulness and reduce stress while making better decisions.**

Why It Works

Zen Leadership is effective because it:

- **Enhances Clarity & Decision-Making** – Leaders approach challenges with calmness, reducing impulsive mistakes.

- **Increases Resilience & Emotional Stability** – Mindfulness **helps leaders manage stress and uncertainty effectively.**

- **Fosters Compassion & Stronger Relationships** – Leaders **prioritize people and create a culture of trust.**

- **Encourages Simplicity & Focus** – Zen practices **eliminate distractions, enhancing productivity and efficiency.**

- **Creates Long-Term Sustainable Leadership** – Leaders **avoid burnout by practicing balance, patience, and self-awareness.**

Studies show that **mindful, self-aware leaders cultivate healthier workplaces, increase employee engagement, and drive long-term success.**

How It Works

Zen Leadership follows a **mindfulness-based, presence-focused approach:**

1. **Practice Daily Mindfulness & Meditation** – Leaders develop self-awareness and emotional stability.

2. **Detach from Ego & Outcomes** – Decision-making is based on wisdom, not personal attachment.

3. **Emphasize Clarity & Simplicity** – Leaders **cut through noise, focusing on what truly matters.**

4. **Lead with Compassion & Understanding** – Leadership **prioritizes relationships and the well-being of others.**

5. **Stay Adaptable & Open-Minded** – Leaders **embrace uncertainty with calmness and flexibility.**

Unlike **command-driven leadership, which forces outcomes, Zen Leadership embraces flow, leading with presence and wisdom.**

Application

Zen Leadership is widely applied in:

- **Corporate Leadership & Innovation** – Companies like **Google and Apple integrate mindfulness into leadership.**

- **Healthcare & Well-Being Organizations** – Mindful leadership **reduces stress in high-pressure industries.**

- **Education & Coaching** – Zen principles **enhance teaching, mentoring, and personal development.**

- **Entrepreneurship & Creative Fields** – Leaders **use Zen techniques for focus, clarity, and creative problem-solving.**

Key Insights

1. **Stillness Enhances Leadership – Great leadership comes from inner peace, not external control.**

2. **Clarity & Simplicity Drive Success – Removing distractions and focusing on the essential leads to better outcomes.**

3. **Presence & Awareness Create Stronger Leaders – Mindful leaders make better decisions and foster trust.**

4. **Ego-Free Leadership Builds Sustainable Success – True leaders serve, adapt, and grow without attachment to power.**

Zen Leadership proves that **leaders who cultivate mindfulness, self-awareness, and simplicity inspire teams, drive innovation, and lead with wisdom and compassion.**

83. Existential Leadership

Existential Leadership: A Breakdown

Theory

Existential Leadership is a leadership model rooted in **existential philosophy**, emphasizing **authenticity, personal responsibility, meaning-making, and individual freedom.** It is based on the idea that **leaders must confront uncertainty, make meaningful choices, and help others find purpose in their work and lives.**

Influenced by the works of **Jean-Paul Sartre, Viktor Frankl, Søren Kierkegaard, and Friedrich Nietzsche,** Existential Leadership acknowledges that **life and leadership are filled with ambiguity, and it is the leader's role to create meaning and inspire others to take ownership of their choices.** Unlike traditional leadership models that focus on **efficiency and authority, Existential Leadership is deeply personal, philosophical, and reflective.**

Key characteristics of **Existential Leadership**:

1. **Authenticity & Self-Awareness** – Leaders **embrace their true selves, acting with honesty and integrity.**

2. **Freedom & Responsibility** – Leaders **acknowledge that with freedom comes the responsibility to make ethical choices.**

3. **Meaning & Purpose-Driven Leadership** – Leadership **focuses on creating purpose for individuals and organizations**.

4. **Embracing Uncertainty** – Existential leaders **accept ambiguity and make decisions despite uncertainty**.

5. **Encouraging Personal Growth** – Leaders **inspire others to take responsibility for their actions and growth**.

Unlike **transactional leadership, which prioritizes structure and control, Existential Leadership is introspective, purpose-driven, and focused on the deeper aspects of human experience**.

Example

A powerful example of **Existential Leadership** is **Viktor Frankl**, a Holocaust survivor and author of *Man's Search for Meaning*. Frankl developed **Logotherapy**, a psychological approach that emphasizes **finding meaning in suffering**. His leadership philosophy teaches that **leaders must help others discover purpose, even in hardship**.

Another example is **Howard Schultz, the former CEO of Starbucks**, who built Starbucks not just as a coffee company but as a **brand cantered on community, experience, and purpose**. Schultz led with **authenticity, vision, and a deep belief in personal responsibility**, shaping Starbucks into a global leader while maintaining its cultural ethos.

Why It Works

Existential Leadership is effective because it:

- **Inspires Purpose & Meaning in Work** – Employees feel more engaged when their work has deeper significance.

- **Builds Resilient & Adaptive Leaders** – Leaders develop the ability to navigate uncertainty and difficult choices.

- **Encourages Personal Responsibility & Ownership** – Team members **take accountability for their actions and growth.**

- **Fosters Authentic Leadership & Trust** – Authenticity **builds credibility and stronger relationships.**

- **Promotes Ethical & Value-Based Decision-Making** – Leaders **act based on deeply held values, not external pressures.**

Studies show that **leaders who cultivate meaning, authenticity, and personal responsibility build stronger, more engaged, and purpose-driven teams.**

How It Works

Existential Leadership follows a **self-reflective, purpose-driven approach**:

1. **Cultivate Self-Awareness & Authenticity** – Leaders understand their beliefs, values, and personal mission.

2. **Create Meaning & Purpose for Others** – Organizations **align their vision with deeper human aspirations**.

3. **Encourage Responsibility & Freedom of Choice** – Employees **are empowered to take ownership of their work and actions**.

4. **Embrace Uncertainty & Complexity** – Leaders **navigate ambiguity with confidence and philosophical insight**.

5. **Lead with Ethical Integrity & Courage** – Decision-making **is guided by ethics, authenticity, and existential values**.

Unlike **directive leadership, which imposes authority**, **Existential Leadership empowers individuals to find their own path and take responsibility for it**.

Application

Existential Leadership is widely applied in:

- **Corporate & Business Leadership** – CEOs like **Howard Schultz and Satya Nadella emphasize purpose and personal growth**.

- **Education & Personal Development** – Teachers and coaches **help individuals discover their purpose and potential.**

- **Healthcare & Therapy** – Logotherapy and meaning-based leadership **support patient and employee well-being.**

- **Social Movements & Nonprofits** – Leaders **drive change by helping people connect with larger existential goals.**

Key Insights

1. **Leadership is About Helping Others Find Meaning** – **Organizations thrive when leaders inspire purpose beyond profits.**

2. **Authenticity Builds Stronger Leadership** – **Being true to oneself creates trust, credibility, and lasting impact.**

3. **Freedom Requires Responsibility** – **Leaders and employees must take ownership of their choices and actions.**

4. **Navigating Uncertainty is a Core Leadership Skill** – **Great leaders embrace complexity and make decisions with conviction.**

Existential Leadership proves that **leaders who embrace authenticity, purpose, and responsibility create resilient, engaged, and ethically driven organizations.**

84. Maverick Leadership

Maverick Leadership: A Breakdown

Theory

Maverick Leadership is a leadership model that focuses on **bold, unconventional, and independent thinking**. Maverick leaders **challenge the status quo, take calculated risks, and inspire change through their visionary and disruptive approaches**. Unlike traditional leadership models that emphasize hierarchy and stability, **Maverick Leadership thrives on innovation, autonomy, and breaking norms to drive progress**.

Rooted in **Transformational Leadership, Entrepreneurial Leadership, and Disruptive Innovation Theory**, this model suggests that **true leaders do not just follow trends—they create them**. Maverick leaders often have **strong convictions, a high tolerance for uncertainty, and a willingness to take unpopular stands**.

Key characteristics of **Maverick Leadership**:

1. **Unconventional Thinking** – Leaders **challenge norms and bring fresh perspectives**.

2. **High-Risk, High-Reward Mentality** – Decisions **are bold and calculated, with a willingness to disrupt industries**.

3. **Independence & Autonomy** – Mavericks **trust their instincts and lead with conviction, often rejecting bureaucracy.**

4. **Resilience & Adaptability** – Failure **is seen as a stepping stone, not an endpoint.**

5. **Inspiring & Charismatic Leadership** – Leaders **influence others through passion, vision, and confidence.**

Unlike **bureaucratic leadership, which follows established processes, Maverick Leadership is about challenging norms and creating new paths to success.**

Example

A classic example of **Maverick Leadership** is **Elon Musk.** His approach to **Tesla, SpaceX, and Neuralink** has been unconventional, pushing boundaries in electric vehicles, space travel, and AI. Musk has consistently **challenged industries, taken enormous risks, and introduced groundbreaking innovations that others doubted.** His ability to **inspire teams, defy traditional business models, and execute visionary ideas embodies Maverick Leadership.**

Another example is **Richard Branson, founder of Virgin Group**, who built his empire by **disrupting industries such as music, airlines, and telecommunications.** Branson's leadership style is **playful, rebellious, and customer-focused,** proving that **mavericks can succeed across** multiple industries by embracing bold ideas and taking calculated risks.

Why It Works

Maverick Leadership is effective because it:

- **Drives Breakthrough Innovation** – Disruptive thinking leads to industry-changing solutions.

- **Inspires Teams with Vision & Passion** – Employees rally behind leaders with bold, ambitious missions.

- **Encourages Risk-Taking & Resilience** – Failure is embraced as part of the journey to success.

- **Breaks Bureaucratic Constraints** – Organizations become more agile, adaptive, and competitive.

- **Creates New Market Opportunities** – Maverick leaders see possibilities where others see limitations.

Studies show that **companies led by bold, unconventional thinkers often outperform competitors in innovation and market influence**.

How It Works

Maverick Leadership follows a **bold, visionary, and risk-tolerant approach**:

1. **Challenge Industry Norms** – Leaders **constantly ask, "Why not?" and push for new ways of thinking.**

2. **Take Calculated Risks** – Mavericks **make bold moves but use data and intuition to guide them.**

3. **Empower & Inspire Teams** – Leadership **focuses on rallying people behind a compelling vision.**

4. **Stay Resilient in the Face of Failure** – Setbacks **are treated as learning opportunities, not roadblocks.**

5. **Remain Independent & Authentic** – Leaders **trust their instincts and maintain their unique leadership style.**

Unlike **compliance-driven leadership, which emphasizes following rules, Maverick Leadership thrives on breaking barriers and forging new paths.**

Application

Maverick Leadership is widely applied in:

- **Entrepreneurship & Startups** – Founders **disrupt traditional industries with bold ideas.**

- **Technology & Innovation Companies** – Leaders like **Elon Musk and Steve Jobs redefined entire industries.**

- **Corporate Turnarounds & Transformations** – Maverick CEOs **revitalize stagnant organizations with bold strategies.**

- **Entertainment & Creative Industries** – Filmmakers, musicians, and writers **challenge norms and shape cultural trends.**

Key Insights

1. **Disruptive Thinking Drives Progress** – Industries evolve when leaders challenge conventional wisdom.

2. **Risk-Taking is Essential for Breakthroughs** – Success often requires stepping outside comfort zones.

3. **Authenticity & Independence Strengthen Leadership** – Mavericks build loyal followings by staying true to their vision.

4. **Resilience & Adaptability Define Success** – Great leaders embrace failure as part of the innovation process.

Maverick Leadership proves that **leaders who defy convention, take risks, and inspire through bold vision create lasting impact and industry-defining change.**

85. Paradoxical Leadership

Paradoxical Leadership: A Breakdown

Theory

Paradoxical Leadership is a leadership model that focuses on **embracing and balancing opposing forces in leadership and decision-making**. It acknowledges that **leaders must manage contradictions—such as stability and change, control and empowerment, tradition and innovation— rather than choosing one over the other**.

Rooted in **Dialectical Thinking, Complexity Leadership, and Adaptive Leadership**, Paradoxical Leadership suggests that **effective leaders thrive in uncertainty by navigating competing demands simultaneously**. This approach is especially valuable in today's fast-changing, ambiguous, and complex work environments.

Key characteristics of **Paradoxical Leadership**:

1. **Balancing Stability & Change** – Leaders **preserve core values while driving innovation**.

2. **Embracing Control & Empowerment** – Leaders **set clear direction while allowing autonomy**.

3. **Managing Short-Term & Long-Term Goals** – Immediate performance **is balanced with sustainable success**.

4. **Being Both Decisive & Open-Minded** – Leaders **act with confidence but remain flexible to new insights**.

5. **Balancing Personal Humility & Strong Presence** –
   Leaders **stay humble while demonstrating
   confidence and vision**.

Unlike **traditional leadership, which often seeks linear
solutions, Paradoxical Leadership thrives in complexity,
allowing leaders to leverage contradictions for better
outcomes**.

Example

A strong example of **Paradoxical Leadership** is **Satya
Nadella, CEO of Microsoft**. He transformed Microsoft by
**balancing continuity with change—respecting the
company's legacy while shifting towards cloud
computing, AI, and open-source collaborations**. He also
**combined strong leadership with humility, encouraging a
culture of learning and adaptability**.

Another example is **Jeff Bezos, founder of Amazon**, who
managed the paradox of **customer obsession and
operational efficiency**. He maintained **long-term strategic
vision while driving short-term innovation and
experimentation, balancing risk-taking with strong
execution**.

Why It Works

Paradoxical Leadership is effective because it:

- **Enhances Adaptability & Resilience** – Leaders
  **navigate uncertainty without being trapped by
  rigid thinking**.

- **Encourages Both Stability & Innovation** – Organizations **evolve while maintaining foundational strengths.**

- **Increases Employee Engagement & Trust** – Teams **benefit from clear direction while feeling empowered.**

- **Improves Decision-Making Under Complexity** – Leaders **analyse multiple perspectives rather than seeking simplistic solutions.**

- **Fosters Sustainable Growth** – Balancing **short-term wins with long-term strategy ensures continuous success.**

Studies show that **leaders who can embrace contradictions and balance competing forces create more innovative, agile, and enduring organizations.**

How It Works

Paradoxical Leadership follows a **dual-minded, integrative approach:**

1. **Recognize & Accept Paradoxes** – Leaders **acknowledge rather than resist contradictions.**

2. **Think Both-And, Not Either-Or** – Decision-making **integrates opposing perspectives for better solutions.**

3. **Encourage Flexibility & Structure** – Teams **have autonomy within well-defined strategic boundaries**.

4. **Balance Confidence & Learning** – Leaders **act decisively while staying open to evolving insights**.

5. **Foster a Culture of Dialogue & Experimentation** – Organizations **continuously explore and refine their approach**.

Unlike **binary leadership models that force trade-offs, Paradoxical Leadership thrives on integrating opposites for dynamic, sustainable success.**

Application

Paradoxical Leadership is widely applied in:

- **Corporate & Tech Leadership** – Companies like **Microsoft, Amazon, and Google navigate disruption while maintaining stability**.

- **Government & Public Policy** – Leaders **balance economic growth with environmental sustainability**.

- **Healthcare & Education** – Institutions **combine traditional knowledge with modern advancements**.

- **Entrepreneurship & Innovation** – Startups **blend agility with long-term strategic thinking**.

Key Insights

1. **Embracing Contradictions Strengthens Leadership – Great leaders manage tensions instead of choosing sides.**

2. **"Both-And" Thinking Drives Innovation – Leaders succeed by integrating competing demands, not eliminating them.**

3. **Resilient Leaders Navigate Complexity Without Fear – Uncertainty is a leadership advantage, not a limitation.**

4. **Sustainable Success Requires Balance – Organizations thrive when they merge tradition with transformation.**

Paradoxical Leadership proves that **leaders who embrace contradictions, think flexibly, and integrate opposing forces can create stronger, more innovative, and future-ready organizations.**

86. Wisdom-Based Leadership

Wisdom-Based Leadership: A Breakdown

Theory

Wisdom-Based Leadership is a leadership model that emphasizes **deep insight, ethical decision-making, and long-term thinking**. It is rooted in the idea that **true leadership is not just about knowledge and expertise but about applying wisdom to navigate complexity, uncertainty, and human dynamics effectively**.

Drawing from **philosophy, ethical leadership, and reflective decision-making**, this model integrates **intellectual intelligence (IQ), emotional intelligence (EQ), and moral intelligence (MQ)** to guide leaders toward sound, ethical, and sustainable choices. Wisdom-Based Leadership prioritizes **understanding over reaction, long-term impact over short-term gains, and people over mere profit**.

Key characteristics of **Wisdom-Based Leadership**:

1. **Deep Reflection & Insight** – Leaders **think critically before making decisions, considering long-term implications**.

2. **Ethical & Values-Driven Decision-Making** – Choices are guided by integrity, morality, and fairness.

3. **Holistic Thinking** – Leaders **consider multiple perspectives, understanding the bigger picture**.

4. **Balance of Logic & Emotion** – Wisdom integrates **rational thinking with human compassion**.

5. **Adaptability & Open-Mindedness** – Leaders **continuously learn, evolve, and embrace new perspectives**.

Unlike **Transactional Leadership, which focuses on short-term efficiency**, **Wisdom-Based Leadership fosters deep, sustainable impact by combining knowledge, ethics, and emotional depth**.

Example

A strong example of **Wisdom-Based Leadership** is **Mahatma Gandhi**, who led India's independence movement through **principled, ethical, and non-violent leadership**. Gandhi understood the **complexity of social change, balancing pragmatism with moral vision**, proving that wisdom-driven leadership can create profound, lasting impact.

In the corporate world, **Warren Buffett** is an example. Buffett **emphasizes patience, ethical investing, and long-term value over short-term gains**. His leadership style demonstrates **prudence, ethical responsibility, and a deep**

understanding of economic and human behaviour, making him a model of wisdom-driven leadership.

Why It Works

Wisdom-Based Leadership is effective because it:

- **Encourages Ethical & Sustainable Decisions** – Leaders **prioritize integrity over short-term profits.**

- **Reduces Impulsive & Poor Judgment Calls** – Wisdom fosters **thoughtful, balanced decision-making.**

- **Strengthens Organizational Resilience** – Wise leadership **navigates uncertainty with clarity and stability.**

- **Builds Trust & Credibility** – Employees and stakeholders **respect leaders who act with wisdom and fairness.**

- **Fosters Long-Term Success** – Organizations led by wisdom-based leaders **avoid short-sighted pitfalls and build lasting legacies.**

Studies show that **leaders who practice wisdom-based decision-making create more ethical, stable, and high-performing organizations.**

How It Works

Wisdom-Based Leadership follows a **reflective, principle-driven approach:**

1. **Develop Self-Awareness & Deep Thinking –** Leaders **prioritize reflection before making key decisions.**

2. **Seek Multiple Perspectives –** Wise leaders **consult diverse viewpoints before acting.**

3. **Prioritize Ethical & Sustainable Choices –** Decisions **are made with long-term impact in mind.**

4. **Balance Rationality with Compassion –** Leaders **use both logic and empathy in leadership.**

5. **Continuously Learn & Adapt –** Wisdom **is a lifelong pursuit, requiring openness to growth.**

Unlike **autocratic leadership, which relies on authority, Wisdom-Based Leadership fosters respect through integrity, understanding, and careful decision-making.**

Application

Wisdom-Based Leadership is widely applied in:

- **Politics & Social Movements –** Leaders like **Gandhi, Mandela, and the Dalai Lama prioritize wisdom in decision-making.**

- **Corporate Leadership –** CEOs like **Warren Buffett and Satya Nadella lead with long-term vision and ethical responsibility.**

- **Education & Thought Leadership –** Professors and researchers **influence with wisdom rather than authority.**

- **Healthcare & Public Policy** – Wise leaders **balance science, ethics, and human well-being in decision-making.**

Key Insights

1. **Wisdom is the Highest Form of Leadership – Knowledge alone is not enough; wisdom guides the best decisions.**

2. **Ethics & Integrity Define Great Leaders – True leadership is about doing what's right, even when it's difficult.**

3. **Long-Term Thinking Creates Stronger Organizations – Wisdom ensures sustainable success over short-term gains.**

4. **The Best Leaders Listen & Reflect Before Acting – Patience, deep thinking, and emotional intelligence are key traits.**

Wisdom-Based Leadership proves that **leaders who prioritize ethical, thoughtful, and long-term decision-making create enduring success, trust, and positive change in organizations and society.**

87. Dialectical Leadership

Dialectical Leadership: A Breakdown

Theory

Dialectical Leadership is a leadership model based on **the ability to navigate and integrate opposing ideas, perspectives, and tensions to find balance and innovation**. It originates from **dialectical thinking, a concept in philosophy (Hegel) and psychology (Marxist dialectics and cognitive flexibility theory)**, which suggests that **progress and growth emerge from reconciling contradictions rather than choosing between extremes**.

This leadership model acknowledges that **complex environments require leaders to hold multiple, sometimes contradictory, truths at once**. Instead of viewing challenges as **"either-or" dilemmas, Dialectical Leadership finds "both-and" solutions**, fostering **adaptability, critical thinking, and continuous learning**.

Key characteristics of **Dialectical Leadership**:

1. **Embracing Contradictions – Leaders see tensions as opportunities for growth rather than conflicts to resolve.**

2. **Balancing Opposing Forces** – Leadership **integrates stability and change, control and autonomy, tradition and innovation.**

3. **Encouraging Open Dialogue & Multiple Perspectives** – Decision-making **incorporates diverse viewpoints for deeper insight.**

4. **Continuous Learning & Adaptation** – Leaders **reassess and refine their understanding as new information emerges.**

5. **Pragmatism Over Dogma** – Instead of rigid beliefs, leaders **adapt strategies to fit evolving realities.**

Unlike **authoritarian leadership, which enforces a single perspective, Dialectical Leadership thrives on ambiguity, complexity, and flexibility.**

Example

A powerful example of **Dialectical Leadership** is **Nelson Mandela.** Rather than choosing between **revenge or passivity** after apartheid, Mandela **balanced justice with reconciliation,** allowing South Africa to transition peacefully. His leadership embraced **both accountability and unity, fostering long-term national stability.**

In the corporate world, **Satya Nadella at Microsoft** demonstrated Dialectical Leadership by **preserving Microsoft's traditional strengths (enterprise software) while radically shifting its culture toward openness, cloud computing, and collaboration (embracing Linux and open-**

source software). Instead of viewing **legacy and innovation as incompatible, he integrated them for sustained success.**

Why It Works

Dialectical Leadership is effective because it:

- **Enhances Problem-Solving & Innovation** – Leaders synthesize opposing views into creative solutions.

- **Builds Organizational Resilience** – Companies adapt better to change by balancing short-term needs with long-term goals.

- **Encourages Inclusivity & Collaboration – Diverse perspectives strengthen team decision-making.**

- **Prepares Leaders for Uncertainty** – Leaders become comfortable navigating ambiguity and paradoxes.

- **Reduces Conflict & Strengthens Teams** – By integrating perspectives, leaders **build stronger alignment and trust.**

Studies show that **organizations led by dialectical thinkers are more innovative, resilient, and successful in complex environments.**

How It Works

Dialectical Leadership follows an **adaptive, integration-focused approach:**

1. **Identify & Acknowledge Opposing Forces** – Leaders **recognize contradictions instead of suppressing them**.

2. **Engage in Open Dialogue & Deep Listening** – Teams **explore different viewpoints without bias**.

3. **Find Integrative Solutions ("Both-And" Thinking)** – Instead of choosing one extreme, **leaders seek balanced approaches**.

4. **Experiment, Reflect, & Adapt** – Leadership **evolves continuously based on new insights**.

5. **Encourage Critical Thinking in Teams** – Organizations **foster cultures where complex, dialectical thinking is the norm**.

Unlike **linear leadership models that enforce binary choices**, **Dialectical Leadership allows for flexibility, nuanced decision-making, and continuous learning**.

Application

Dialectical Leadership is widely applied in:

- **Politics & Social Change** – Leaders like **Mandela and Obama balanced opposing social forces for long-term unity**.

- **Corporate Strategy & Innovation** – Companies like **Microsoft and Apple balance legacy products with disruptive technologies**.

- **Science & Technology** – AI ethics leaders **integrate progress with responsibility.**

- **Crisis Management & Policy Making** – Governments **balance economic growth with environmental sustainability.**

Key Insights

1. **Contradictions Can Be Productive** – Great leaders **find synthesis instead of avoiding complexity.**

2. **Balanced Thinking Leads to Sustainable Success** – **Rigid, one-sided strategies create long-term failure.**

3. **Wisdom Lies in Integration, Not Extremes** – **Leaders who combine structure with flexibility create lasting impact.**

4. **Adaptability is the Core of Leadership in Complexity** – **In a fast-changing world, the best leaders embrace paradoxes rather than resist them.**

Dialectical Leadership proves that **leaders who master the art of integrating contradictions, balancing competing needs, and thinking flexibly create stronger, more adaptive, and forward-thinking organizations.**

88. Spiritual Leadership

Spiritual Leadership: A Breakdown

Theory

Spiritual Leadership is a leadership model that integrates **values, purpose, and inner fulfilment into leadership practices**. It focuses on **inspiring and guiding teams by fostering a sense of meaning, connection, and personal growth**. Unlike traditional leadership models that prioritize efficiency and profit, **Spiritual Leadership emphasizes well-being, ethical decision-making, and service to others**.

Rooted in **Servant Leadership, Transformational Leadership, and Purpose-Driven Leadership**, this model suggests that **leaders should nurture both the professional and spiritual dimensions of employees, helping them align their work with their deeper purpose and values**.

Key characteristics of **Spiritual Leadership**:

1. **Purpose & Meaning** – Leaders **help employees find deeper significance in their work**.

2. **Compassion & Empathy** – Leadership is **grounded in kindness, understanding, and ethical responsibility**.

3. **Inner Peace & Mindfulness** – Leaders **cultivate self-awareness and balance, leading with calmness and wisdom.**

4. **Service to Others** – Leadership is about **serving employees, communities, and society rather than personal power.**

5. **Alignment of Values & Actions** – Decisions **reflect ethical principles and long-term well-being, not just short-term gains.**

Unlike **authoritarian leadership, which focuses on power and control, Spiritual Leadership creates a culture of trust, well-being, and collective success.**

Example

A great example of **Spiritual Leadership** is **Dalai Lama, a global spiritual leader who promotes compassion, peace, and ethical leadership.** His teachings on **kindness, mindfulness, and service-based leadership have inspired millions, including business and political leaders.**

In the corporate world, **Howard Schultz, former CEO of Starbucks,** applied **Spiritual Leadership by embedding ethical sourcing, employee well-being, and community service into Starbucks' mission.** He prioritized **people over profit, ensuring fair wages, healthcare benefits, and educational programs for employees, which strengthened Starbucks' culture and brand loyalty.**

Why It Works

Spiritual Leadership is effective because it:

- **Inspires Employee Engagement & Commitment** – Employees **feel connected to a larger purpose**.

- **Enhances Workplace Well-Being** – A culture of **compassion reduces stress and burnout**.

- **Builds Trust & Ethical Leadership** – Organizations **prioritize integrity, fairness, and responsibility**.

- **Encourages Long-Term Success** – Companies **balance profit with people and planet, ensuring sustainability**.

- **Strengthens Team Collaboration & Unity** – Shared values **create a cohesive, motivated workforce**.

Studies show that **workplaces that integrate purpose and well-being see increased productivity, employee satisfaction, and long-term financial success**.

How It Works

Spiritual Leadership follows a **values-driven, holistic approach**:

1. **Define & Communicate a Clear Purpose** – Leaders **help employees see the deeper impact of their work**.

2. **Lead with Compassion & Integrity** – Decisions **are made ethically, considering long-term consequences**.

3. **Cultivate Mindfulness & Self-Reflection** – Leaders **develop inner balance, setting an example for their teams**.

4. **Foster a Culture of Service & Growth** – Organizations **support employee well-being and professional development**.

5. **Measure Success Beyond Profits** – Companies **track impact on people, communities, and ethical standards**.

Unlike **profit-first leadership models, Spiritual Leadership balances financial performance with purpose, well-being, and ethical impact**.

Application

Spiritual Leadership is widely applied in:

- **Corporate & Ethical Businesses** – Companies like **Starbucks, Patagonia, and Google integrate purpose-driven leadership**.

- **Nonprofits & Social Enterprises** – Leaders **focus on service, ethics, and social change**.

- **Education & Healthcare** – Schools and hospitals **prioritize emotional intelligence, care, and personal growth**.

- **Government & Policy-Making** – Leaders **use ethical decision-making to benefit communities and long-term societal well-being**.

Key Insights

1. **Leadership is About Service, Not Power – The best leaders inspire and uplift others.**

2. **Work Must Have Meaning Beyond Profit – Employees and organizations thrive when driven by purpose.**

3. **Compassion & Ethics Build Trust – Integrity leads to stronger relationships and lasting impact.**

4. **Success is Holistic—Personal, Professional & Ethical – True leadership balances financial, emotional, and social well-being.**

Spiritual Leadership proves that **leaders who integrate purpose, ethics, and well-being into their organizations create sustainable success, motivated teams, and a positive global impact.**

89. Historical Leadership Lessons

Historical Leadership Lessons: A Breakdown

Theory

Historical Leadership Lessons is a leadership model that derives insights from **past leaders, events, and civilizations to inform modern leadership practices.** This model suggests that **by analysing historical successes and failures, contemporary leaders can develop strategies for resilience, decision-making, and ethical leadership.**

Rooted in **Lessons from History, Strategic Leadership, and Transformational Leadership**, this approach emphasizes that **history provides timeless wisdom about power, strategy, ethics, and human nature.** Effective leaders **study history to avoid past mistakes, replicate successful strategies, and adapt enduring principles to modern challenges.**

Key characteristics of **Historical Leadership Lessons:**

1. **Learning from Past Leaders & Events** – Examining **both great successes and catastrophic failures.**

2. **Applying Timeless Leadership Principles** – Using **proven leadership traits such as vision, resilience, and adaptability.**

3. **Understanding Power & Strategy** – Studying **historical conflicts, negotiations, and governance for modern leadership insights.**

4. **Avoiding Repeated Mistakes** – Identifying **patterns of failure, ethical dilemmas, and poor decision-making**.

5. **Adapting Historical Wisdom to Contemporary Challenges** – Translating **historical lessons into practical modern leadership strategies**.

Unlike **trend-driven leadership models that focus solely on present-day strategies, Historical Leadership Lessons emphasize the continuity of human leadership challenges and solutions across centuries**.

Example

A powerful example of **Historical Leadership Lessons** is **Abraham Lincoln**, whose leadership during the American Civil War demonstrated **resilience, moral clarity, and strategic decision-making**. Lincoln's ability to **navigate national division, inspire a shared vision, and balance diplomacy with decisive action remains a leadership benchmark**.

In business, **Winston Churchill's wartime leadership has been studied by CEOs and military strategists alike**. His **ability to rally a nation, communicate with conviction, and persist through adversity** has inspired corporate and political leaders facing crises.

Why It Works

Historical Leadership Lessons are effective because they:

- **Provide Tested Leadership Principles** – Leaders learn from real-world historical successes and failures.

- **Enhance Strategic Thinking** – History **teaches leaders about power, conflict, and long-term impact**.

- **Promote Resilience & Adaptability** – Studying past crises **helps leaders develop crisis management skills**.

- **Encourage Ethical & Visionary Leadership** – Lessons from history **reinforce the importance of integrity and long-term thinking**.

- **Reduce Costly Mistakes** – By **analysing past failures, leaders can avoid repeating historical errors**.

Studies show that **leaders who understand history are better equipped to navigate complex challenges and make informed decisions**.

How It Works

Historical Leadership Lessons follow a **study-adapt-apply approach**:

1. **Study Historical Leaders & Events** – Analyse leaders like Lincoln, Churchill, Mandela, and global civilizations.

2. **Extract Core Leadership Lessons** – Identify universal principles such as perseverance, strategy, and ethical leadership.

3. **Apply Insights to Modern Leadership** – Use historical examples to inform business, political, and organizational decisions.

4. **Learn from Past Mistakes** – Recognize **failures in leadership (e.g., poor crisis management, ethical lapses) to avoid repeating them.**

5. **Adapt Historical Wisdom to Contemporary Issues** – Integrate **historical strategies into modern leadership challenges.**

Unlike **static leadership models that rely on rigid frameworks, Historical Leadership Lessons evolve with changing contexts, providing adaptable wisdom for modern leaders.**

Application

Historical Leadership Lessons are widely applied in:

- **Political Leadership & Governance** – Leaders **study past rulers and revolutions to shape modern policies.**

- **Corporate & Business Strategy** – CEOs **use historical case studies for decision-making and crisis management.**

- **Military & Strategic Planning** – Armed forces **apply military history to modern defence strategies.**

- **Crisis Leadership & Resilience Building** – Organizations **learn from historical crises to prepare for uncertainty.**

Key Insights

1. **History Repeats Itself—Wise Leaders Learn from It** – Avoiding past mistakes leads to better leadership decisions.

2. **Resilient Leaders Adapt, Not Just React** – Historical leaders thrived by adjusting to change, not resisting it.

3. **Ethical Leadership Stands the Test of Time** – Leaders who prioritize integrity leave lasting positive legacies.

4. **Visionary Leaders Think Long-Term** – Great historical leaders didn't just react to the present—they shaped the future.

Historical Leadership Lessons prove that **leaders who study and apply wisdom from history develop better strategic thinking, avoid costly mistakes, and create lasting impact in their organizations and societies.**

90. Transcendent Leadership

Transcendent Leadership: A Breakdown

Theory

Transcendent Leadership is a leadership model that **goes beyond conventional leadership by integrating personal growth, ethical responsibility, and a higher purpose into leadership practices**. It is rooted in the idea that **leaders should not only focus on organizational success but also elevate the people, culture, and values of the communities they serve**.

This model draws from **Servant Leadership, Transformational Leadership, and Spiritual Leadership**, emphasizing **self-awareness, moral integrity, and a vision that extends beyond individual or organizational gain**. Transcendent leaders **operate on a higher plane of leadership, balancing personal fulfilment, societal impact, and business excellence**.

Key characteristics of **Transcendent Leadership**:

1. **Higher Purpose & Vision** – Leaders **align their mission with a purpose greater than themselves**.

2. **Holistic & Ethical Decision-Making** – Choices **consider not only business success but also social and moral impact**.

3. **Self-Actualization & Personal Growth** – Leaders continually evolve, seek wisdom, and develop emotional intelligence.

4. **Empowerment & Collective Success** – Leadership prioritizes developing others, ensuring collective well-being.

5. **Long-Term Impact Over Short-Term Gains** – Decisions **focus on sustainability, legacy, and transformational change.**

Unlike **transactional leadership, which is focused on immediate results, Transcendent Leadership prioritizes the holistic growth of individuals, organizations, and societies.**

Example

A strong example of **Transcendent Leadership** is **Mahatma Gandhi,** who led India's independence movement **not just with political strategy but through a moral and spiritual vision of nonviolence and justice.** His leadership was not about personal gain but about **uplifting an entire nation and creating a long-lasting legacy of peace and ethical resistance.**

In the business world, **Paul Polman, former CEO of Unilever,** exemplified Transcendent Leadership by **shifting Unilever's strategy towards long-term sustainability, ethical sourcing, and social responsibility while still maintaining strong financial performance.** His leadership transformed Unilever into a purpose-driven company with a lasting positive impact on society.

Why It Works

Transcendent Leadership is effective because it:

- **Inspires Deep Commitment & Loyalty** – Employees and followers **connect to a purpose greater than profit**.

- **Encourages Ethical & Sustainable Leadership** – Leaders **prioritize fairness, responsibility, and long-term impact**.

- **Fosters Innovation & Organizational Growth** – A higher vision **creates a culture of inspiration and creativity**.

- **Builds a Legacy Beyond Business Success** – **Transcendent leaders leave a lasting mark on people and society**.

- **Enhances Personal & Professional Fulfilment** – Leaders **experience deeper meaning in their work and relationships**.

Studies show that **leaders who operate with a higher purpose create stronger, more sustainable, and highly engaged organizations**.

How It Works

Transcendent Leadership follows a **values-driven, purpose-oriented approach**:

1. **Develop a Higher Purpose & Vision** – Leaders identify a mission that benefits society, not just their organization.

2. **Practice Ethical & Mindful Leadership** – Decisions align with principles of fairness, sustainability, and human dignity.

3. **Empower & Inspire Others** – Leaders **focus on lifting others up, fostering collective success.**

4. **Lead with Self-Awareness & Personal Growth** – Leaders **continuously refine their values, character, and wisdom.**

5. **Think Beyond Profit—Focus on Impact** – Success is measured **not just by financial results, but by social and ethical contributions.**

Unlike **ego-driven leadership models, which prioritize authority and self-interest**, Transcendent Leadership **creates lasting transformation by balancing personal integrity with societal progress.**

Application

Transcendent Leadership is widely applied in:

- **Social Movements & Political Leadership** – Figures like **Gandhi, Nelson Mandela, and Martin Luther King Jr. led with moral conviction.**

- **Corporate & Ethical Business Models** – Leaders like Paul Polman (Unilever) and Yvon Chouinard (Patagonia) prioritized sustainable leadership.

- **Nonprofits & Global Change Organizations** – Leaders in **human rights, climate action, and education drive meaningful change.**

- **Personal Development & Coaching** – Transcendent leaders **help others achieve purpose-driven success.**

Key Insights

1. **Leadership Must Serve a Higher Purpose – True leadership transcends personal ambition and seeks greater good.**

2. **Ethics & Integrity Define Long-Term Success – Sustainable impact comes from morally guided leadership.**

3. **Self-Awareness & Growth are Essential – The best leaders continuously evolve, reflect, and learn.**

4. **Legacy Matters More Than Immediate Wins – Transcendent leaders create movements, not just profits.**

Transcendent Leadership proves that **leaders who embrace purpose, ethical responsibility, and collective success leave a meaningful and lasting impact on the world.**

Experimental & Unconventional Leadership Models

91. Improv Leadership

Improv Leadership: A Breakdown

Theory

Improv Leadership is a leadership model inspired by the principles of **improvisational theatre (improv)**, where leaders **adapt, collaborate, and navigate uncertainty with agility and creativity.** This model is built on the belief that **effective leadership requires flexibility, quick thinking, and the ability to build upon ideas in real-time rather than relying solely on rigid structures and pre-planned strategies.**

Rooted in **Agile Leadership, Adaptive Leadership, and Creative Problem-Solving**, Improv Leadership emphasizes **spontaneity, active listening, and team synergy.** Instead of dictating rigid plans, improv leaders **embrace uncertainty, encourage experimentation, and foster environments where innovation thrives.**

Key characteristics of **Improv Leadership**:

1. **"Yes, And" Mentality** – Leaders **build on ideas rather than shutting them down, fostering collaboration and momentum.**

2. **Adaptability & Agility** – Leaders **thrive in uncertainty, quickly adjusting to changing circumstances**.

3. **Active Listening & Presence** – Leadership **prioritizes being fully engaged in conversations and open to new insights**.

4. **Encouraging Experimentation & Risk-Taking** – Leaders **create a safe space for failure and continuous learning**.

5. **Building Trust & Psychological Safety** – Teams **feel comfortable contributing ideas without fear of judgment**.

Unlike **hierarchical leadership, which focuses on strict planning and authority**, **Improv Leadership thrives in uncertainty, enabling leaders to react, adapt, and create solutions on the spot**.

Example

A strong example of **Improv Leadership** is **Elon Musk**, whose leadership at **Tesla and SpaceX** has been defined by **quick pivots, rapid experimentation, and an openness to evolving ideas**. His ability to **embrace failure, iterate, and rapidly adapt strategies embodies the principles of improv leadership in high-stakes innovation**.

Another example is **Tina Fey**, a leader in the entertainment industry who applied improv skills from her days at *Saturday Night Live* to build successful creative teams and lead productions with flexibility, humour, and quick decision-making.

Why It Works

Improv Leadership is effective because it:

- **Enhances Agility & Resilience** – Leaders **can navigate unexpected challenges with confidence.**

- **Fosters Team Collaboration & Innovation** – Teams **feel more engaged, creative, and motivated.**

- **Encourages Quick, Smart Decision-Making** – Leaders **develop the ability to assess and respond instantly.**

- **Builds a Culture of Trust & Experimentation** – Employees **feel empowered to take risks and contribute ideas.**

- **Increases Emotional Intelligence & Presence** – Leaders **improve their ability to connect, listen, and respond in real time.**

Studies show that **organizations that encourage improvisation and adaptability are more innovative and better equipped to handle rapid market changes.**

How It Works

Improv Leadership follows a **dynamic, interaction-driven approach:**

1. **Embrace the "Yes, And" Philosophy** – Leaders **build on ideas rather than shutting them down, fostering momentum.**

2. **Stay Present & Listen Actively** – Leaders **focus fully on conversations and feedback to adapt effectively.**

3. **Encourage Risk-Taking & Experimentation** – Teams **are empowered to test ideas and embrace failure as learning.**

4. **Develop Quick Thinking & Decision-Making Skills** – Leaders **train themselves to react decisively and creatively.**

5. **Foster a Culture of Play & Psychological Safety** – A supportive work environment **allows creativity to flourish.**

Unlike **rigid leadership structures that depend on pre-set strategies, Improv Leadership enables leaders to make real-time decisions and create adaptive solutions in unpredictable situations.**

Application

Improv Leadership is widely applied in:

- **Startups & Entrepreneurial Ventures** – Founders **pivot rapidly based on market feedback.**

- **Corporate Innovation Teams** – Companies like Google and IDEO encourage spontaneous idea generation.

- **Crisis Management & Emergency Response** – Leaders **must make fast, decisive, and adaptive choices.**

- **Creative & Media Industries** – Writers, directors, and producers **use improv principles for storytelling and team collaboration.**

Key Insights

1. **Flexibility & Adaptability Define Great Leaders** – **Rigid thinking limits growth, but improv leaders embrace change.**

2. **The Best Ideas Emerge from Collaboration** – **"Yes, And" builds innovation, while rejection shuts it down.**

3. **Quick Thinking & Presence Strengthen Leadership** – **Effective leaders react in the moment, making confident, creative choices.**

4. **Failure is an Essential Part of Growth** – **Improv Leadership creates safe environments where risks lead to breakthroughs.**

Improv Leadership proves that **leaders who embrace spontaneity, collaboration, and adaptability can drive innovation, inspire teams, and navigate uncertainty with confidence and creativity.**

92. Gamification Leadership

Gamification Leadership: A Breakdown

Theory

Gamification Leadership is a leadership model that **applies game mechanics and principles to motivate, engage, and develop employees**. This approach leverages **competition, rewards, challenges, and real-time feedback to drive performance and innovation**.

Rooted in **Behavioural Psychology, Motivation Theory (Self-Determination Theory), and Digital Leadership**, Gamification Leadership suggests that **leaders can create a more engaging and high-performing work environment by integrating elements of play, incentives, and achievement into organizational culture**.

Key characteristics of **Gamification Leadership**:

1. **Clear Goals & Progress Tracking** – Employees **understand their objectives and receive feedback on performance.**

2. **Rewards & Incentives** – Systems **recognize achievements, from badges and leaderboards to tangible benefits.**

3. **Healthy Competition & Collaboration** – Teams engage in challenges that foster both competitive spirit and teamwork.

4. **Instant Feedback & Continuous Improvement** – Leaders **provide real-time insights to drive motivation and learning.**

5. **Personalization & Engagement** – Work **becomes more interactive and tailored to employee strengths.**

Unlike **traditional leadership, which relies on hierarchy and routine processes, Gamification Leadership transforms work into a dynamic, engaging, and rewarding experience.**

Example

A strong example of **Gamification Leadership** is **Google**, which uses **game mechanics in its workplace culture to encourage innovation and productivity.** Google employees participate in **hackathons, internal competitions, and performance-based incentives that foster engagement and creativity.**

Another example is **Salesforce's Trailhead**, a gamified learning platform that **rewards employees with badges, points, and rankings based on their training progress**, making professional development **more engaging and motivating.**

Why It Works

Gamification Leadership is effective because it:

- **Boosts Employee Motivation & Engagement** – Employees **respond positively to rewards, challenges, and recognition**.

- **Increases Productivity & Performance** – Game mechanics **drive goal achievement and continuous improvement**.

- **Enhances Learning & Skill Development** – Interactive challenges **improve knowledge retention and growth**.

- **Encourages Collaboration & Teamwork** – Gamified systems **promote healthy competition and peer support**.

- **Improves Retention & Workplace Satisfaction** – Employees **feel a sense of achievement and purpose**.

Studies show that **organizations using gamification see higher employee engagement, lower turnover rates, and increased innovation**.

How It Works

Gamification Leadership follows a **motivation-driven, interactive approach**:

1. **Set Clear Objectives & Reward Progress** – Employees **see their goals and track their performance**.

2. **Incorporate Game Mechanics (Points, Badges, Leaderboards)** – Systems **offer incentives for achievements.**

3. **Use Real-Time Feedback & Challenges** – Employees **receive instant recognition and new opportunities to grow.**

4. **Encourage Competition & Collaboration** – Teams **engage in friendly challenges that foster teamwork.**

5. **Personalize the Experience** – Leadership **aligns gamification strategies with individual strengths and goals.**

Unlike **traditional leadership models focused on rigid evaluation, Gamification Leadership makes performance tracking interactive and rewarding.**

Application

Gamification Leadership is widely applied in:

- **Sales & Performance-Based Roles** – Companies like **SAP and Salesforce use gamified sales targets.**

- **Corporate Learning & Development** – Organizations **gamify training programs to boost learning engagement.**

- **Innovation & Problem-Solving Initiatives** – Hackathons **and idea competitions drive creativity.**

- **Customer Loyalty & Engagement Programs** – Brands **gamify customer interactions for higher retention.**

Key Insights

1. **Motivation is Driven by Rewards & Challenges** – Employees perform better when their efforts are recognized.

2. **Engagement Increases with Interactive Work Environments** – People respond positively to progress tracking and competition.

3. **Learning & Growth Are More Effective When Gamified** – Gamification makes professional development fun and rewarding.

4. **Gamified Leadership Boosts Productivity & Innovation** – Teams become more engaged, creative, and motivated to excel.

Gamification Leadership proves that **leaders who integrate game mechanics into the workplace create higher engagement, productivity, and motivation, making work more rewarding and effective.**

93. Reverse Leadership

Reverse Leadership: A Breakdown

Theory

Reverse Leadership is a leadership model that **challenges traditional top-down leadership structures by empowering employees at all levels to lead and influence organizational decisions.** It emphasizes **learning from subordinates, fostering bottom-up innovation, and distributing leadership responsibilities across the organization.**

Rooted in **Servant Leadership, Participative Leadership, and Agile Leadership**, Reverse Leadership suggests that **leaders should actively seek input from frontline employees, creating an environment where knowledge, decision-making, and influence flow in both directions rather than just from the top down.** This approach recognizes that **employees often have insights that executives lack, especially in customer-facing roles or specialized functions.**

Key characteristics of **Reverse Leadership**:

1. **Bottom-Up Influence** – Employees **are empowered to shape company strategy and operations.**

2. **Learning from Subordinates** – Leaders **seek knowledge from those closest to customers and processes.**

3. **Decentralized Decision-Making** – Authority **is distributed to those with the most relevant expertise.**

4. **Innovation & Agility** – Organizations **become more adaptable by incorporating diverse insights.**

5. **High Trust & Employee Engagement** – Employees **feel valued, increasing motivation and retention.**

Unlike **traditional leadership, which follows a command-and-control model**, Reverse Leadership fosters a dynamic, learning-focused culture where leadership is shared and constantly evolving.

Example

A strong example of **Reverse Leadership** is **Pixar Animation Studios**, where executives and directors **actively solicit feedback from animators, designers, and junior staff, treating everyone as a valuable creative contributor.** This approach has led to **continuous innovation and groundbreaking films.**

Another example is **Jack Welch's leadership at General Electric (GE)**, where he encouraged **"reverse mentoring"**, having senior executives learn about emerging technology and modern workplace trends from younger employees. This initiative helped GE **stay competitive in an evolving digital landscape.**

Why It Works

Reverse Leadership is effective because it:

- **Unlocks Innovation & Problem-Solving** – Employees **on the ground often have the best insights into inefficiencies and opportunities.**

- **Encourages Knowledge Sharing & Collaboration** – Leaders and employees **learn from each other, leading to smarter decisions.**

- **Empowers & Engages Employees** – Employees **feel heard, which boosts motivation and commitment.**

- **Improves Organizational Agility** – Companies **respond faster to change by decentralizing authority.**

- **Builds a Stronger Leadership Pipeline** – Employees **develop leadership skills early, strengthening succession planning.**

Studies show that **organizations that embrace bottom-up leadership models see higher employee satisfaction, innovation, and adaptability.**

How It Works

Reverse Leadership follows a **collaborative, empowerment-driven approach:**

1. **Encourage Employees to Take Ownership** – Leaders **create opportunities for employees to lead projects and initiatives.**

465

2. **Implement Reverse Mentoring Programs** – Senior leaders **learn from younger employees, gaining fresh insights**.

3. **Foster Open Communication & Feedback** – Organizations **break down hierarchies and encourage open dialogue**.

4. **Decentralize Decision-Making** – Leaders **trust employees to make strategic contributions**.

5. **Recognize & Reward Bottom-Up Leadership** – Employees **are acknowledged for their leadership and innovation**.

Unlike **top-down leadership, which limits influence to executives, Reverse Leadership distributes leadership opportunities across all levels, making organizations more inclusive and responsive**.

Application

Reverse Leadership is widely applied in:

- **Technology & Creative Industries** – Companies like Google and Pixar **empower employees to lead innovation**.

- **Corporate Learning & Development** – Firms **use reverse mentoring to bridge generational knowledge gaps**.

- **Agile & Startup Environments** – Startups **thrive on flat hierarchies and employee-driven decision-making.**

- **Customer-Focused Organizations** – Retail and service industries **benefit from insights gathered directly from frontline employees.**

Key Insights

1. **Leadership is Not Limited to Executives** – **Reverse Leadership empowers employees at all levels to contribute.**

2. **Learning Happens in Both Directions** – **Senior leaders gain insights from junior employees, and vice versa.**

3. **Decentralized Decision-Making Increases Innovation** – **Giving employees a voice leads to smarter and faster solutions.**

4. **Engaged Employees Drive Stronger Organizations** – **People work harder and stay longer when they feel valued.**

Reverse Leadership proves that **organizations thrive when they break traditional hierarchies, empower employees, and create a culture of shared leadership and learning.**

94. Tribal Leadership

Tribal Leadership: A Breakdown

Theory

Tribal Leadership is a leadership model that **focuses on the cultural development of an organization by understanding and influencing its "tribes"—the naturally occurring social groups within a workplace**. It suggests that **leadership success is directly tied to the ability to guide a tribe through different cultural stages toward higher performance, collaboration, and innovation**.

Developed by **Dave Logan, John King, and Halee Fischer-Wright**, Tribal Leadership categorizes workplace cultures into **five stages**, each with a distinct mindset and level of effectiveness:

1. **Stage 1 ("Life Sucks")** – A culture of **despair, hostility, and disengagement**.

2. **Stage 2 ("My Life Sucks")** – A culture where **employees feel stuck, undervalued, and unmotivated**.

3. **Stage 3 ("I'm Great")** – A culture of **personal success and competition, but lacks team collaboration**.

4. **Stage 4 ("We're Great")** – A culture of **team-driven success, collaboration, and shared values**.

5. **Stage 5 ("Life is Great")** – A culture of **purpose-driven leadership, innovation, and industry-wide impact**.

The **goal of Tribal Leadership** is to **help organizations move from lower stages (individual-focused and competitive) to higher stages (team-oriented, purpose-driven, and innovative)**.

Example

A strong example of Tribal Leadership is **Zappos**, under the leadership of Tony Hsieh. Zappos built a strong organizational culture that emphasized **values-driven collaboration, customer happiness, and a sense of shared purpose**, elevating the company to **Stage 4 and Stage 5 leadership**. Employees were **empowered to innovate and contribute beyond their roles**, fostering loyalty and business success.

Another example is **Apple under Steve Jobs**, which evolved from **a Stage 3 "I'm Great" individualist culture** to a **Stage 4 team-driven innovation powerhouse**, where shared vision and collaboration drove groundbreaking products.

Why It Works

Tribal Leadership is effective because it:

- **Identifies Workplace Culture & Transforms It** – Leaders **assess and strategically elevate their organization's cultural stage**.

- **Encourages Collaboration & Team Excellence –** Moving from **"I'm Great"** to **"We're Great"** unlocks greater productivity and innovation.

- **Strengthens Employee Engagement & Purpose –** Employees **feel valued when they contribute to a collective vision.**

- **Promotes Long-Term Growth & Innovation –** Stage 5 organizations **influence entire industries, creating lasting impact.**

- **Reduces Workplace Politics & Toxicity –** Healthy, **tribe-oriented cultures minimize conflict and increase alignment.**

Studies show that **companies with strong tribal cultures have higher employee retention, engagement, and overall success.**

How It Works

Tribal Leadership follows a **culture-driven, team-oriented approach:**

1. **Assess the Organization's Cultural Stage –** Leaders **determine where their teams fall within the five stages.**

2. **Encourage Growth to the Next Stage –** Organizations **progress from self-interest (Stage 3) to team-driven purpose (Stage 4 & 5).**

3. **Foster Collaboration & Shared Values** – Leadership shifts focus from individual success to collective achievements.

4. **Empower Employees with a Mission** – Teams **align with a higher purpose that extends beyond financial goals.**

5. **Sustain a High-Performing Culture** – Continuous **reinforcement of shared values and collaboration maintains Stage 4 and 5 success.**

Unlike **traditional leadership, which focuses on hierarchy and control, Tribal Leadership builds leadership from within the culture itself, ensuring sustainable and authentic growth.**

Application

Tribal Leadership is widely applied in:

- **Corporate & Tech Companies** – Organizations like **Google and Apple focus on collaborative, values-driven cultures.**

- **Startups & Entrepreneurship** – Founders **build team-oriented missions to drive innovation and engagement.**

- **Nonprofits & Social Enterprises** – Mission-driven organizations **leverage shared values to maximize impact.**

- **Healthcare & Education** – Leaders **use Tribal Leadership to improve teamwork and morale in high-pressure environments**.

Key Insights

1. **Culture Defines Leadership Success – Leadership isn't just about strategy; it's about shaping a thriving team culture**.

2. **The Most Successful Teams Operate in "We're Great" Mode – Collaboration outperforms individualism in high-functioning organizations**.

3. **Workplaces Evolve Through Cultural Stages – A leader's job is to guide their tribe toward shared success and purpose**.

4. **Values-Driven Leadership Creates Industry Impact – Organizations that reach Stage 5 don't just succeed—they inspire others**.

Tribal Leadership proves that **leaders who understand and elevate workplace culture create engaged, high-performing teams that drive lasting innovation and success**.

95. Hacker Leadership

Hacker Leadership: A Breakdown

Theory

Hacker Leadership is a leadership model that **embraces creativity, problem-solving, and disruption to challenge conventional systems and drive innovation**. It draws inspiration from **hacker culture**, which values **curiosity, experimentation, agility, and the ability to find unconventional solutions to complex problems**.

Rooted in **Agile Leadership, Disruptive Innovation, and Lean Startup Methodology**, Hacker Leadership is about **breaking down inefficient processes, thinking outside the box, and leveraging technology and data to optimize performance**. Hacker leaders are **not bound by hierarchy or bureaucracy but instead focus on adaptability, rapid learning, and continuous improvement**.

Key characteristics of **Hacker Leadership**:

1. **Rapid Experimentation & Iteration** – Leaders **test, tweak, and refine solutions quickly rather than waiting for perfection**.

2. **Challenging the Status Quo** – Leaders **question assumptions, break down traditional structures, and embrace disruption**.

3. **Resourcefulness & Problem-Solving** – Innovation comes from **creative approaches rather than excessive resources**.

4. **Decentralization & Collaboration** – Power **is distributed, and teams operate in flat, agile structures**.

5. **Technology-Driven Decision-Making** – Leaders **leverage data, automation, and AI to optimize efficiency**.

Unlike **traditional leadership models that focus on control and structure, Hacker Leadership thrives on adaptability, open-source collaboration, and continuous learning.**

Example

A strong example of **Hacker Leadership** is **Elon Musk**, who has applied hacker principles to **Tesla, SpaceX, and Neuralink** by **disrupting industries through rapid iteration, open innovation, and bold problem-solving**. Musk's ability to **challenge outdated industry practices and apply first-principles thinking** showcases Hacker Leadership in action.

Another example is **Mark Zuckerberg's early approach to Facebook**, where he and his team used the motto **"Move fast and break things"** to encourage rapid experimentation and aggressive innovation. This philosophy allowed Facebook to **evolve quickly and dominate the social media space**.

Why It Works

Hacker Leadership is effective because it:

- **Accelerates Innovation & Problem-Solving** – Rapid prototyping and continuous testing drive faster breakthroughs.

- **Encourages Agility & Adaptability** – Leaders quickly pivot when faced with new challenges or opportunities.

- **Optimizes Efficiency & Performance** – Technology and automation **enhance productivity and streamline processes.**

- **Reduces Bureaucracy & Encourages Autonomy** – **Flat leadership structures empower employees to take initiative.**

- **Builds a Culture of Experimentation & Learning** – Teams **embrace failure as part of the innovation process.**

Studies show that **companies that prioritize agile, hacker-style leadership outperform competitors in innovation, efficiency, and market adaptation.**

How It Works

Hacker Leadership follows a **fast, iterative, and problem-solving approach:**

1. **Question Everything & Redefine Problems** – Leaders **apply first-principles thinking to identify the root of challenges.**

2. **Prototype & Test Rapidly** – Instead of waiting for perfect solutions, **leaders implement quick iterations and refine them.**

3. **Leverage Data & Technology** – Decision-making **is based on analytics, automation, and technological advancements.**

4. **Empower Teams with Decentralized Decision-Making** – Organizations **allow employees to experiment and innovate.**

5. **Embrace Failure as a Learning Tool** – Mistakes **are seen as necessary steps toward breakthrough solutions.**

Unlike **hierarchical leadership models that resist change, Hacker Leadership embraces disruption, continuous learning, and iterative progress.**

Application

Hacker Leadership is widely applied in:

- **Tech Startups & Innovation Labs** – Companies like **Google, Tesla, and SpaceX drive disruption through hacker culture.**

- **Product Development & Agile Teams** – Teams **use rapid iteration to optimize products and services.**

- **Cybersecurity & Ethical Hacking** – Hackers **apply creative problem-solving to protect digital systems.**

- **Entrepreneurship & Business Transformation –** Leaders **disrupt traditional industries through bold innovation.**

Key Insights

1. **Innovation Comes from Breaking Rules – Hacker leaders challenge existing systems to create better solutions.**

2. **Speed & Agility Outperform Perfection – Iterating quickly leads to faster, more effective innovation.**

3. **Technology & Data Drive Smarter Decisions – Hacker leaders rely on analytics and automation to optimize processes.**

4. **Empower Teams to Experiment & Fail Fast – A culture of trial-and-error fosters breakthrough innovations.**

Hacker Leadership proves that **leaders who embrace disruption, agility, and rapid iteration can transform industries, inspire innovation, and build resilient, future-ready organizations.**

96. Swarm Leadership

Swarm Leadership: A Breakdown

Theory

Swarm Leadership is a decentralized leadership model that **emphasizes collective intelligence, self-organization, and adaptive decision-making without a traditional hierarchy.** Inspired by **nature—such as the way birds, fish, and ants coordinate their movements and decision-making— Swarm Leadership leverages the power of many individuals working together in a fluid, dynamic system.**

Rooted in **Complex Systems Theory, Distributed Leadership, and Agile Leadership**, this model suggests that **leaders should not impose control but instead create an environment where individuals can self-organize, collaborate, and make real-time decisions based on shared purpose and local knowledge.** Instead of relying on one central authority, **leadership emerges through the collective actions of individuals who respond to real-time data and feedback.**

Key characteristics of **Swarm Leadership**:

1. **Decentralized Decision-Making** – Leadership is distributed among individuals rather than controlled by a single authority.

2. **Collective Intelligence & Collaboration** – The group's knowledge and expertise are pooled to find the best solutions.

3. **Self-Organization & Adaptability** – Teams **adjust in real-time based on feedback, similar to how a swarm of birds moves together.**

4. **Speed & Efficiency** – Decision-making **is fast, allowing teams to react quickly to changing circumstances.**

5. **Minimal Bureaucracy** – Leadership **is flexible and situational, reducing hierarchy and rigid structures.**

Unlike **top-down leadership models, which rely on authority and rigid structures, Swarm Leadership fosters agility, adaptability, and real-time problem-solving through collective intelligence.**

Example

A strong example of **Swarm Leadership** is **Wikipedia,** where **thousands of contributors self-organize to create, edit, and maintain one of the world's largest knowledge repositories** without a centralized authority controlling content creation. Instead of a **single leader, leadership is distributed among editors, moderators, and contributors who act based on shared community guidelines.**

Another example is **the Occupy Wall Street movement,** which functioned without a formal leadership hierarchy but still managed to **coordinate large-scale protests, actions, and advocacy through decentralized organization and collective decision-making.**

Why It Works

Swarm Leadership is effective because it:

- **Taps into Collective Intelligence – Harnessing the wisdom of the crowd leads to better decision-making.**

- **Increases Agility & Responsiveness – Teams react faster to change because decisions are made in real-time.**

- **Reduces Bureaucracy & Bottlenecks – Empowering individuals eliminates unnecessary delays and inefficiencies.**

- **Encourages Innovation & Problem-Solving – Diverse perspectives lead to more creative and effective solutions.**

- **Enhances Employee Engagement & Ownership – When employees have a voice, they feel more motivated and invested in outcomes.**

Studies show that **organizations that adopt decentralized decision-making models often outperform rigid hierarchical structures in dynamic, fast-changing environments.**

How It Works

Swarm Leadership follows a **self-organizing, decentralized approach**:

1. **Establish a Shared Purpose & Guiding Principles** – Individuals **work toward a common goal rather than waiting for direct orders.**

2. **Encourage Distributed Decision-Making** – Employees **make decisions based on local knowledge rather than hierarchical approval.**

3. **Foster Open Communication & Transparency** – Information **is shared freely, ensuring everyone is informed and aligned.**

4. **Promote Adaptability & Real-Time Adjustments** – Teams **adjust quickly based on immediate feedback.**

5. **Trust in the Power of Collective Action** – Leaders **empower individuals to contribute based on their expertise and situational awareness.**

Unlike **traditional command-and-control leadership, which relies on central authority, Swarm Leadership distributes decision-making and trusts in the collective intelligence of the team.**

Application

Swarm Leadership is widely applied in:

- **Open-Source Communities** – Projects like **Linux and Wikipedia rely on decentralized collaboration.**

- **Tech & Agile Teams** – Companies like **Spotify use squad-based models to allow teams to self-organize and innovate**.

- **Crisis Response & Emergency Situations** – Disaster relief organizations **coordinate large-scale efforts without a strict hierarchy**.

- **Social & Political Movements** – Decentralized movements **use Swarm Leadership to mobilize large groups efficiently**.

Key Insights

1. **Leadership is Not About Control, But Enabling Collective Action** – Empowering individuals leads to better decision-making.

2. **Decentralized Teams Are More Agile & Innovative** – **Self-organizing teams adapt faster to change than hierarchical ones**.

3. **Trust & Transparency Strengthen Team Coordination** – **Open information sharing keeps everyone aligned and effective**.

4. **Swarm Leadership is Ideal for Fast-Paced, Complex Environments** – **It allows organizations to thrive in unpredictable, rapidly evolving industries**.

Swarm Leadership proves that **leaders who enable decentralized decision-making, trust in collective intelligence, and create adaptable environments build** stronger, more resilient, and high-performing organizations.

97. Benevolent Dictatorship

Benevolent Dictatorship: A Breakdown

Theory

Benevolent Dictatorship is a leadership model where **a single leader holds absolute authority but exercises power with fairness, wisdom, and a focus on the collective good.** Unlike traditional autocratic leadership, **benevolent dictators use their authority to benefit their people, rather than for personal gain or control.**

Rooted in **Authoritarian Leadership, Servant Leadership, and Paternalistic Leadership**, this model suggests that **a strong, centralized leader can make quick decisions, drive efficiency, and implement long-term visions without bureaucratic obstacles.** However, their leadership is **guided by ethical responsibility, care for their people, and a commitment to progress rather than oppression.**

Key characteristics of **Benevolent Dictatorship**:

1. **Centralized Decision-Making** – The leader **has ultimate authority but acts in the best interest of the group.**

2. **Long-Term Vision & Stability** – The leader **focuses on sustainable growth and avoids short-term compromises.**

3. **Ethical & Responsible Leadership** – Power is exercised with fairness, integrity, and a moral compass.

4. **Efficiency & Decisiveness** – Decision-making **is fast and effective without excessive bureaucracy.**

5. **People-Cantered Governance** – The leader prioritizes the well-being, progress, and needs of their followers.

Unlike **pure autocratic leadership, which prioritizes control, Benevolent Dictatorship blends strong authority with ethical stewardship and care for the community.**

Example

A strong example of **Benevolent Dictatorship** is **Lee Kuan Yew, the founding Prime Minister of Singapore.** He ruled with **firm control but transformed Singapore into a global economic powerhouse through strategic policies, strong governance, and a focus on education, infrastructure, and anti-corruption efforts.** Despite centralized power, **his leadership was widely respected because of its fairness and long-term benefits for Singaporeans.**

In the business world, **Steve Jobs at Apple** exemplified this model. He had **unquestioned authority over product development, corporate vision, and decision-making,** yet his leadership resulted in **some of the most innovative products and a thriving corporate culture.** Jobs was known for **demanding excellence while inspiring employees to achieve remarkable breakthroughs.**

Why It Works

Benevolent Dictatorship is effective because it:

- **Eliminates Bureaucratic Inefficiencies** – Decisions are made quickly and executed effectively.

- **Ensures Long-Term Stability & Vision** – Leaders can implement lasting reforms without political gridlock.

- **Provides Clear Direction & Accountability** – The organization or nation follows a single, coherent vision.

- **Encourages High Standards & Innovation** – Strong leaders set ambitious goals and push for excellence.

- **Balances Control with Ethical Responsibility** – Leaders act with fairness, avoiding the pitfalls of pure dictatorship.

Studies show that **organizations and nations led by benevolent dictators often achieve remarkable progress, provided that leaders remain committed to ethical leadership and public welfare.**

How It Works

Benevolent Dictatorship follows a **top-down, ethically guided leadership approach**:

1. **Establish a Clear, Long-Term Vision** – The leader defines a compelling mission for sustainable growth.

2. **Enforce Discipline & High Standards** – **Leaders demand excellence and efficiency in execution.**

3. **Prioritize Ethical & Fair Decision-Making** – Power is **exercised responsibly to benefit people, not exploit them.**

4. **Control Critical Decisions, Delegate Execution** – Leaders **retain authority but allow experts to implement policies.**

5. **Ensure Progress Through Accountability** – The leader **remains focused on measurable outcomes that improve lives.**

Unlike **pure autocracy, which can become oppressive**, **Benevolent Dictatorship requires ethical commitment and a genuine focus on people's well-being.**

Application

Benevolent Dictatorship is widely applied in:

- **Government & Political Leadership** – Examples like **Lee Kuan Yew and Mustafa Kemal Atatürk demonstrate strong, ethical governance.**

- **Corporate & Business Leadership** – Companies like **Apple and Tesla thrive under visionary, centralized leadership.**

- **Military & Crisis Leadership** – In emergencies, centralized, decisive leadership is often necessary for rapid action.

- **Nonprofit & Philanthropic Organizations** – Strong leaders **drive impact while maintaining ethical responsibility.**

Key Insights

1. **Absolute Power Must Be Balanced with Ethical Stewardship – A benevolent dictator must act in the best interest of their people, not personal gain.**

2. **Visionary Leadership Drives Progress – Leaders with long-term strategies achieve more than those focused on short-term wins.**

3. **Bureaucracy Can Hinder Success – Organizations and nations benefit from efficient, decisive leadership.**

4. **The Best Leaders Inspire, Not Just Command – Benevolent dictators succeed by earning respect and fostering loyalty, not fear.**

Benevolent Dictatorship proves that **when strong leadership is guided by ethics, responsibility, and a focus on collective well-being, it can lead to transformational success and long-term stability.**

98. Open Leadership

Open Leadership: A Breakdown

Theory

Open Leadership is a leadership model that **embraces transparency, collaboration, and shared decision-making** to create an inclusive and innovative workplace. It is built on the idea that **leaders should empower employees by giving them access to information, autonomy, and opportunities to contribute meaningfully to decision-making processes.**

Rooted in **Servant Leadership, Participative Leadership, and Open-Source Principles**, Open Leadership is about **removing unnecessary hierarchies and silos, encouraging trust, and fostering a culture where employees feel heard, valued, and motivated to drive the organization forward.**

Key characteristics of **Open Leadership**:

1. **Transparency & Information Sharing** – Leaders **openly communicate strategies, challenges, and company performance.**

2. **Trust & Empowerment** – Employees **are given autonomy and responsibility to make meaningful contributions.**

3. **Collaborative Decision-Making** – Leaders **involve teams in key business decisions rather than relying solely on top-down directives.**

4. **Adaptability & Open Feedback** – Organizations **embrace feedback, continuously improve, and stay agile.**

5. **Authenticity & Vulnerability** – Leaders **are open about challenges and welcome diverse perspectives.**

Unlike **traditional leadership, which relies on control and** secrecy, **Open Leadership fosters trust, engagement, and shared responsibility, making organizations more resilient and innovative.**

Example

A strong example of **Open Leadership** is **Satya Nadella at Microsoft.** When Nadella took over as CEO, he transformed Microsoft's culture from a **competitive, closed system to an open, learning-oriented organization.** He emphasized **collaboration, transparency, and empathy,** shifting Microsoft's strategy to embrace **open-source software, cloud computing, and cross-industry partnerships.** This openness helped **drive innovation, increase employee engagement, and improve Microsoft's global reputation.**

Another example is **Buffer, a social media management company,** which practices radical transparency by **publicly sharing employee salaries, revenue, and decision-making** processes. This approach has built **trust among employees and customers, fostering a culture of openness and shared purpose**.

Why It Works

Open Leadership is effective because it:

- **Builds Trust & Employee Engagement – Transparency and inclusion make employees feel valued and invested in success.**

- **Encourages Innovation & Collaboration – Open discussions and knowledge sharing drive creativity and problem-solving.**

- **Increases Organizational Agility – Employees respond faster to challenges when they have full access to information.**

- **Reduces Hierarchical Barriers – Decentralized leadership fosters a more engaged and productive workforce.**

- **Strengthens Brand & Customer Loyalty – Organizations that practice openness gain trust from customers and stakeholders.**

Studies show that **companies with high levels of transparency and employee empowerment experience better retention, innovation, and financial performance**.

How It Works

Open Leadership follows a **collaborative, trust-driven approach**:

1. **Embrace Transparency & Open Communication** – Leaders **share information openly to empower employees.**

2. **Encourage Employee Participation in Decisions** – Organizations **listen to employees' input and act on valuable insights.**

3. **Foster a Learning-Oriented Culture** – Leaders **promote continuous learning and adaptability.**

4. **Trust Employees with Responsibility** – Teams **are given autonomy and accountability for their work.**

5. **Lead with Authenticity & Vulnerability** – Leaders **admit mistakes, seek feedback, and build genuine relationships.**

Unlike **top-down leadership models that control information, Open Leadership thrives on shared knowledge, empowerment, and participative decision-making.**

Application

Open Leadership is widely applied in:

- **Technology & Innovation Companies** – Organizations like **Microsoft and Google embrace open collaboration.**

- **Startups & Agile Teams** – Founders **empower teams by decentralizing decision-making.**

- **Remote & Hybrid Work Environments** – Open leadership **ensures clarity and trust when teams are geographically dispersed.**

- **Nonprofits & Community Organizations** – Transparency **builds trust among stakeholders and donors.**

Key Insights

1. **Transparency Builds Trust & Engagement** – **Employees perform better when they understand leadership's vision and challenges.**

2. **Empowered Employees Drive Innovation** – **When employees have ownership, they contribute more creatively and proactively.**

3. **Collaboration Strengthens Decision-Making** – **Open discussions lead to smarter, more effective solutions.**

4. **Authentic Leaders Inspire Loyalty & Performance** – **Vulnerability and honesty create stronger teams and work cultures.**

Open Leadership proves that **leaders who embrace transparency, trust, and shared decision-making build more engaged, innovative, and resilient organizations.**

99. Peer Leadership

Peer Leadership: A Breakdown

Theory

Peer Leadership is a leadership model that emphasizes **collaboration, mutual influence, and shared responsibility among individuals of the same hierarchical level**. Instead of leadership being imposed from the top down, **peer leaders guide, inspire, and support their colleagues by leveraging trust, respect, and shared goals rather than authority**.

Rooted in **Collaborative Leadership, Distributed Leadership, and Team-Oriented Leadership**, this model suggests that **leadership is not confined to a title or rank but can emerge from anyone within a group who demonstrates influence, expertise, and initiative**. In peer leadership, **team members hold each other accountable, provide feedback, and contribute equally to decision-making and problem-solving**.

Key characteristics of **Peer Leadership**:

1. **Mutual Influence & Shared Authority** – Leadership is distributed rather than concentrated in a single figure.

2. **Collaboration & Teamwork** – Teams **operate through trust, support, and shared responsibilities**.

3. **Respect & Accountability** – Peers **hold each other accountable and support collective goals**.

4. **Knowledge Sharing & Continuous Learning** – Leadership **emerges from expertise and willingness to share knowledge**.

5. **Adaptive & Flexible Leadership** – Leadership **roles shift based on situational needs rather than fixed hierarchy**.

Unlike **hierarchical leadership, which relies on power structures**, Peer Leadership is built on mutual respect, influence, and shared goals.

Example

A strong example of **Peer Leadership** is **Spotify's Squad Model**, where teams (squads) **self-organize without a central leader**. Each squad consists of **cross-functional peers who collaborate, make collective decisions, and hold each other accountable**. This model has allowed Spotify to **stay agile, innovative, and highly adaptable**.

Another example is **Wikipedia**, where content creation and editing are **led by peer contributors without a formal hierarchy**. Volunteers **collaborate, review each other's work, and uphold content standards through collective leadership**, demonstrating how peer-led models can sustain large-scale, high-quality outputs.

Why It Works

Peer Leadership is effective because it:

- **Enhances Collaboration & Team Cohesion** – Teams work together with a sense of shared purpose and responsibility.

- **Fosters Innovation & Creativity** – Ideas flow freely when leadership is not limited to a few individuals.

- **Builds Trust & Psychological Safety** – Peers **feel valued and respected, increasing engagement and morale.**

- **Encourages Accountability & Ownership** – Team members **feel a stronger sense of responsibility for success.**

- **Increases Adaptability & Responsiveness** – Teams **quickly adjust to challenges without waiting for hierarchical approval.**

Studies show that **organizations that implement peer leadership see higher employee engagement, improved problem-solving, and stronger team performance.**

How It Works

Peer Leadership follows a **collaborative, trust-based approach:**

1. **Create a Culture of Shared Responsibility** – Organizations **foster environments where leadership emerges naturally.**

2. **Encourage Open Communication & Feedback** – Peers **regularly exchange insights, guidance, and constructive criticism**.

3. **Rotate Leadership Roles Based on Expertise** – Leadership **is fluid, allowing different members to take the lead when needed**.

4. **Foster Mutual Accountability** – Team members **hold each other accountable without relying on hierarchical oversight**.

5. **Promote Knowledge Sharing & Skill Development** – **Everyone contributes their expertise to improve collective performance**.

Unlike **top-down leadership models, where authority is rigid**, Peer Leadership thrives on shared decision-making, flexibility, and collective responsibility.

Application

Peer Leadership is widely applied in:

- **Tech & Agile Work Environments** – Companies like **Spotify and Google use peer-led teams to drive innovation**.

- **Startups & Entrepreneurial Teams** – Small, **self-directed teams maximize efficiency and adaptability**.

- **Academia & Research Groups** – Scientists and scholars **collaborate as equals to advance knowledge**.

- **Nonprofits & Grassroots Organizations** – Volunteer-led initiatives **use peer leadership to drive collective action**.

Key Insights

1. **Leadership is Not About Titles—It's About Influence – Peer Leadership proves that leadership can come from anyone within a team**.

2. **Collaboration Outperforms Command-Based Leadership – Teams with shared leadership innovate faster and work more effectively**.

3. **Accountability is Stronger Among Peers – When leadership is collective, members take greater ownership of outcomes**.

4. **Organizations That Embrace Peer Leadership Are More Agile – Decentralized decision-making enables rapid adaptation**.

Peer Leadership proves that **by distributing leadership across a team, organizations can achieve greater collaboration, innovation, and collective success**.

100. Holographic Leadership

Holographic Leadership: A Breakdown

Theory

Holographic Leadership is a leadership model that **distributes knowledge, decision-making, and adaptability throughout an organization, much like a hologram, where each part contains the whole**. Instead of relying on a single leader or hierarchical structure, **Holographic Leadership ensures that leadership is embedded at every level, allowing teams to function independently while maintaining alignment with a shared vision.**

Rooted in **Systems Thinking, Distributed Leadership, and Agile Organizations**, this model suggests that **leaders should focus on creating self-sustaining teams where every member understands and embodies the organization's mission, values, and goals.** By doing so, **leadership is no longer confined to specific roles but is instead shared across the organization.**

Key characteristics of **Holographic Leadership**:

1. **Decentralized Leadership & Self-Sufficiency** – Every individual **understands and can embody leadership principles**.

2. **Shared Vision & Collective Intelligence** – The entire organization **operates based on a unified purpose**.

3. **Agility & Adaptability** – Teams **respond quickly to change without waiting for top-down direction.**

4. **Resilience & Redundancy** – The organization **remains stable even if key leaders are absent or replaced.**

5. **Collaborative & Knowledge-Sharing Culture** – Information and expertise **are distributed, empowering everyone to lead.**

Unlike **traditional leadership models that centralize authority**, Holographic Leadership distributes leadership capabilities throughout the system, ensuring continuity, flexibility, and resilience.

Example

A strong example of **Holographic Leadership** is **the Mondragon Corporation**, a federation of worker cooperatives in Spain. In Mondragon, **every employee is considered both a worker and a decision-maker**, ensuring that leadership and decision-making are **fully embedded within the workforce rather than centralized at the top.**

Another example is **the Linux open-source community**, where leadership is distributed among contributors rather than dictated by a single authority. Developers worldwide **collaborate based on shared goals, and leadership emerges organically based on expertise and contribution rather than rank.**

Why It Works

Holographic Leadership is effective because it:

- **Increases Organizational Agility & Resilience –** Teams adapt and make decisions independently without waiting for hierarchical approval.

- **Strengthens Employee Engagement & Accountability – When leadership is shared, employees take greater responsibility for outcomes.**

- **Reduces Bottlenecks & Improves Innovation –** Ideas and decision-making are not limited to a select few, leading to faster problem-solving.

- **Ensures Long-Term Stability –** Organizations do not collapse when a single leader leaves because leadership is embedded in the system.

- **Encourages Knowledge Sharing & Continuous Learning –** Employees continuously grow, making the organization more intelligent as a whole.

Studies show that **organizations that implement decentralized leadership structures experience higher adaptability, innovation, and employee satisfaction.**

How It Works

Holographic Leadership follows a **distributed, systems-oriented approach:**

1. **Create a Clear, Shared Vision** – Every member understands the organization's mission and values.

2. **Empower Teams with Knowledge & Decision-Making** – Leadership **is not confined to executives but spread across the organization.**

3. **Encourage Self-Sufficiency & Autonomy** – Teams **are equipped to solve problems without waiting for direction.**

4. **Develop Redundancy & Cross-Training** – Employees **are trained in multiple areas to ensure organizational resilience.**

5. **Foster Open Communication & Collaboration** – Knowledge **flows freely, ensuring alignment and shared responsibility.**

Unlike **hierarchical leadership, which relies on command-and-control, Holographic Leadership creates self-sustaining teams where leadership emerges naturally.**

Application

Holographic Leadership is widely applied in:

- **Worker Cooperatives & Democratic Workplaces** – Organizations like **Mondragon ensure leadership is embedded at all levels.**

- **Tech & Open-Source Communities** – Projects like **Linux and Wikipedia thrive on decentralized, knowledge-based leadership.**

- **Agile Organizations & Startups** – Companies like **Spotify use self-organizing teams that function independently.**

- **Crisis Management & Disaster Response** – Distributed teams **can respond without waiting for central command.**

Key Insights

1. **Leadership Should Be Embedded, Not Concentrated – When leadership is shared, organizations become more resilient and adaptive.**

2. **A Strong, Shared Vision Aligns Decentralized Teams – Holographic Leadership works best when all members understand the big picture.**

3. **Organizations Function Best When Everyone Can Lead – Empowered employees make faster, smarter decisions.**

4. **Eliminating Bottlenecks Improves Innovation & Agility – When leadership is decentralized, decision-making becomes faster and more effective.**

Holographic Leadership proves that **by distributing leadership throughout an organization, teams become more resilient, adaptable, and high-performing.**

BEST OF LUCK APPLYING THESE LEADERSHIP MODELS IN YOUR ORGANISATION

OTHER BOOKS IN THIS 100 SERIES – SCAN HERE

100 COGNITIVE AND MENTAL MODELS TO HELP YOUR CAREER: Mental Shortcuts for Smarter Choices, Sharper Thinking, and Success

-

ANOTHER 100 MENTAL MODELS TO HELP YOUR CAREER - VOLUME 2: Another 100 Powerful Mental Models for Clarity, Confidence, and Climbing the Career Ladder

-

100 HEURISTICS AND HEURISTIC MODELS: The Hidden Rules of Smart Thinking Used by Experts, Entrepreneurs, and Machines

-

100 GAME THEORIES AND DECISION MODELS FOR RATIONAL DECISION MAKING IN COMPETITIVE SITUATIONS: 100 Winning Strategies for Rational Thinking in High-Stakes Scenarios

-

100 BUSINESS STRATEGIES PROVEN TACTICS FOR GROWTH, INNOVATION AND MARKET DOMINATION: Actionable Strategies to Scale, Disrupt and Lead in Any Industry

-

100 LEADERSHIP MODELS AND STRATEGIES FOR EFFECTIVE DECISION-MAKING FOR ORGANIZATIONAL SUCCESS: Empowering Your Leadership, 100 Proven Strategies and Models to Enhance Decision-Making & Drive Success

-

100 BUSINESS GROWTH HACKS AND STRATEGIES TO GROW PROFIT AND INCREASE YOUR COMPETITIVE ADVANTAGE: Proven Techniques to Scale Faster, Boost Revenue, and Dominate Your Market with Actionable Growth

-

100 ECONOMIC THEORIES DEMYSTIFIED : A Guide To The World's Most Influential Economic Ideas From Keynesian Economics To Debt-deflation Theory

-

100 PASSIVE INCOME STREAM SIDE HUSTLES, MASTERING SIDE HUSTLES AND SMART INVESTMENTS: How to Make Money While You Sleep and Secure Your Financial Future

-

WHILST YOU ARE HERE , WHY NOT SCAN THIS TO SEE IF THERE ARE ANY MORE BOOKS PUBLISHED YET

OR FOLLOW ME AT @DANDANMUSICMAN ON X AND @DANDANMUSICMANUK ON INSTAGRAM

PROVEN TACTICS FOR GROWTH, INNOVATION, AND MARKET DOMINATION

100 BUSINESS STRATEGIES
BY DAN WAITE

REFERRAL PROGRAM STRATEGY	CUSTOMER-CENTRIC STRATEGY	BOOTSTRAPPING STRATEGY
VENTURE CAPITAL STRATEGY	CROWDFUNDING STRATEGY	PRIVATE EQUITY STRATEGY
DEFENSIVE STRATEGY	HYPERLOCAL STRATEGY	DROPSHIPPING STRATEGY
AUTOMATION STRATEGY	SURPRISE & DELIGHT STRATEGY	HYPERAUTOMATION STRATEGY
REVERSE LOGISTICS STRATEGY	SIX SIGMA STRATEGY	GAMIFICATION STRATEGY
HYPER-PERSONALIZATION STRATEGY	ECOSYSTEM STRATEGY	JUST-IN-TIME (JIT) STRATEGY

100 BUSINESS STRATEGIES

BLUE OCEAN EXPANSION	BLOCKCHAIN STRATEGY	UPSELLING STRATEGY
WEB3 STRATEGY	METAVERSE STRATEGY	SEO STRATEGY
BLUE OCEAN STRATEGY	GLOBAL EXPANSION STRATEGY	CONGLOMERATE STRATEGY
HORIZONTAL INTEGRATION	VERTICAL INTEGRATION	FIRST-MOVER ADVANTAGE
FAST-FOLLOWER STRATEGY	PLATFORM STRATEGY	COST LEADERSHIP STRATEGY
DIFFERENTIATION STRATEGY	ORGANIC GROWTH STRATEGY	GROWTH HACKING STRATEGY
OMNICHANNEL STRATEGY	LOYALTY PROGRAM STRATEGY	VIRAL MARKETING STRATEGY
STORYTELLING STRATEGY	NOSTALGIA MARKETING STRATEGY	AND MANY, MANY MORE

100 GAME THEORIES AND DECISION MODELS

GAME THEORY
BY DAN WAITE

MUTUALLY ASSURED DESTRUCTION	DOLLAR AUCTION	HAWK-DOVE GAME
VOLUNTEER'S DILEMMA	SILENT DUEL	AI ALIGNMENT GAME
BAYESIAN GAME	TIPPING POINT GAME	SOCIAL INFLUENCE
TIT-FOR-TAT IN EVOLUTION	DIVIDE THE DOLLAR GAME	MONTY HALL PROBLEM
DIFFUSION OF RESPONSIBILITY	FREE RIDER PROBLEM	FLOCKING BEHAVIOUR
PARASITE-HOST GAME	CYBERSECURITY GAME	PREDATOR-PREY GAME

100 GAME THEORIES
RATIONAL DECISION-MAKING IN COMPETITIVE SITUATIONS

EVOLUTIONARILY STABLE STRATEGY	LIMITED WAR GAME	SECURITY DILEMMA
TRUST GAME	SUNK COST GAME	SHAPLEY VALUE
TERRORIST VS. GOVERNMENT	SPY VS. SPY GAME	DETERRENCE THEORY GAME
COLONEL BLOTTO GAME	WAR OF ATTRITION	MARKET FOR LEMONS
MORAL HAZARD GAME	PRINCIPAL-AGENT PROBLEM	JOB MARKET SIGNALLING
SOCIAL MEDIA VIRALITY GAME	SPAM DETECTION GAME	ADVERSE SELECTION GAME
BERTRAND COMPETITION	CASCADING FAILURE GAME	EL FAROL BAR PROBLEM
SELF-DRIVING CAR DILEMMA GAMES	MECHANISM DESIGN THEORY	AND MANY, MANY MORE

ORGANIZATIONAL SUCCESS AND EFFECTIVE DECISION-MAKING

100 LEADERSHIP MODELS AND STRATEGIES
BY DAN WAITE

GAMIFICATION LEADERSHIP	NONPROFIT LEADERSHIP	IMPROV LEADERSHIP
HACKER LEADERSHIP	SWARM LEADERSHIP	TECH LEADERSHIP
GREAT MAN THEORY	SITUATIONAL LEADERSHIP	AGILE LEADERSHIP
HOLOGRAPHIC LEADERSHIP	TRANSFORMATIONAL LEADERSHIP	PEER LEADERSHIP
LAISSEZ-FAIRE LEADERSHIP	AUTOCRATIC LEADERSHIP	BENEVOLENT DICTATORSHIP
POLITICAL LEADERSHIP	MILITARY LEADERSHIP	LEVEL FIVE LEADERSHIP

100 LEADERSHIP MODELS

RESONANT LEADERSHIP	COACHING LEADERSHIP	EMPATHETIC LEADERSHIP
AI-INTEGRATED LEADERSHIP	MAVERICK LEADERSHIP	IMPROV LEADERSHIP
VISIONARY LEADERSHIP	PACESETTING LEADERSHIP	SUSTAINABLE LEADERSHIP
PARADOXICAL LEADERSHIP	INFLUENCER LEADERSHIP	OPEN-SOURCE LEADERSHIP
STOIC LEADERSHIP	ZEN LEADERSHIP	STARTUP LEADERSHIP
EXISTENTIAL LEADERSHIP	DIALECTICAL LEADERSHIP	SPIRITUAL LEADERSHIP
HUMAN-CENTERED LEADERSHIP	CRISIS LEADERSHIP	HOLACRACY LEADERSHIP
SPORTS LEADERSHIP	DATA-DRIVEN LEADERSHIP	AND MANY, MANY MORE

100 ECONOMIC THEORIES DEMYSTIFIED

ECONOMIC THEORIES
BY DAN WAITE

MERCANTILISM	GIG ECONOMY THEORY	SAY'S LAW
MALTHUSIAN THEORY	JAPAN'S ECONOMIC MODEL	MARXIST ECONOMICS
RICARDIAN EQUIVALENCE	UTILITY THEORY	MARGINAL UTILITY THEORY
D.O.G.E. DEPARTMENT OF GOVERNMENT EFFICIENCY	GENERAL EQUILIBRIUM THEORY	RANDOM WALK THEORY
PRICE ELASTICITY OF DEMAND	CONSUMER SURPLUS	CLASSICAL ECONOMICS
THEORY OF THE FIRM	PIGOUVIAN TAXES	KEYNESIAN ECONOMICS

100 ECONOMIC THEORIES DEMYSTIFIED

EVOLUTIONARILY STABLE STRATEGY	LIMITED WAR GAME	IRRATIONAL EXUBERANCE
PHILLIPS CURVE	DEBT-DEFLATION THEORY	SHAPLEY VALUE
PERMANENT INCOME HYPOTHESIS	VEBLEN GOODS	BRETTON WOODS SYSTEM
MORAL HAZARD	MARKET STRUCTURE THEORY	DUTCH DISEASE
ADVERSE SELECTION	NETWORK EFFECTS	HARROD-DOMAR GROWTH MODEL
GLOBALIZATION THEORY	GRAVITY MODEL OF TRADE	NEW TRADE THEORY
CONVERGENCE THEORY	HECKSCHER-OHLIN MODEL	SOLOW-SWAN GROWTH MODEL
CREATIVE DESTRUCTION	BIG PUSH THEORY	AND MANY, MANY MORE

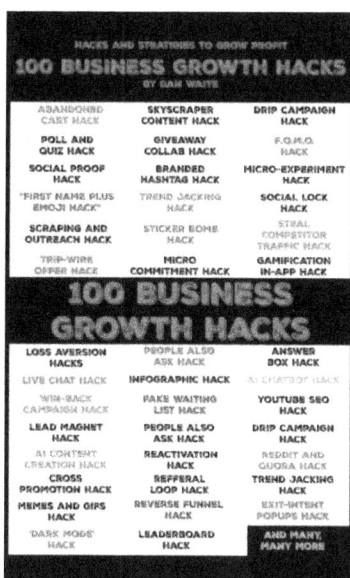

HACKS AND STRATEGIES TO GROW PROFIT

100 BUSINESS GROWTH HACKS

BY DAN WAITE

ABANDONED CART HACK	SKYSCRAPER CONTENT HACK	DRIP CAMPAIGN HACK
POLL AND QUIZ HACK	GIVEAWAY COLLAB HACK	F.O.M.O. HACK
SOCIAL PROOF HACK	BRANDED HASHTAG HACK	MICRO-EXPERIMENT HACK
"FIRST NAME PLUS EMOJI HACK"	TREND JACKING HACK	SOCIAL LOCK HACK
SCRAPING AND OUTREACH HACK	STICKER BOMB HACK	STEAL COMPETITOR TRAFFIC HACK
TRIP-WIRE OFFER HACK	MICRO COMMITMENT HACK	GAMIFICATION IN-APP HACK

100 BUSINESS GROWTH HACKS

LOSS AVERSION HACKS	PEOPLE ALSO ASK HACK	ANSWER BOX HACK
LIVE CHAT HACK	INFOGRAPHIC HACK	AI CHATBOT HACK
WIN-BACK CAMPAIGN HACK	FAKE WAITING LIST HACK	YOUTUBE SEO HACK
LEAD MAGNET HACK	PEOPLE ALSO ASK HACK	DRIP CAMPAIGN HACK
AI CONTENT CREATION HACK	REACTIVATION HACK	REDDIT AND QUORA HACK
CROSS PROMOTION HACK	REFFERAL LOOP HACK	TREND JACKING HACK
MEMES AND GIFS HACK	REVERSE FUNNEL HACK	EXIT-INTENT POPUPS HACK
'DARK MODE' HACK	LEADERBOARD HACK	AND MANY, MANY MORE

www.ingramcontent.com/pod-product-compliance
Lightning Source LLC
Chambersburg PA
CBHW060112200326
41518CB00008B/806